THREADS of IDENTITY

THREADS of IDENTITY

Maya Costume of the 1960s in Highland Guatemala

Patricia B. Altman ⚙ Caroline D. West

FOWLER MUSEUM OF CULTURAL HISTORY

University of California, Los Angeles

This Catalog and associated exhibition
were supported by funding from
The Ralph B. Lloyd Foundation
Elizabeth and Richard Rogers
Elizabeth Lloyd Davis
Carter Hawley Hale
The Ahmanson Foundation
The National Endowment for the Humanities
and Manus, the support group of the Fowler Museum of Cultural History

Front and Back Covers: Costume of Patzún.
Page 1: Women in Sololá.
Pages 2,3: Festival in Sololá.
Page 4: Embroidered neckline of a huipil from Patzún.
Page 192: Santa Apolonia woman.

Fowler Museum of Cultural History
University of California, Los Angeles
405 Hilgard Avenue
Los Angeles, California, USA 90024-1549

Printed and bound in Hong Kong by Pearl River Printing Company.

Library of Congress Cataloging-in-Publication Data

Altman, Patricia, 1917-
    Threads of identity : Maya costume of the 1960s in Highland
    Guatemala / Patricia Altman, Caroline West.
        p. cm.
    Includes bibliographical references.
    ISBN 0-930741-23-4 (hardbound) — ISBN 0-930741-24-2 (softbound)
    1. Mayas—Costume and adornment. 2. Mayas—Textile industry and fabrics.
3. Mayas—Ethnic identity. 4. Costume—Guatemala—History—20th century.
5. Hand weaving—Guatemala. I. West, Caroline, 1915-   . II. University of
California, Los Angeles. Fowler Museum of Cultural History. III. Title.
F1435.3.C69A44 1992
391'.0097281'09046—dc20   92-72523
                                                          CIP

Contents

Foreword

Research on dress and textiles has long been a priority of the Fowler Museum of Cultural History. Clothing traditions, whether they constitute the focus of a given study or just one of many elements of culture under investigation, have invariably been interpreted here as a fundamental component of a society's expressive culture. This volume significantly affirms such an interpretation.

The Fowler Museum first displayed Guatemalan Maya textiles at UCLA in 1975 with a modest exhibition and catalogue titled *Guatemala: Quetzal and Cross*. That project was based upon material collected in the field between 1962 and 1972 and later donated to the Museum by Caroline and Howard West. Caroline, as committed patron, valued associate, and energetic volunteer, has been active in Museum programs ever since our founding in 1963. Since the 1975 exhibition, she has worked with tireless dedication, building and analyzing the Museum collection in preparation for this volume and its accompanying exhibition. We are greatly indebted to her.

Patricia Altman has been the Museum's Curator of Textiles and Folk Art since 1967, a position we are delighted she continues to hold despite her carefully camouflaged "retirement" in 1990. Pat is one of the best friends this museum has ever had, and the present project is just one in the long line of Pat's distinguished contributions to the Museum's development. Much of our past and present success can be directly traced to her efforts. She has our sincerest gratitude.

As always the Museum staff, listed at the back of this volume, performed with their usual excellence. Special thanks go to Henrietta Cosentino, Senior Editor, Danny Brauer, Director of Publications, Denis Nervig, Photographer, David Mayo, Exhibition Designer, and Betsy Quick, Director of Education. Their careful attention to the demands of this project is greatly appreciated.

This publication was made possible by a substantial grant from the Ralph B. Lloyd Foundation. We would like to thank Elizabeth and Richard Rogers and Elizabeth Lloyd Davis for their support on our behalf. Additional funding was supplied by Carter Hawley Hale and by Manus, the support group of the Fowler Museum of Cultural History.

Christopher B. Donnan, Director
Doran H. Ross, Deputy Director

Preface

A remark made by Lilly de Jongh Osborne, doyenne of Guatemalan textiles, sent us on the search that results in this publication. She said that Guatemalan Maya "textiles were their books and each one wrote his own."* The ability of costume to tell a full and complex story about the wearer was an intriguing idea, and provided a vital stimulus for our research. An interested public has customarily identified Guatemalan Maya costumes, or their separate parts, according to the village where they are worn and/or made, or characterized them according to the textile process. We felt it was time to apply a larger perspective. One of us was particularly interested in unexplored aspects of costume history, while the other was intrigued by costume similarities transcending village borders.

One avenue of investigation began with a look backward — at highland costume before the Spanish Conquest, and at colonial records charting some of the changes in costume, particularly men's costume, in the centuries following Alvarado's arrival. It led beyond those records, however, and into the vast realm of Spanish costume. Old books were combed for documentation of clothing in the Spanish countryside in the effort to trace some of the rarer and more interesting elements of men's costume back to their sources. The results of these investigations are presented in Chapters One and Two.

It was the costumes themselves that directed the other part of the work — how they looked, how they were made. Using the Museum collection, costumes were grouped and compared according to their stylistic traits such as colors used, background treatment, arrangement of supplementary design areas, types and repetition of motifs. Construction techniques were also analyzed and classified, including loom type, number of webs, neckline treatment, length and width, nature of edges and side openings, supplementary fibers, foreign findings, and embroidery. Although all parts of the costume were considered, huipils provided the most useful material for comparative purposes. Two hundred and two huipils were analyzed — approximately the same number considered by Lila M. O'Neale in her definitive study of the 1930s.

A wide-angle visual scan of costumes showed up groups that seemed to belong together. Others seemed to stand alone. The question was, why? Sometimes the

*This remark appears on the back of Ann Pollard Rowe's 1981 publication, *A Century of Change in Guatemalan Textiles.*

reasons were obvious: the villages were neighbors sharing language, geography, and/or cultural history. Sometimes the reasons were puzzling, and only a line in history provided the pertinent clue. It was evident that costumes worn by people who spoke the same language and inhabited the same area would be similar, and those similarities were easily charted. But as we looked more closely at the costumes, a deeper layer suggested itself. These "textile books" even seemed to acknowledge ancient tribal movements in patterns still evident in costumes worn during the 1960s. This called for a perusal of historic, ethnographic, linguistic, anthropological, even archaeological resources to understand the factors on which costume similarities (or dissimilarities) could hinge. Chapters Four, Five, and Six of this volume examine costume in ways that take us beyond the village boundary.

As we worked with these costumes, it seemed to us that the 1960s might well be regarded as a recent "classic" period in Guatemalan costume history. Many village costumes worn in that decade showed no change in color or basic styling from those of the 1930s described by O'Neale in her classic study. The indigo skirt still predominated in most villages as it had since the turn of the century. Village weavers still used natural fibers, particularly cotton, but also silk and wool as a design accent or for additional warmth. Acrylics and lurex had not yet pervaded their world. Local vendors and markets offered a wide choice in colors and qualities of cotton thread, and it was affordable. The weaver, freed from the laborious and time-consuming aspects of spinning and dyeing, could direct her energy to other aesthetic considerations, but she was still bound by a tradition that demanded village-specific styles. It was unthinkable for a woman of that time to wear the huipil of a village not her own.

In the 1960s a confident and exuberant hand was at work elaborating on a repertoire of motifs that harked back to before the Conquest. Guatemalan weaving began to be seen and valued outside the highlands by collectors and artists. These orchestrations of clear marvelous color began to find a market in the cities of the world. It gives us great pleasure to be able to explore what is recorded (in many cases for the last time) in these costumes of the 1960s. We hope you will find it as interesting as we did to discover what these "textile books" had to say to us.

Patricia B. Altman and Caroline D. West

Acknowledgments

The person trying to write meaningfully about Guatemala burns candles in thanks to the many who were earlier at that task. The old, the middle, and the young stalwarts of Guatemalan costume (O'Neale, Osborne, Delgado, Rowe) provide fresh information and new insights at every reading. Pom is burned to the field studies which illuminate specific towns, areas, and eras (Annis, Bunzel, Carmack, Fox, Lovell, Orellana, MacLeod, McBryde, Reina, Tax, Wagley, the Ixchel Museum monographs, and many more). Aguardiente is poured for all those who helped, whether through patient answering of questions or hours spent measuring, translating, sketching, counting threads, researching, tying *cintas*, reading manuscripts, programming computers, providing field photographs, dressing mannequins, and such.

The following museums (and individuals) were gracious and helpful in allowing one or both of us to view their Guatemalan holdings: Museo Ixchel (Cherri Pancake and Linda Asturias de Barrios); Museo Nacional de Arqueología y Etnología de Guatemala (Dora Guerra de González and Axel Orlando García); the Peabody Museum of Archaeology (Rosemary Joyce); the Taylor Museum of the Colorado Springs Fine Arts Center (Jonathan Batkin); the Robert H. Lowie Museum of Anthropology; the Museum of Man in San Diego (Grace Johnson); the Pitts River Museum (Lynne Williamson); and the Victoria and Albert Museum (J.W. Weardem).

The mannequins used for the photographs in this publication were created by Pauline Zima and generously donated by Thomas McLaughlin. We are very grateful for the authenticity of these models, which were based on photographs of actual highland individuals. They were especially valuable in that they enabled costumes from different villages to be brought together for close range comparison.

Due to building delays, the gestation of this project was a long one and the Museum staff was particularly helpful in smoothing out the difficulties. Barbara Underwood and Betsy Escandor enabled years of communications while Millicent Besser oversaw accounting. Emily Woodward helped us focus our ideas in the early stages. Sarah Kennington, Owen Moore, and Paulette Parker tracked textiles for us over the years and through the move, facilitating our work at many points. Robin Chamberlin oversaw the conservation of the textiles; Eileen Hocker vacuumed and packed up most of the textiles, and Margaret Dennis and Barbara Sloan unpacked, folded, and relocated them. Kristin Calla organized initial lists and textiles for exhibition, and Barbara Sloan organized them for photography and permanent storage. Betsy Quick developed the interpretive aspects of the exhibition as well as all public programming. Mary Kay

Kendall worked on many aspects of the project, from perfecting object lists to refining labels. George Kershaw made helpful comments on parts of the manuscript, as did Susan Masuoka, who read the manuscript thoughtfully at many stages. Susan also drew on her field work abilities to conduct in-depth video interviews for the exhibition and Grace Barnes lent her skill as a film-maker. David Mayo was responsible for the exhibition design, ably realized by Gene Riggs, Victor Lozano, and in particular Don Simmons and Patrick White who created wonderful props. Denis Nervig photographed many textiles, and Danny Brauer worked his magic on the publication design. Our most important staff thanks go to Henrietta Cosentino, our editor, who combed and cajoled our material into a presentable fabric.

The contributions of certain individuals were especially valuable because of their crucial timing. Gwendolin Ritz read an early manuscript and offered encouragement along with her comments and suggestions. Axel García ferreted out at their source those costume parts necessary to complete sixties' costumes. Eva de Smith and Pedro Sun shared unstintingly their vast knowledge of Guatemalan textiles. Christopher Lutz suggested important bibliographic material, both personally and through CIRMA, which he founded and maintains. Frieda Whitman Ellsworth provided a home base in Guatemala and the photographic archives of her late husband Irving Whitman, which are a valuable resource for sixties' research. Howard West, Caroline's husband, made it possible for her to pursue her investigations in Guatemala and elsewhere, and Andrew Dawley West, their son, photographed the mannequin plates and hundreds of other textiles as his contribution to the effort.

Others whose help made this publication possible are listed according to the nature of their contributions. *Research:* Sam Bright, Harriette Crocker, Henry DuFlon, James Louckey, Louise Lyon, Susan Masuoka, David L. Morrill, John Watanabe. *Translation:* Giselle Flores Cordero, Fresia Brenes Dunlap, Yoana Walschap. *Computer Programming:* Carter Hawley Hale Data Center, Vincent Conant, Don McClelland, Alexander Smith. *Weaving:* James Bassler, Bernard Kester, Dorothy Laupa, Mary Jane Leland, Roger Wolfe. *Field Photographs:* Polly Blank, John Blanton, Dan Clement, Richard Dunlap, Laurie Levin, Susan Masuoka, Susan Turner, Jane Ullman. *Mannequin Dressers:* Robin Chamberlin, Sharon Donnan, Roy Dowell, Susanna Meiers, Paula Williams, Claire Witherspoon. *Costume Sketches:* Shirley Hulsey. *Maps:* Tony Kluck.

None of the above is responsible for the sins of omission and commission occurring through the ignorance or carelessness of

The Authors

CHAMÁ MOUNTAINS

COBÁN
Cahabón River
San Pedro Carchá
San Juan Chamelco

Chixoy O Negro River
San Cristóbal Verapaz
Tamahú
Tactic
Tucurú
Polochic River

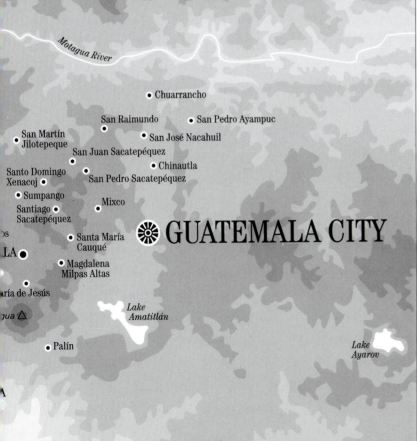

Rabinal
San Miguel Chicaj
SALAMÁ

CHUACÚS MOUNTAINS

baj

Motagua River

Chuarrancho
San Raimundo
San Pedro Ayampuc
San Martín Jilotepeque
San José Nacahuil
San Juan Sacatepéquez
Santo Domingo Xenacoj
Chinautla
San Pedro Sacatepéquez
Sumpango
Mixco
Santiago Sacatepéquez
GUATEMALA CITY
Santa María Cauqué
Magdalena Milpas Altas
ría de Jesús
Lake Amatitlán
jua
Lake Ayarov
Palín
LA
os

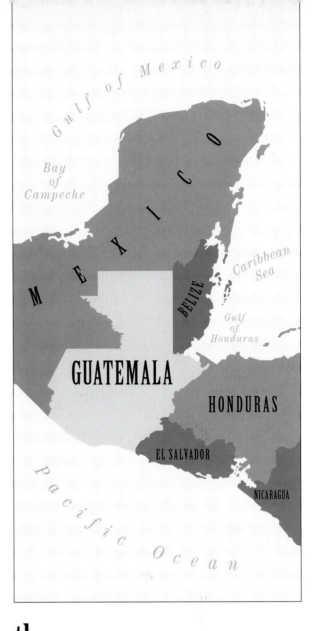

Gulf of Mexico
Bay of Campeche
MEXICO
Caribbean Sea
BELIZE
Gulf of Honduras
GUATEMALA
HONDURAS
Pacific Ocean
EL SALVADOR
NICARAGUA

the Highlands of Guatemala

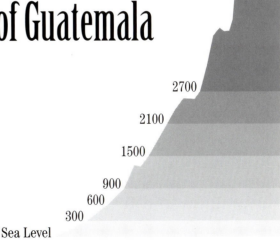

3600
2700
2100
1500
900
600
300
Sea Level

ELEVATION IN METERS

Map showing settlement of the Guatemalan highlands during the Classic period (A.D. 250-900).

CHAPTER 1

Maya Costume and Culture in the Guatemalan Highlands

T he costume of the Guatemalan highland people is rooted partly in the ancient culture of the Maya, and partly in the transformations that occurred in that culture as a result of the Spanish Conquest. In order to understand the contexts that produced highland costume of the 1960s, one needs to have a sense of the long sweep of Maya history.

A proto-Maya culture emerged in the lowlands of southern Mexico and Central America at least 11,000 years ago. The earliest occupants of this area lived as migrant hunters and gatherers, but by the beginning of the Preclassic Period (2000 B.C.), they were practicing agriculture, making pottery, and trading for scarce and regional materials such as obsidian, jade, and salt. Mayan languages gradually differentiated until there were more than twenty separate but related languages in the area of present-day Guatemala. Although linguistically differentiated, these Maya groups retained a strong core of shared culture.[1]

The flowering of Maya high civilization, known as its Classic Period, took place in the Petén lowlands of Guatemala, and parts of Chiapas, Campeche, and Quintana Roo, in Mexico (map, opposite). Lasting from approximately A.D. 250-900, this civilization produced elaborate settlements, public architecture, monumental carvings adorned with advanced hieroglyphic writings, extensive trade, and an accurate knowledge of mathematics and astronomy. At the head of a sharply stratified society stood the ruler, surrounded by aristocrats who controlled trade, religion, and war, and whose lives are depicted on the Classic sculpture performing ceremonies or taking captives. Below them was a class of craftsmen and occupational specialists. The lives — and clothing — of the elite were documented in monumental carvings. Those of the common people were less well documented, but we know that they lived humbly and paid tribute to their lords.

By A.D. 1000, for reasons which are not clear, the Maya high civilization had collapsed. The cities were largely abandoned and the population had decreased. New centers arose in the northern highlands, especially in the Yucatán, and dominated the area. As in the south, the nobles controlled politics, commerce, and religion, craftspeople and minor merchants formed a middle class, and the common people farmed *milpas* (cornfields). These centers did not, however, attain the degree of central control or elaborate culture of the high civilization.[2]

In the late Classic and Postclassic Periods, the Guatemalan highlands absorbed many influences from the outside — often from what is now Mexico. Trade was one agent of culture contact and change; warfare was another. In 1524, Pedro de Alvarado arrived with his small army and proceeded, on behalf of the Spanish crown, to conquer the area now known as Guatemala.

At the time of the Conquest, the highlands were dominated by the Quiché. Prior to Alvarado's arrival, the Quiché had expanded their dominion, pushing back the Mam people of Huehuetenango. They were also at war with the Cakchiquel and the Tzutujil, people who spoke languages closely related to Quiché, and with whom the Quiché had aligned themselves in earlier wars. When Alvarado's army invaded the Guatemalan highlands, they found allies. Cakchiquel and Tzutujil peoples, resentful of Quiché domination, willingly joined the conquistadors, just as the Tlaxcalans had allied themselves with Cortés in the Mexican highlands. Some say that many of the Maya who fought with Cortés and Alvarado felt they were fighting for liberation from oppression by their neighbors rather than in aid of the Spaniards. Thus small bands of Spaniards were able to conquer and take control of the highlands in spite of fierce resistance.[3]

The impact of Spanish control was great and its effects were far-ranging. The Spaniards built cities and designed them to a European plan, with a church dominating a central plaza. Above all, they profoundly altered the lives of the indigenous people. Maya living in scattered settlements were brought to towns so that they could be controlled, taxed, and indoctrinated. Maya labor was exploited for colonial ends. Hand in hand with the colonial administration came its most effective agent of control, the Catholic church. With local labor, churches were constructed throughout the highlands, and Spanish friars proceeded to convert the so-called "pagans." In the face of these cataclysmic changes, the inherited rank that had characterized Maya society and costume before the Conquest did not survive.[4]

A Reconfigured World

More profound for Maya culture than any other single change was the transformation of the belief system. The religion that grew from the Maya encounter with their Spanish conquerors was a syncretic mixture of European Catholic and ancient Maya beliefs. Its formal aspects revolved around the Catholic Godhead, the Virgin Mary, and the Saints. At the same time, many features of Maya religion, being compatible with those of sixteenth-century Spanish Catholicism, syncretized easily: for example, drinking and dancing at religious fiestas, the adornment of idols for public procession, fasting and abstention from sexual relations before holy days, the confession of sins, and the use of multiple holy names were common to both religions. There is ample evidence that the fusions were not involuntary.[5]

Certain features not familiar to Spaniards survived as well, including the Prehispanic calendar, the practice of divination, and, at least in limited form for a short time, bloodletting and animal sacrifice. In this blended religion, various ancient deities, such as nature gods controlling the weather, still commanded attention. Prayers could be addressed to a saint at the church altar and, in almost the same terms, to a Maya deity at a shrine in the mountains. At the same time, the Catholic saints themselves were Mayanized. *Santos* would often be dressed, for example, in the local village costume, as can still be seen today (fig. 1). These practices as they evolved were not a series of isolated acts, traceable to one past or another. Rather they formed an integrated network of practices, deeply felt, carefully observed, and central to the Maya community.[6]

Cofradías. As part of their effort to support and encourage Catholic practice in the highlands, the colonial missionaries introduced religious brotherhoods, *cofradías*, which became central to the institutional structure of village life. At first, New World *cofradía* chapters were located only in urban areas and had a Spanish membership. They were modeled after their Spanish counterparts and functioned as mutual support groups (members helping each other in times of need) and also maintained the cult of the patron saint. As early as 1570, however, *cofradías* were starting to be established for the Maya (in Chiapas, for instance). They were often eagerly embraced — in part, as a result of the amazing zeal displayed by Christian missionaries and the profound religious character of the pre-Conquest Maya. By the seventeenth century the *cofradías* had become widespread and their primary function had shifted from self-help to the cult of the saints.[7]

In the 1960s, although traditional religion with its *cofradía* activity was losing ground in some areas to Protestant sects and other forces, it was still strong. The *cofradías* were still dedicated to the care of saint figures, *santos*, to be clothed, venerated, and paraded on festival days (fig. 2). And so it generally continues today. Any man who wants to gain respect in his community must serve several ranks in one or more *cofradías*. The brotherhoods vary greatly from place to place, but all are rigidly hierarchical. In some towns, the *cofradía* includes female participants, while in others, wives often have important ceremonial roles (women's offices, titles, and duties differ substantially from one area to another). Other family members may be involved as well — for example cooking ritual food and dressing saints' figures.

Cofradía involvement is a major financial commitment, for a great deal of money must be expended on a host of ceremonial expenses such as food, liquor, flowers, and candles. Not the least of these is the cost of the special ceremonial textiles which are obligatory for the *cofradía* official, and can serve to identify his or her status in the community. The church mass, the rental of performance masks and costumes, the hiring of a dance teacher, and the fireworks that mark every phase of the special celebrations are costly as well. Extensive outlays of time and money for the *cofradía* help to build status, although the profits are not always passed on to the Maya community.

1. Santos in the church in Santiago Atitlán, dressed in local village costume.

2. *Cofradía festival in Sololá.*

3. Men at a gathering of municipal officers from Todos Santos. Two (one at far left, one at center) wear Ladino Western-style clothing; the others wear the traditional traje of Todos Santos.

Maya or Ladino? A Question of Identity. The Mayas' adoption of the cultural elements brought by the Spaniards was highly selective. The ultimate question was whether to remain Maya at all. Even from the early days of the Conquest some Maya, frequently those with an admixture of European blood, embraced the ways of the conquerors rather than those of their own people. They wore European-style clothing, lived in European-style houses, spoke Spanish, aspired to literacy, and forsook their heritage. Europeanized Maya, stratified on the basis of birth and wealth, were generally accorded a higher social status. They became what is now termed *Ladino*, and the process of "Ladinoization" continues today (fig. 3).[8]

Nevertheless, in the 1960s a vast number of highland people had retained their Maya identity. Wherever they had adopted elements of European culture and religion, they had "Mayanized" them. In contrast to the urbanized Ladinos, who looked outward to the national center and embraced change, the Maya remained strongly attached to their land, their *milpas*, and their collective traditions or *costumbre*. Ladinos might be farmers and value their land, but such farming was not essential to their identity. For the Maya, however, to be a man was to grow corn; that was fundamental to the Maya identity.[9]

The individual also had a public duty to celebrate the saints and observe the holy days, to serve in the *cofradías* and/or civilian posts, and to respect the elders. Within this larger context were the myriad acts of custom and ritual that synthesized the spiritual life and helped maintain the community. Of these acts, the most visible was the wearing of traditional costume, or *traje*.

Impact of the Conquest on Costume

Like their religious practices, the clothing traditions of the Maya underwent substantial change in the wake of the Conquest. Some changes were the direct result of colonial and church policies. Although the Crown professed disinterest in traditional native dress, this did not extend to permitting what was perceived as indecent exposure. The sole garment of lower-rank Maya men in Prehispanic times was the loincloth. This lack of covering was unacceptable to the Spaniards and legs were soon concealed in various styles of trousers. Even before the conquest of Guatemala, the Spanish crown had dictated — in a 1513 amendment to the Laws of Burgos — how the colonized people of the Americas should dress: "Also we order and command that within two years the men and women shall go about clad." In 1618 this was reiterated by King Philip III, perhaps indicating that the first laws had not been observed. At the same time, the crown seems to have forbidden the use of certain garments. Until the end of the sixteenth century, indigenous people of ordinary rank were not permitted to wear Spanish styles, though chiefs *(caciques)* and elders *(principales)* were sometimes granted that right.[10]

The church influenced costume development in two respects. First, it was especially concerned with promoting decency, and passed ordinances regulating dress. For the sake of cost, clothing should be without adornment or color and made at home to save tailoring expense. To prevent jealousy and discord, all dresses were to conform to all others. In Michoacán, Mexico, Bishop Quiroga passed an ordinance that clothes should be white, clean, and modest. As all over Latin America, the Bishop stipulated that women's heads should be covered with a veil of white cotton especially for church attendance. Thus in general the church encouraged modest attire. At the same time, special costumes were developed in the context of the religious fraternities, for use by *cofradía* officials and sometimes their spouses on festival days. Not surprisingly, these were the most elaborate costumes to evolve in the centuries following the Conquest.[11]

Changes in dress code were also instituted locally. In 1880, for example, a Ladino official ordered the men of Chichicastenango to wear shirts under their decorative woolen jackets; the omission was penalized with a fine. At about the same time, in the town of Salamá, a German physician noted that a "chief" had forbidden the wearing of the native dress in this town. Women were ordered to dress as Ladinas; this probably meant blouse with sleeves, full gathered skirt and possibly sandals. (Maya dress is not worn in Salamá now.) Sometimes change was reinforced even within the household. Osborne reports, for example, that "…a young woman whose mother wore a tight skirt [a native, wrapped skirt] said her father wished her to be civilized and therefore obliged her to wear the pleated skirt."[12]

Some alterations in dress were the by-products of new materials (wool, linen, silk) and new technology, which brought differences in style, costume construction, and decoration. Steel needles, scissors, and spinning wheels all greatly facilitated textile processes. So did the foot-powered treadle loom, which allowed the weaver to warp many yards at a time and to increase weaving speed and fabric width. Scissors were useful and the existence of a needle factory in Mexico City only sixty years after the Conquest suggests that the steel sewing needle presented advantages over agave spines.[13]

In some cases, indigenous people no doubt altered their dress voluntarily in imitation of the ruling class, for they had the opportunity to see Spanish clothing styles, especially in urban areas. During the first few decades of the Conquest, clothing and textiles made up a very large part of the merchandise in ships coming from Spain. Not only did six or seven Spanish tailors come with the first conquistadors, but ship after heavily laden ship arrived. Some 2,805 vessels sailed to the New World between 1504 and 1555 alone. While these clothes were intended for the Spaniards, not the native people, they would have been widely seen and possibly perceived as models of clothing by the latter.[14]

At some time probably following the Conquest, highland dress became village-specific. Each village acquired its own unique *traje* (costume), with stylistic features distinguishing it. When and how this happened has been the subject of much speculation. Many claim that village dress styles were mandated by Spanish officials and missionaries. Others theorize that colonial landowners *(encomenderos)* forced the Maya to wear distinctive clothing. While this would account for the local differences from town to town, there are no known records to prove that this was the case.[15]

Spanish colonization did not have equal impact on both genders. Women's dress survived the Conquest without substantial alteration. Men's dress, on the other hand, changed early under the influence from Spanish clothing, and the "traditional" *traje* that emerged was as syncretic in its way as the highland Catholicism described above. Detective work, presented in Chapter Two, is needed to trace the origin of certain men's costume elements whose trails lead back to northern provinces of Spain.

4. *Female, probably of lower rank, depicted on a Late Classic period Jaina ceramic sculpture, wearing sarong-like garment.*

© Copyright 1985 Justin Kerr.

5. *Woman of high rank, possibly a ruler, depicted on a typical panel that may have come from El Cayo in the Usumacinta Valley.*

The Unbroken Traditions of Women's Dress

Most native garments worn by highland Guatemalan women today owe their shapes to Prehispanic Maya costume. The search for origins need not be confined to that dress worn at the time of the Conquest, for their antecedents can be seen in the various media (vase painting, monumental sculpture, codices and ceramic sculpture) depicting women of earlier periods in the Maya past. Although the Maya high civilization collapsed in most areas around A.D. 900, certain elements of feminine costume have persisted relatively unchanged, along with the various Maya languages, world view and mythology.

Remnants of that high civilization, discovered by archaeologists beginning in the nineteenth century, provide evidence of the Prehispanic costume of Maya women. The great monuments and sculptures from the Classic Period depict the rulers and the elite, commemorating ritual events such as royal accession, celebrations of success in warfare, royal bloodletting, and other significant occasions. Such scenes portray high ranking retainers of the court, male warriors, and captives, often ready for sacrifice and stripped of garments. High-ranking males depicted in these sculptures are so heavily adorned that it is often difficult to find their faces or interpret the elements of their clothing. Female clothing, however, is somewhat clearer. Typical is a panel that may have come from El Cayo in the Usumacinta Valley (fig. 5), showing a woman of high rank, possibly a ruler. Despite the ornateness of her jewelry and headdress, her clothing is visible.[16]

6. *Woman depicted on Yaxchilan lintel 32, clad in a wide huipil with what appears to be an all-over brocaded design. The concentric diamonds recall present-day patterns used in the costumes of Santa María de Jesús.*

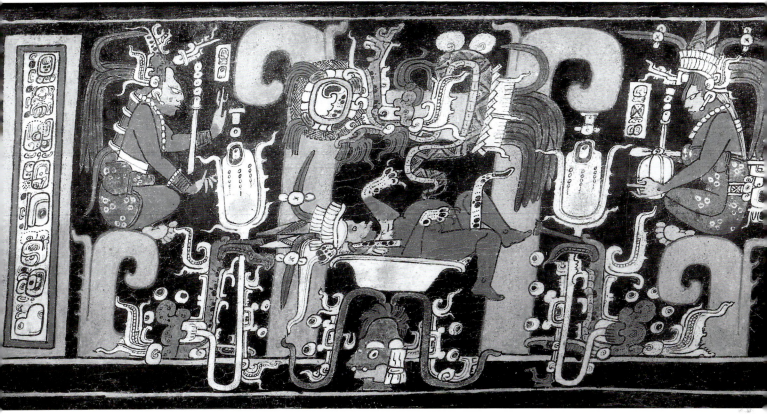

7. *Male and female figures (far left and far right) on a black background vase, dressed in patterned cloth that may be tie-dyed.*

It is clear from such monuments that the basic garments of female royalty were the huipil and skirt. The former was (and in most places remains) an untailored sleeveless dress or blouse, the length and width of which depended on occasion, regional preference, and loom width. The classic Maya huipil, made of fine cotton, was long enough to show a few inches of the long skirt beneath. It was heavily decorated with motifs and a border at the bottom; we do not know whether such decorations were made in the weaving or embroidered after the textile was finished. Few larger pieces survive; but cloth fragments probably dating from Middle to Late Classic and found in the Sacred Cenote of Chichén Itzá prove that the Maya were capable weavers. Monumental carvings show motifs which to some degree resemble supplemental weft brocade. For example, lintel 32 at Yaxchilán (fig. 6) shows concentric diamond patterns reminiscent of those appearing at Santa María de Jesús (fig. 269). A further similarity is noted at the seam areas of the huipil. Like the *randa* on modern huipils, the seam is overworked with decorative stitches (fig. 8).[17]

Women of lower rank do not often appear on monumental sculpture. Therefore we must turn to other media, such as ceramics, for such depictions. On these, it seems that one of the more common garments was a "sarong" style skirt. It appeared on pottery figurines (fig. 4) and on at least one black background vase (fig. 7). The female seen at the far right of the vase painting is dressed in fabric with circular patterns that may have been created by tie-dyeing.[18]

Sometimes the skirt appears as the sole garment, leaving the upper body uncovered. On other occasions, again on a painted cylindrical vessel, we see a wide sash or fitted

8. *High-ranking woman seen on the Bonampak Stela 2 (circa A.D. 790), with decorative seam much like the decorative join, or randa, seen on many present-day highland Guatemalan costumes.*

9. *Female depicted on a painted cylindrical vessel from Late Classic period (exact provenance unknown) wearing a wide band of cloth knotted between the breasts, unlike any extant huipil.*

band of cloth, which Schele and Miller define in *Blood of the Kings* as an "upper body huipil," with the ends of the cloth knotted between the breasts. This garment (fig. 9) is unlike any that still exists, and it differs in every way from a huipil: it is form-fitting, knotted in the front, and does not extend over the shoulder.

Whether elite women wore belts is unclear. If they did, their belts do not show under the huipil, so we cannot compare them with those worn now. Today's belts and sashes are intended to support the wrapped skirt; but it appears that sashes were not used for that purpose in the Classic Period.[19]

There is some evidence that the rectangular shawl, an item now worn by women of almost all Guatemalan towns, has Prehispanic origins. A shawl-like garment is depicted on a Late Classic period figurine from Alta Verapaz, illustrated in Clancy et al. Another such garment is visible on one of the Lagartero figurines illustrated in Morris. This proves at least that shawls were not unknown in Prehispanic times; perhaps their use was widespread.[20]

The distinctive woman's hairwrap *(cinta)* once worn in at least forty-four highland towns probably also has origins in Prehispanic headpieces. In fact, the similarities between the headdresses seen on Precolumbian Maya figurines and those worn by contemporary Maya women suggest that the *cinta*, like the huipil, has Prehispanic origins, although the evidence is not entirely clear. The elaborate, feathered ornamental tuft depicted in Maya monumental sculptures is surely not the source.

On the other hand, many small pottery figurines, probably depicting women of more ordinary status, show hairstyles reminiscent of those seen today in the highlands (figs. 10-13). This is true of several figurines yielded by the Lagartero refuse find in Chiapas, which show women's heads with square-cut "bangs" or hair parted in the center, and surmounted by turban-like rolls which could well be wrapped hair. One head, especially, seems to demonstrate the ribbon-wrapped hair of a *cinta*. An example from Quiriguá in Guatemala (fig. 10) looks very much like the *cinta* still occasionally worn in Santiago Atitlán (fig. 11). Two other small, simple pottery pieces show headdresses which resemble more baroque modern examples. One, a complete figurine, is wearing a knotted, puffy headdress (fig. 12) like that currently worn in Nebaj (fig. 104). The other, a head fragment, appears to have huge tassels falling from a puffy headdress (fig. 13). This is reminiscent of the *cinta* of Santa María Chiquimula (fig. 231). Wrapped braids reminiscent of hairwraps in many highland areas appear on a picture of an engaged girl from Aragón in northern Spain (fig. 14). This shows that different cultures can arrive independently at similar solutions to a problem.[21]

10. *Figurine, probably from the Late Classic period, from Quiriguá, wearing a headwrap much like the one still worn occasionally in Santiago Atitlán.*

11. *Women in the market at Santiago Atitlán wearing headdresses much like the one depicted in a ceramic figurine probably of the Late Classic period.*

12. *Prehispanic female depicted in ceramic figurine from Guatemala with a knotted, puffy headdress like that worn currently in Nebaj (cf. fig. 163).*

13. *Ceramic fragment, possibly from Guatemala, showing a puffy headdress with huge tassels that fall beside the cheeks, reminiscent of the black head tie of Santa María Chiquimula.*

14. *Headdress of an engaged girl from Aragón, Spain, composed of wrapped braids remarkably like hairwraps in several highland areas.*

The Role of Weaving in the Maya Cosmos

Maya married couples consider themselves partners, yet each with a clearly defined sphere. That of the man is the *milpa*, the cornfield; that of the woman, the house with the many activities centered in it. Together they provide the essentials of food, clothing, and shelter for the family. Woman's domain includes the hearth with three stones on which cooking pots rest. In San Pedro la Laguna a baby girl's umbilical cord is placed under one of these stones so that she will stay home when she is grown. A boy's umbilical cord is hung in the granary near the corn so he will tend his field.[22]

In Quiché cosmology there are strong connections between the *milpa*, the house, and the textile. All have four corners and four sides, and all are reflections of the "skyearth": the four corners and sides bounding earth and sky. The emergence of the skyearth is recounted in the *Popul Vuh*, a repository of Quiché myth and ritual said to have been written by Quiché overlords shortly after the Conquest. This event is expressed in the language of textiles and, as Barbara and Dennis Tedlock have noted, can be "read as metaphor for weaving technology."[23]

Weaving, as one of the most important activities of women, has two patronesses in Maya cosmology. One is Ix Chebel Yax, wife of the principal deity, the creator. The other is the moon goddess Ixchel (or Ix Chel), known in the Yucatán and other Maya areas. The relationship between these two is unclear, but both are said to have been the first weavers and neither is actually said to have taught weaving to Maya women. Both seem to share a number of attributes, being patronesses of childbirth, procreation, and medicine, and both are known as wanton. While there are in the codices numerous illustrations of goddesses, there are no sculptures, so far as I can find, portraying either of these deities in the process of weaving. There is, however, a series of Jaina pottery figurines depicting females at their looms (fig. 17).[24]

There are indications that weaving had religious significance in Prehispanic times, traces of which persist into the present. According to J.E.S. Thompson, the Prehispanic Maya considered weaving a sacred undertaking. Prehispanic Quiché Maya stone deity figures were clothed in actual textiles (like the *santos* of modern times). The same was true of Aztec sacred images. An infant Aztec girl was surrounded during her first important ritual bath by "all the equipment of a woman": a little reed basket, a spindle whorl, a spinning bowl, skeins of thread, and the weaving batten or beater (fig. 15). Although the purpose of this juxtaposition is not clear, we can extrapolate from a similar ritual performed in modern times. In San Pedro la Laguna during the 1970s, a girl child was given a ritual bath on the eighth day following birth, after which the sticks of a loom were held over her head so she might become a good weaver.[25]

Further evidence from the present, although scattered, is impossible to discount. One of the most telling pieces of information comes from Chichicastenango in the 1930s. Ruth Bunzel writes that skill in weaving was women's counterpart to men's public service, thus an almost inescapable religious and civic duty. In Chichicastenango during the 1930s a woman's weaving tools were buried with her. In the 1960s, highland Guatemalan women still offered a prayer before starting a new textile.[26]

Beyond the ritual significance of weaving, clothing itself has ritual importance at festivals and in rites of passage such as births, weddings, and funerals. Clothing was the traditional gift of godparent to godchild in several Guatemalan towns. At weddings in Chichicastenango, according to one report, a father was expected to give his daughter a trousseau of five complete, new costumes. Another report from the same town states that the girl takes with her only her clothes when she leaves her father's house for her husband's. In several areas of Guatemala, a woman from one town who marries a man from another town retains the garments of her natal place. Given that town-specific costume testifies to civic solidarity, one must wonder why a woman and, in some cases also her daughter, keep the old costume. It is possible that, at least in the Quiché Maya area, the custom might have Prehispanic origins.[27]

In several areas of Guatemala, new clothes are made for burials. In Colotenango, as a woman approaches old age she usually prepares an *ajuar* or dowry for death — a costume in which to be buried. In Cobán, although much latitude is allowed in daily dress at present, a woman still feels she must be buried in traditional dress: handwoven white huipil, blue skirt, and striped shawl. In addition, all available space in the coffin of the deceased is filled with her belongings, especially clothing. This happens in other areas as well, for example Sololá (fig. 16). In Cobán, so important

15. The paraphernalia of weaving surrounded an infant Aztec girl during her first ritual bath, as depicted in the Florentine Codex. "And if a girl was to be bathed, they prepared for her all the equipment of women — the spinning whorl, the batten, the reed basket, the spinning bowl, the skeins, her little skirt and her little shift."

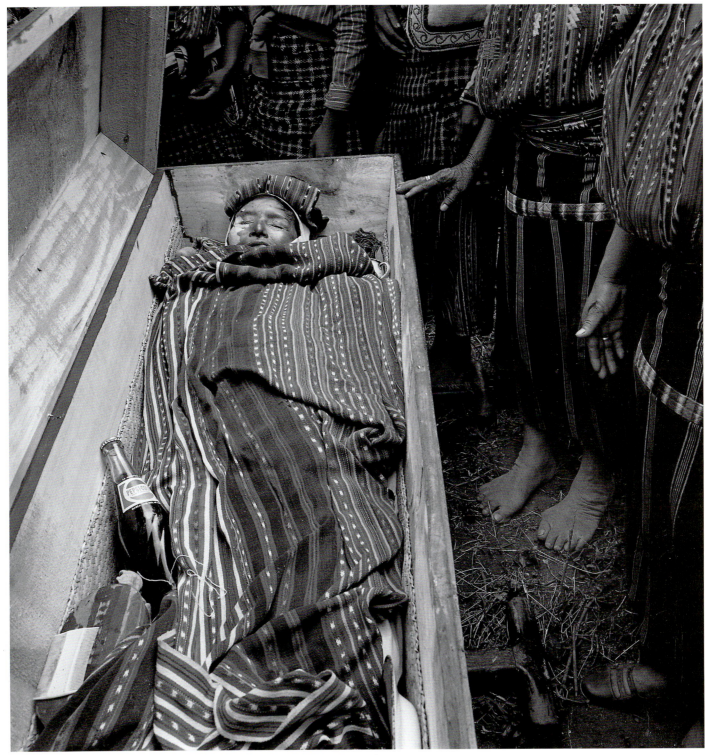

16. Sololá woman buried with her garments.

is the burial of the deceased's clothing that garments which cannot fit in the coffin are buried at the end of the novena (the nine days of prayer) in a separate grave dug behind the ranch house.[28]

Considering the importance accorded to woven clothes and weaving, it is not surprising that until recently in almost all areas of Guatemala it was said that a girl was hardly marriageable without weaving skill. Indeed in the first half of this century, at least in one town in Huehuetenango department, girls who could not weave were assumed by the parents of boys to be either stupid or badly trained. Until recently when ready-made clothes were available in large quantities, families depended on their women to keep them clothed.

17. *Jaina pottery figurine depicting a female at what appears to be backstrap loom like those still used in the Guatemala highlands.*

Weaving Technology

The Backstrap Loom. Before the Conquest it was women who made all the clothing for themselves and their families on the backstrap loom. After the Conquest the Spaniards introduced new modes of production and brought some men into weaving. And yet, in the 1960s, some of the most beautiful clothes (including most of the pieces seen in this volume) were still being made by women on the backstrap loom, which continues in use up to the present. The loom is called, in Spanish, *palos* (sticks) or sometimes *telar de palitos* (loom of little sticks). It is also known as *telar de cinta* (literally, belt loom).

The backstrap loom has no fixed parts and only becomes a loom when it is strung with the warp threads that will be woven into cloth. Its permanent parts consist merely of five essential sticks and the belt which passes behind the weaver when the loom is in use. Thus while capable of producing elaborate textiles, it is a relatively simple and inexpensive device, whose parts can be cut and whittled in less than an hour. The only other prerequisites are a stable place to fasten one end of the loom and adequate space to extend the warp. Being portable, it can be used inside or outside in the courtyard, where the women of the household may gather to weave with friends. When the weaver is ready to stop her weaving, she merely rolls it up and puts it aside, out of the way — a very practical feature in a small house.[29]

On the *telar de cinta*, the end beams hold the warp threads under tension in a very simple manner. If the weaver wishes a textile finished on all four sides, she attaches a strong cord to each of the end beams and passes her warp around this cord at both ends, rather than around the beams. The loom is attached by rope to a house post or a tree and the other end is held by the backstrap. With the strap around her hips, the weaver may kneel, sit on her haunches, sit on the ground with legs stretched out in front, or even, although rarely, stand up. Whatever her position, she uses the backstrap to maintain tension on the warp threads. After weaving an inch or two to set the warp, she reverses the loom, fastening the woven end to a post or tree, and then begins weaving from the end now near her. Ultimately she reaches the part first woven. Using successively smaller bobbins and batten, she weaves in the weft, at last using a needle for the final threads. Judicious use of the fingernails can almost obliterate the loose section of weaving that results from the final rows not being able to be firmly packed. In some towns women make little effort to achieve this result, leaving a section with a threadbare appearance.[30]

This technique, native to Latin America, produces a textile that is finished not just at the side selvedges, but on all four sides — hence, a web. The textile can thus be woven to size; and instead of cutting the warp off the loom the weaver can simply untie the end cords holding it to the end sticks. Without having to cut cloth, a weaver can combine various sizes of finished four-selvedge webs to form almost any Guatemalan costume part.

A weaver's training is not a formal education, but rather a process of enculturation which probably starts at around the age of eight. Younger girls do not generally have the physical development or endurance to weave even a small cloth. A girl is taught informally, in a familiar setting, with one-on-one instruction — usually by her mother or a female relative (fig. 18). Since she has been present at weaving situations since birth and has watched her mother at work almost as long, she is already well prepared for the learning process. She is permitted to start a small textile and proceed as far as she can by imitation. Lessons are given primarily by demonstration. Rather than verbally correcting an error the mother usually takes the loom to demonstrate the correct technique which the child then attempts. By age twelve to fourteen a girl is usually a competent weaver.[31]

Not all women in every village weave, and there are surely many reasons for this, economic and otherwise. By 1960, some towns had abandoned traditional dress. In other areas still retaining the *traje*, women invested much energy in vegetable growing activities to the neglect of their weaving skills. Whether or not they weave, however, women take a keen interest in the quality of textiles. Reports from several areas mention that women and girls spend a great deal of time discussing weaving and textiles. Judgements are frequently made on the basis of the firmness and regularity of weave, or the number of decorative motifs executed.[32]

A Guatemalan highland weaver's training tends to foster continuity of tradition and repetition of learned models. To conform to traditional patterns is to do something the "true" way. Our assessment of the degree of conformity that exists in Maya women's textiles may be exaggerated, however. A more accurate statement comes from Wilhite,

18. Woman and girl, probably mother and daughter, sitting together at their backstrap looms. Town unknown.

19. Market day in Santiago Atitlán.

who observed weavers in two Cakchiquel villages: "Designs are traditional and not subject to innovation although considerable variation is allowed." Nevertheless, in the 1960s and even more recently, people in a costume-weaving town on market day appeared homogeneous in their dress (fig. 19). Certainly no two huipils were exactly alike despite their similarities; how much variation was due to regional differences and how much to independent creativity is difficult to assess. A recent study of the town of Colotenango points out that, in addition to design differences from town to town, a local observer can distinguish differences between the dress of a town and its hamlet or *aldea.* Thus it is likely that on market day every woman would recognize the town and hamlet affiliation of every other woman, simply by her dress.[33]

20. *A Todos Santos man at a foot loom.*

The Foot Loom. Shortly after the Conquest, the Spaniards established small textile factories *(obrajes)* which were outfitted with foot-powered treadle looms, or foot looms. They employed local men — often forcibly — to operate the looms. In using men rather than women as weavers, the colonizers followed a Spanish model of industry. While the foot loom is not mechanically powered, it enables the weaver to produce cloth in considerably greater quantity than with a backstrap loom. As Anawalt points out, the pattern established by the Spaniards has perpetuated men in the role of quantity weavers of commercial cloth (fig. 20), leaving home production of dress and household goods to women. Several thousand highland men, both Maya and Ladinos, chiefly in the departments of Totonicapán and Quezaltenango, derive most if not all of their income from this profession.[34]

A male weaver is usually born into the profession. He generally starts his weaving education at an early age, observing his father weaving and performing various related chores such as winding thread on bobbins, dyeing, or starching threads. A boy has to be near adult height, however, to reach the foot pedals. Male weavers used to serve an apprenticeship of two to seven years; more recently it is said to be from two to eighteen months.[35]

The quantity of garment yardage that can be woven in a day on a foot loom depends on the simplicity or elaboration of designs on the textile. Cloth is measured in *varas*, each *vara* being 33 inches long. In most towns, six *varas*, or 198 inches, are enough for one skirt length. A foot loom can hold a warp long enough for several skirt lengths, but often for economic reasons the weaver does not weave the entire warp before removing it from the loom and cutting into lengths. Rather, he finishes the six *varas* needed for one skirt, cuts them off and sells them; then he re-attaches the warp ends to the beam at the front of the loom and continues weaving.

On the same loom the weaver may work with individual shuttles to produce elaborate huipil designs (a process very much slower, of course, than plain weave). A special class of huipil is woven in quantity on the foot loom, often in styles reminiscent of one town or another, and sometimes in "generic" styles. Requiring less of an outlay in time and money than backstrap-woven huipils, the generic styles tend to be worn in towns where women don't weave, and elsewhere by those seeking an alternative to the traditional town-specific garment.

The Perseverance of Maya Culture

Guatemalan culture has been subject to change for millennia. A woman's costume, however, manifests the impact of the colonial encounter far less than that of her mate. Women's dress, though always evolving in color and design, retains age-old forms and evokes the continuity of Maya life in the highlands. Men's traditional *traje*, with its multiple debts to European costume, reflects a history of change and adaptation. In this volume we focus on the men's and women's costume as they existed during the 1960s, when the highland village seemed poised for a moment, before the latest onslaught of change. At the same time, we cannot help but contemplate the future.

For many years now, observers have deplored the changes in Guatemalan costume. Of the women's costumes known to exist in the 1960s, only a small number are still worn today. Traditional men's dress is even rarer; it is worn probably in no more than ten villages. One can expect that beautiful garments will continue to be lost and there will be further changes in Maya lives. Still, to put these changes in perspective, one has only to think what vicissitudes the Maya have weathered to reach this period with their essential spirit alive. Guatemala still presents a Maya face to the world.

No single reason can explain this persistence. In large part, the fact that Guatemala was peripheral to Mexico protected it from some of the worst Spanish pressures. Lacking mineral wealth, the land was rich only in manpower and fertile soil. Using these two assets, the Spaniards came to take land grants *(encomiendas)* and stayed to exploit the local resources. Most of these products were already traditional Maya industries, such as cochineal, indigo, cacao, and cotton. Others — the production of sugarcane and coffee and the mining of gold — were initiated by the Spaniards.

The Spaniards underestimated the past accomplishments of the Maya whose Classic period in the Petén was long gone, its monuments concealed by tropical growth. By the time of the Conquest, the Maya of Yucatán and those of the Guatemalan highlands, though strong foes, appeared less well organized politically and less economically advanced than their Aztec neighbors to the north. But heavy as the burden of Conquest was on the Maya, they had endured similar situations in the past. Throughout history, outsiders had invaded Maya society — some coming peacefully, to settle, and others as enemies, to conquer. Thus, in marked contrast to the Mexican Aztecs, they were accustomed to absorbing foreign influx.[36]

A further and perhaps more important reason for Maya persistence may be found in the cultural propensity for accepting new ideas in a non-exclusive, cumulative way. Madsen, like several authorities, has noted that the Maya "...retained paganism as the meaningful core of their religion which became incremented with varying degrees of Catholicism." Barbara Tedlock has said that the Quiché felt they did not need to resist innovations, "but that they should be added to older things rather than replacing them." This applies to new agricultural technology, which was added to traditional *milpa* techniques, as well as to new religious deities, which were added to the old. Tedlock expresses this best: "The net result of this attitude is that the burdens of time do not so much change as accumulate — even gods overthrown in previous ages remain a part of later pantheons." Thus geographical situation, relative Spanish indifference, and Maya adaptave abilities have combined to contribute to the survival of Maya culture. But what of the future?[37]

Almost fifteen years ago it was said that from two to six of every thousand Maya were found each year to forsake their heritage and to become Ladinos. The number is accelerating rapidly due to increased impingement from the outside world, and the massive displacement due to civil strife unanticipated fifteen years ago. One might think, therefore, that the future of the Maya is at risk.[38]

But those who deplore the passing of traditional native costume must be cautious about identifying Maya-ness only in terms of dress or even language alone. At one time these were reliable markers, and generally this is the case even today. Still, the Quiché of Momostenango, despite an almost total abandonment of traditional Maya dress, openly pursue their religious rites. The town has, it is said, more than ten thousand men and women known as day keepers *(ajk'ij)*, who acquire their calendar and divination knowledge from priest shamans. The Quiché will not lightly abandon ritual knowledge thoroughly understood by so large a body of people. It has, after all, survived the years since the Conquest.[39]

Just as the Maya have preserved the distinctive Maya calendar from generation to generation, so may they also continue to weave beautiful textiles into meaningful patterns, and shape them into dazzling garments — using new materials, colors, and styles to affirm the threads of identity.

Notes

1. The exact number of Maya languages depends on whether certain tongues are classified as languages or dialects, and linguists are not in agreement regarding many points of classification. We take Terrence Kaufman 1976 as our authority.

2. According to one theory Maya high civilization collapsed because the delicate lowland ecology could not support the dense population in some areas.

3. Archaeologists are still working on the problem of how Mexican influence might have come, whether directly, or from groups who settled in the Mexican Gulf coast area, and later continued their eastward trek. On the Spanish Conquest of Mexico and Guatemala, see Beals 1967 (p. 452) and Carmack 1986 (pp. 56,58).

4. H.F. Cline's essay in the *Handbook of Middle American Indians* (1972, vol. 12) is a good source of information on church policy in the colonial era. He remarks, "For historical reasons the Catholic Church was considered an arm of Spanish government, supreme in spiritual matters but subordinated to other organs for administrative concerns" (p. 26).

5. On syncretism, see Madsen 1967 (p. 370). This, in differing proportions, can be said of any Mesoamerican area. Citing H.G. Barnett, Madsen speaks of the "conscious adaptation" of alien forms to an indigenous counterpart (p. 369). La Farge 1947 (p. XI), Tedlock 1985 (pp. 43,149) and Carmack 1981 (p. 316) all add interesting amplification of this concept. Various Prehispanic customs are found in Orellana 1984 and J.E.S. Thompson 1972. The 16th-century Catholic customs are to be found in Christian (1981), a source pointed out to me by anthropologist John Watanabe (pers. com., July 1989).

6. Saints as represented in Central American Maya imagery differ from the intent of the Roman Catholic Church. Though scholarly interpretations vary, most agree that saints' images were intended primarily to arouse reverence and to render intelligible the attributes and appearance of the saint, especially to an illiterate congregation. Among Central American Maya, as among European peasants, the representation of the saint is perceived as the actual saint. Prayers are directed to the image, not to God through the saint. Sometimes the *santos* are even addressed in the local Mayan language as well. For example, according to John Watanabe, in Santiago Chimaltenango, Huehuetenango, the favorite image of Santiago, the town's patron saint, is prayed to in Mam (pers. com., July 1989). This strongly suggests the town's acceptance of Santiago as a Maya. For a good analysis of Maya cosmology, see Reina 1966.

7. For a description of *cofradías* in 17th-century Spain see MacLeod 1983b (pp. 64-67). Re *cofradías* in Spain today, see Foster 1960 (p. 183). Siegel 1941 (pp. 63-66) says, "As a matter of fact, religion was perhaps most vitally affected by the early impact of Spanish influences."

8. A decree of General Barrios (elected to the Guatemalan presidency in 1873) granted to those natives of San Pedro Sacatepéquez (SM) who would wear white cotton trousers and shirt the right to assume the name Ladino (Holleran 1949, p. 222). This decree was repealed in the 1930s. Regarding the status of Ladinos, see Lincoln 1945 (p. 66).

9. See Fuente 1967 (pp. 435-38), Maynard 1963 (p. 124), and Gillin 1957 on the contrast between Indian and Ladino value systems. The Maya "loves the land and feels himself less than a man if he doesn't have some available on which to work." (Gillin, p. 12). Typically the Maya feel that the variations between them and the Ladinos "represent a series of differences which are natural and impossible to eradicate, based on the different biological heredity" (Fuente, p. 435).

10. Regarding the impact of colonial policy on clothing, consult Charles Gibson 1964 and 1967. Writing not of the Maya but of the Aztecs, Gibson notes: "It was not the intention of Spaniards to interfere in the more prosaic aspects of native commodity production. Indian housing, clothing, and food all were features of a native substratum beneath the notice of colonists. However disruptive Spanish demands may have been in other respects, they required no fundamental transformations in these areas of native economy" (Gibson 1964, p. 335). See also Simpson 1960 (p. 44), who

cites amendments to the Law of Burgos. At the end of the 15th and throughout the 16th and 17th centuries the Crown, beset by debts incurred in wars, tried to limit the costs of upper class dress through sumptuary laws restricting the use of precious metals, costly embroidery and brocade.

11. See Arriaga Ochoa 1938 (pp. 53-54) regarding the policy of Bishop Quiroga.

12. Tax 1947 discusses dress ordinances in Chichicastenango in the 1880s (see f. 240). See Stoll 1886 regarding the town of Salamá at that same era. On the young women whose father wanted her to be "civilized," see Osborne 1975 (p. 73).

13. Benítez 1946 is a good resource on imports, resources, and technology introduced by the Spaniards (see p. 28, re the needle factory).

14. On the tailors who accompanied the first conquistadors, see Benítez 1946 (pp. 27-38). See Torre Revello 1943 (pp. 773-80) for an analysis of what the ships brought. Ships' manifests exist for 33 of them, and clothing and textiles make up by far the largest class of merchandise listed. Imported garments ranged from *apretadores* (waistcoats) to *zapatos* (shoes) of various kinds and included caps, stockings, shirts, cloaks, gloves, belts, etc. The tailors were supplied with an international assortment of rich fabrics in varying colors.

15. See Osborne 1975 (p. 211) re opinions as to the origins of the village-specific *traje*.

16. The panels illustrated in Schele & Miller 1986 (eg. p. 76) are a rich source of information.

17. Coggins & Shane 1984 show some interesting cloth fragments (e.g. p. 143).

18. The theory that the circular pattern may indicate tie-dye is that of Bruhns 1988, whose article is a good source for illustrations of ceramics (e.g. pp. 111-15). Bruhns also suggests that such designs might identify palace servants.

19. An interesting Late Classic figurine (A.D. 700-800) from Alta Verapaz shows a woman in a wrapped, unbelted skirt. One edge is tucked in, just as it is today at Santiago Atitlán, where skirts are also worn without belts. Walter F. Morris, Jr. Ms. (betw. pp. 4 & 5) states that there were no feminine belts before the Conquest.

20. See Clancy et al. 1985 (p. 137, fig. 65) and Morris Ms. (fig. 4). While most shawls worn in the highlands today are long and narrow, those of Zunil and Sololá, for example, are exceptional, being large and nearly square.

21. For hairwraps depicted on Lagartero figurines, see Ekholm 1979 (fig. 10-2, a,b,c,g,j). Mary Butler 1935 (fig. 4G) shows only one.

22. On ritual for girl children in San Pedro la Laguna in the 1970s, see Lois Paul 1974 (p. 284).

23. An excellent resource on Quiché mythology is Tedlock & Tedlock 1985 (see pp. 127-28 on the emergence of the "skyearth").

24. According to Irmgard Johnson (1959, vol. I, p. 439), Ix Chebel Yax is the daughter of Ixchel and patroness of embroidery. Hilda Delgado Pang is the excavator of one of the Jaina figures; she does not identify them as deities, though in the same article she illustrates an Aztec weaving deity/patroness. Her 1969 article is an excellent source of information on Maya cosmology (see p. 148 on Ix Chebel Yax). Pang notes the presence of birds on the stump to which the Jaina figurines have attached their looms as well as on the tree to which the Aztec patroness has fastened hers. J.E.S.Thompson 1972 (p. 337) offers iconographic information which might possibly have some bearing: various birds were frequently offered as sacrifices and a bird was perched on each of the four world directional trees, thus on the supports of the earth and sky. The codices — documents written by Maya for Maya and collected in the colonial period — are of course invaluable in reconstructing Maya life at the time of the Conquest.

25. See J.E.S. Thompson 1966 (p. 211) on sacredness of weaving in Prehispanic Maya culture. Sahagún 1950-69, vol. 6, deals with Aztec material (see pp. 201,205). See L. Paul 1974 (p. 284) for a description of the ritual bath in San Pedro La Laguna.

26. Bunzel 1967 and Tax 1947 are basic sources of information on Chichicastenango in the 1930s. See Bunzel (p. 61) and Tax (f. 575). J.E.S. Thompson 1966 (p. 211) describes the pre-weaving prayer still offered in the '60s.

27. According to Robert Carmack 1981 (p. 63), the early Quiché held women who married into a lineage as outsiders, calling them *c'ulel* or enemies. Perhaps they were forced to maintain their natal costume as well.

28. See Tax 1947 (p. 537) and Bunzel 1967 (p. 28) regarding trousseau customs in Chichicastenango. On the *ajuar* or death costume, see Mejía de Rodas et al. 1987 (p. 122) and Dieseldorff 1984 (p. 33).

29. The batten or sword used to separate the shed and to pack the weft threads tightly is usually well worked. Bunzel 1952 (p. 62) discusses the parts of the loom and the availability of battens in the early '50s. Hagan 1972 (p. 40) mentions prices in the late 1960s, and states that a backstrap loom complete with spare loom sticks, batten, warping frame, rope, and belt and even spindle whorl could cost as little as Q5.38 — that is, considerably less than the foot loom. In the 1950s, the supply of battens for Chichicastenango was made somewhere in the mountains by only two or three experts. For further information on the technology of weaving and the backstrap loom, see the many good descriptions in: O'Neale 1945; Bjerregaard 1977; M. Anderson 1978; Sperlich & Sperlich 1980.

30. It is not necessary to reverse the loom after weaving the first inch or two, and while most weavers do so, it is not universal. The Tzutujil weavers of Santiago Atitlán only do so when weaving infants' garments, which according to Prechtel & Carlsen 1988 (p. 124) shows the close connection between the backstrap weaving and birth in that town.

31. Childs & Greenfield 1980, Greenfield & Lave 1982, Nash 1958, and Wagley 1949 all discuss the training of weavers. An element of fear of embarrassment is involved in this hands-off teaching system. The learner fears being thought stupid and is also reluctant to annoy or challenge the teacher (Greenfield & Lave, p. 187). Public reprimand shames the learner (Nash, p. 30). Wagley relates that in Santiago Chimaltenango a mother said her daughter made many mistakes at first in weaving but she would not correct the beginner" (p. 34). She learned by watching me weave," the mother stated.

32. In Palín in the early 1960s about half the Central Pokomam women wove and no opprobrium seems to have been attached to the non-weavers because there was general recognition that not all women have the personality nor the ability to weave (Maynard 1963, pp. 185-6). In Panajachel, for example, as long ago as 1935 only 63 women in that town of 133 families knew how to weave (Tax 1953, p. 152). Tax does not give the exact figure when he writes further, "Not all the women who know how to weave know how to work the designs on the woman's huipils, a weaver at this point in the process finds a specialist to complete her huipil." With respect to the question of fashion, coauthor West and I questioned a young woman about the use of lurex in her huipil and she answered: "Do you think we want to look like our grandmothers?"

33. On tradition and the "true" way see Childs & Greenfield 1980 (p. 283). Wilhite's comments on allowable variation appear on p. 62 in her 1977 publication. On the Colotenango study, see Mejía de Rodas et al. 1987 (p. 54).

34. For the impact of Spanish commercial patterns on gender roles in weaving see Anawalt 1979 (p. 179).

35. For information on foot loom weavers see Hagan's 1972 dissertation on the hand weaving sector of the Guatemalan economy, based on a study conducted during the late 1960s. On the amount that can be woven in a day, see p. 70. On the length of apprenticeship in the '60s, see p. 52. On being born into the profession, see p. 172. At the time of Hagan's study, a second-hand foot loom cost more than four times the *telar de cinta*. Some 64% of those polled learned weaving from their fathers — some deriving their entire livelihood from this occupation, others having additional sources such as agriculture, tailoring, and so forth. O'Neale 1945 (p. 55) met a twelve-year-old boy in Quezaltenango who said he had been weaving for three years, so while it may be difficult for a boy to weave before reaching adult height, perhaps it is possible.

36. The Aztecs were used to playing the role of invading conquerors, and during their short history had reached a dominant position almost without opposition. To find themselves invaded and conquered was more destructive to the Aztecs than to the Maya; a civilization such as the Aztec, whose chief God was a war god, could not survive intact as a subject people.

37. Though Madsen was speaking of the Yucatán Maya, his observations are generally applicable to the Maya. With regard to Yucatán Maya paganism, see Madsen 1967 (p. 370) and Farriss 1984 (pp. 23,24,320). Tedlock's observations appear in Tedlock 1985 (pp. 176-7).

38. On the forsaking of indigenous heritage, see Early 1983 (p. 77).

39. On daykeepers, see Tedlock 1985 (p. 36).

CHAPTER 2

Men's Dress

Maya men's clothing, unlike women's, began to change soon after the Spaniards arrived in the highlands. Compared with women's dress, men's *traje* of the 1960s is more of a puzzle, for its origins are not as obvious. Many elements are certainly derived from European sources, although when and how is not so clear. Others are probably rooted in Prehispanic dress. To disentangle the separate skeins, one must start with the hypothetical Prehispanic dress and trace the possible steps in its transformation, while also considering the Spanish costume elements that probably contributed to this change.[1]

Prehispanic Costume. There are no records of dress just prior to Conquest and few from the Postclassic period (A.D. 1000 to 1524). To find substantial documentation one must look back to depictions from the Classic Period, some 600 years earlier. Classic documents record mostly the clothing of the upper classes — priests, rulers, and warriors — which may bear little relationship to the dress of the common man. Nevertheless they do give us some notion of the garments worn by commoners. Although the political structures of that civilization collapsed six centuries before the Conquest, there is no reason to believe that this would have changed the basic clothing of the ordinary Maya man.

Let us therefore imagine a man of the Late Classic Period. He would have worn four or five garments, the most important being the loincloth. In the Classic Period this was a rectangle long enough to wrap more than once around the waist or hips and pass between the legs (fig. 21). All men wore the loincloth, and class distinctions were marked by differences in material (cotton for upper classes, maguey fiber for lower classes) and in amount and type of decoration. Such differences were sometimes shown in the manner of wearing garments; for example the average man wore a mantle which passed under one arm and was tied on the opposite shoulder.

21. The Precolumbian Maya loincloth was a rectangle long enough to wrap around the waist and between the legs, as in this scene on a Classic period panel (A.D. 692) from Palenque, Chiapas, depicting a newly installed ruler, seated on bench, with three nobles of high rank. Here the ruler accepts the Jester God headband, emblem of his accession.

22. Man from Todos Santos in his capixay.

23. Cofradía members from Sololá in European-style jackets.

24. Man and boy from Santiago Atitlán wearing traditional bandas.

Men of high rank wore a mantle tied in front under the chin. Again the material, size, and decoration varied by rank. Some men also wore a kilt wrapped around their hips; sometimes it was square, folded to form a triangle, worn with a point falling behind and the ends tied at the front or side. There is some indication that this and other kilts may have been supported by a belt. Sandals again marked distinctions in rank: simple untanned hide for those commoners who were shod (many were not) and very elaborate two-thonged sandals for upper-rank men. Varied headdresses and items of jewelry have been omitted from our account because they probably did not continue after the Conquest.

The items ordinarily forming the traditional Guatemalan men's costume of the 1960s — and to a lesser extent today — include, from head to toe: hat *(sombrero)*; shirt *(camisa)*; European-style open-front jacket *(saco, chaqueta)*; utility cloth *(tzute)*, pants *(pantalones)*, belt and/or sash *(banda)*; and sandals *(caïtes)*. In some towns a bag *(morral)* is part of the *traje*. In addition, three garments of particular interest to the researcher are now of limited distribution but may once have been widely dispersed throughout the highlands. These are the closed-front overgarments *(capixay* and *cotón)*, split overtrousers *(sobrepantalones rajados)*, and hipcloth *(rodillera* or *ponchito)*. Not all garments are used in every village: for example, the traditional *traje* might include either a *capixay* or a European-style jacket, but rarely both (figs. 22,23). In the 1960s, overtrousers were worn in only one town for daily use, and the hipcloth and bag were not ubiquitous. But all were within the current costume repertoire of the Maya male. Of the Prehispanic costume, only remnants survive: sashes and stiff belts, sandals, and utility cloths all have clear Prehispanic origins. The rest appear to have emerged out of Spanish forms.

Prehispanic Survivals

Waist Sashes or Belts (Bandas). In many towns women weave *bandas* for their husbands (for example, in Santa María de Jesús, San Martín Sacatepéquez, and Chichicastenango). In some areas, rather stiff, commercially woven belts or sashes can be seen hanging from nails in markets; they are made in a single color such as red, yellow, orange, and have knotted fringed ends. When tightly wrapped, they are said to form a corset-like support for men engaged in heavy manual labor such as tree cutting.

In shape, *bandas* are rather long and frequently wrapped several times around the body, following the Prehispanic pattern for loincloths. Any designs brocaded on them are town specific. So, too, is the manner of wearing them. In some towns they are wrapped, then knotted, and the ends permitted to fall to the front (fig. 27) or

25. *Man from San Pedro Necta wearing a tzute on his head.*

26. *Traditional sandals similar to those worn in Precolumbian times.*

to the back. Elsewhere they are merely wrapped one or two more times around the body, and the ends tucked in. The opposite extreme occurs in Chichicastenango, where the heavy *bandas* are knotted, then their ends turned back and finally tucked in, the whole forming an ungainly roll. In general, the appearance of a man's belt or sash contrasts strongly with that of the woman's, which tends to be neat and primly wrapped, with fringes or ends carefully tucked in.

There are 167 men's costume parts in the Fowler Museum of Cultural History collection. Of these, nearly a fourth — 42 pieces — are *bandas*. This is significant because it underlines the fact that men, when they adopt Ladino-style shirt and trousers, often keep the sash as the sole remaining native garment. The loincloth, though its function was taken over by pants, was still being worn by Chichicastenango men as an undergarment at least until the 1930s or 1940s. I think the man's sash is Precolumbian because it is the last garment abandoned in many towns. Others have reached the same conclusion for different reasons. Anthropologist Marta Turok feels it is the excessive length of some men's sashes that betrays their origin in the very long loincloth. Textile expert Walter F. Morris, Jr. feels the Maya turned their loincloths into sashes merely as a means of supporting the pants they had been forced by the Spaniards to wear.[2]

Sandals (Caïtes). Sandals seem to be of Prehispanic origin. They once were of leopard and other skins, then of leather. In some areas men have retained the traditional Maya sandals with high-cupped backs (fig. 26). In Huehuetenango, for example, men from San Juan Atitán are known as makers of such footwear, going to the Todos Santos market to practice their craft. Some men's sandals resemble Prehispanic depictions except that now they have one thong passing between the toes instead of two. A relatively recent development is the use of rubber from worn-out tires as sole material.

The wearing of sandals has long been associated with Maya-ness. In the 1960s, Ladinos wore shoes, whereas Maya men tended to wear sandals if they were shod at all. Missionaries encouraged the adoption of shoes from early on. A pamphlet published in 1798 by Fray Matías de Cordóva, for example, advocated putting natives in European dress and shoes, stating that all kinds of benefits would accrue through this action. It would improve the economy by increasing the number of artisans and would give the natives happiness, respect, and health. Fray Matías's wish to see the Maya in shoes is coming to pass; but whether this has resulted in the benefits he envisioned is another story.[3]

Utility Cloths (Tzutes). In some towns, men still wear a *tzute*, either slung over one shoulder, or sometimes covering their heads (figs. 25,27). Now it is usually only the old men who wear *tzutes*. Many former uses of this garment were superseded

27. *Young men from San Juan Atitlán wearing tzutes over their shoulders.*

28. One of the earliest depictions of Guatemalan people after the Conquest, showing how early the changes in men's dress occurred. The men are already clothed in European-style pants. The women, by contrast, are wearing Maya dress.

even in the 1960s by factory-made bandannas. But in San Juan Atitán, on a cool fall morning in 1981, most of the men we saw in the market place wore their *tzutes* over their heads, under their hats and falling in back to shield their necks. Men from Colotenango used to signify their age by the way they wore their *tzutes*. Pubescent boys in the 1950s folded theirs in half diagonally and tied them around the waist with the knot in front (shades of Prehispanic hipcloths); youths also folded theirs, but wore them across one shoulder and under the other arm, tied on the chest. Each age was clearly marked, ending with the old men who wore them wrapped around the head and tied at the nape of the neck.[4]

Clothing with Spanish Antecedents

Except for sandals, loincloths (now vestigial) and utility cloths, Spain can claim credit for the rest of the modern Maya man's clothing styles: the hat *(sombrero)*, the shirt *(camisa)*, jackets *(cotón* and *capixay)*, pants *(pantalones)* and slit overpants *(sobrepantalones)*, and even the kilt *(rodillera)* can be traced to Spanish models. It is not easy to see the steps by which this came about; however one can begin by scrutinizing colonial records, which provide at least a few clues to the puzzle.

Spanish colonial records are sparse. They deal in generalities about indigenous clothing when they touch on the matter at all, lack good descriptions of individual garments, and have failed to indicate the regional distinctions which must have existed. No matter how sincere their regard for native souls or labor, neither missionary nor colonist was much interested in Maya dress.

Sixteenth-century references to clothing, while numerous, are usually brief and uninformative. The following, which dates from 1599 in Mexico, is typical: "the common Indian's garments barely cover his shame, he wears a breech clout but no shoe. A chief, who has more money, wears a cotton shirt and tight short drawers." The Spanish author of this reference went to Mexico and observed people at work. Some of his pictures show Spanish men in hats and cloaks, Maya men in shirts and pants, and Maya women in huipils (fig. 28).[5]

Written reports made in 1580 for King Felipe (Philip) II are somewhat more informative than most reports from the sixteenth century. According to these, the costume of Guatemalan male nobility included a white shirt; thin, fine, transparent white pants reaching mid-calf; and, over them, ornamented pants which came only to the knees thus allowing the inner pants to show. On their feet were sandals of sisal from the agave plant. At the waist they wore a large, colored *toalla* (literally "towel" in Spanish) resembling a sash, tied at the front. Over the shoulders like a cape hung a *tilma* of transparent white cloth (fig. 29) embroidered with lions and birds in white thread. A drawing by Fuentes y Guzmán, made at the end of the seventeenth century, is based on the description in the 1580 report, as well as on old paintings and, apparently, old textiles. It is extremely revealing: except for the absence of a hat and use of a *tilma,* which is Prehispanic, everything is in the Spanish style. Particularly striking is the fact that overpants are shown being worn at this period. Even if Fuentes y Guzmán erred in his drawing, which is probable, and really depicted seventeenth-century styles rather than those of the late sixteenth, it is still the first mention of such pants. The sandals are specifically described as being like *alpargatas* — that is, fiber-soled and with one thong between the toes in the Spanish mode. Such early colonial references show how soon and how readily some Maya males adopted Spanish styles.[6]

Seventeenth-century descriptions of the dress of various highland people range from brief to detailed. Fray Antonio Remesal, who worked among the Ixil people during the first quarter of the seventeenth century, reports that they wore hats, shirts, and pants as well as colored mantles called *mantas, tilmas,* or *ayates.* This would probably have described the costume of other highland groups as well. [7]

The 1630 report of Thomas Gage, who lived in Guatemala in the Valley of Mixco for some years, is more interesting. Perhaps he described the Mixco costume or that of San Pedro Sacatepéquez or San Juan Sacatepéquez when he wrote:

> Their ordinary clothing is a pair of linen or woolen drawers broad and open at the knees, without shoes…or stockings…a coarse shirt which reaches a little below their waist and for a cloak a woollen or linen mantle (called *ayate*) tied with a knot over one shoulder, hanging down on the other side almost to the ground. They also wear a twelve penny or two shilling hat.[8]

This description reveals that the man is dressed more or less in the Spanish mode, with hat, shirt, and pants. The latter are described as "open at the knees," most likely meaning not slit, but, rather, loose — that is, unrestricted at the knee.

A painting done in 1678 depicts a crowd scene in front of the Guatemala cathedral, which Luis Luján Muños has analyzed for its view of local clothing. As he describes it, male natives are shown wearing short overpants which seem to be of wool and are open at the knee. Under these are longer, white pants. They wear white shirts with sleeves rolled to the elbows. Some of the Maya wear a woolen *capixay* (which is not described; presumably it is similar to the current overgarment of that name). Others wear a type of *tilma,* or mantle. They also wear felt or reed hats and are unshod.[9]

Eighteenth-century descriptions are lacking. During the mid-nineteenth century Guatemala was included in one of the two volumes of John L. Stephen's monumental travel book, *Incidents of Travel,* but it is notable for its lack of dress description. The author reports that in Tecpán, Guatemala, he observed "…Indians, the first we had seen in picturesque costume." He further notes having seen twenty or thirty local officials in full suits of blue cloth, the trousers open at the knees, and cloaks with hoods like the Arab burnoose.[10]

Dr. Otto Stoll, an ethnologist who worked in Guatemala in the late nineteenth century, described the average Maya as wearing a single garment which was more holes than fabric and which he wore rain or shine. Those who were more prosperous had a few garments for a change or for fiesta. The people of Retalhuleu wore white cotton pants, a white shirt-like garment, and sandals but no socks.[11]

The color now so apparent in Guatemalan dress is noticeably lacking in early descriptions. It also appears that if ethnic distinctions in dress had once existed, these were lost under colonization or were not noted by foreign observers. Probably the gathering of rural Maya to be placed under church control left them without a dress indicative of village affiliation, a lack remedied over the centuries since that time.

In contemporary Guatemala there is no trace of the early sixteenth-century styles worn by the conquistadors. Portraits of Cortés and Alvarado show stalwart proud figures in armor or partial armor. Alternatively they wore the upper-class styles of the era — ruffed necklines, armor-shaped upper garment, padded sleeves and sleek legs in hose, perhaps with upperstocks above them like rudimentary puffed short pants. Garments like these continued to be worn by noblemen and landowners

29. 17th-century rendering of what was thought to be late 16th-century costume in Guatemala, based on colonial written reports from 1580.

30. *Man and boys wearing Sololá shirts with vestigial tab collars and dangling cuffs.*

31. *Early 20th-century Spanish costume of Huesca, Aragón including a jacket similar to that of Sololá.*

following the Conquest. No doubt many indigenous people saw such clothes, but it is unlikely they would have copied them given cost, royal prohibition against their use, difficulty of tailoring and probably lack of inclination. In any case, upper-class Spanish styles were never adopted by the Maya.[12]

The kind of overtrousers and pants mentioned in the few sixteenth- and seventeenth-century accounts of native dress do not appear in pictures of the conquistadors. Rather, these and other garments appear to have been modeled on the clothing of the lower-class Spanish male of the period. This is logical, for in fact the majority of Spaniards who arrived in the sixteenth and seventeenth centuries were from the lower classes and even riffraff. Shortly after setting foot on American soil, this group of average and lower-class citizens became the upper class thanks to colonial class lines dividing Spaniards from the native population.[13]

Garments Derived from Spanish Prototypes

Highland people must have been exposed to a variety of Spanish styles. Itself an amalgam of many diverse sources, Spanish costume comprised both national and regional dress traditions. Both ultimately contributed features to highland male costume. Components of highland dress traceable to pan-Spanish (indeed, pan-European) traditions include the hat, shirt, and sleeved jacket.

Hats (Sombreros). It is certain that the whole idea of the hat is transplanted from Spain, for the thousands of elaborate Prehispanic headdresses had no such mundane function as protection from sun or rain; they were ceremonial or indicated status. It seems that Maya men took easily to the wearing of Spanish style hats, although it was some time before these came to be part of the highland male costume. One of the first recorded exchanges of clothes between the Spaniards and the natives took place in what is now Mexico as a prelude to the meeting of their leaders. The Aztec ruler sent Cortés "ten loads of fine mantles of white cotton adorned with plumage" as well as the even more desirable gold. Cortés sent Moctezuma a crimson cap. After all these centuries the present Guatemalan hat is called *sombrero.* The word itself, which is now generic, can be traced to thirteenth-century Seville; however, I have found no exact regional prototype for current Guatemalan hats.[14]

Shirts (Camisas). Sleeved shirts were certainly brought by the Spanish colonists. The idea of a shirt with sleeves and collar did not exist among the Maya; it is essentially European. Nevertheless the 1960s version owes something to Guatemalan looms. Backstrap-woven shirts are made of two webs joined together. Separately woven sleeves (one web cut in half) are sewn onto the shoulder edge of the body. This addition of sleeves to a two-web body resembles an afterthought, suggesting a step not far from huipil construction. While such shirts are mostly made at home, ready-to-tailor lengths of material *(cortecitos)* can be purchased in some areas. For example, the Tzutujil women of San Pedro la Laguna, in the Lake Atitlán area,

32 (left). Men's costumes from Chichicastenango (left), Nebaj (center), and Soloma (right).

33. Typical saco of Joyabaj.

weave *cortecitos* in a variety of village-specific stripe patterns. In Nahualá, the town's striped red shirt yardage is produced on the foot loom and sold by the *vara*.[15]

In several areas, shirts have collars and cuffs which are woven separately, for example San Juan Atitán and Todos Santos. In Sololá the collar has little relation to the human neck since it is merely attached to a small gathered portion at the back of the shirt. It could be a non-functional version of the kind seen on seventeenth- or eighteenth-century European shirts. Similarly the cuffs there and in San Juan Atitán (fig. 30) are certainly misunderstood from a European point of view, not being large enough to surround the wrist; they flop uselessly near the hand. No doubt the gussets which make some shirts and also trousers more adaptable to movement were also learned from the Spaniards.[16]

Jackets (Sacos, Chaquetas). Guatemalan sleeved jackets, too, are generally in the European style, although not as intricately tailored as their Spanish prototypes. The distinctive jackets from Sololá, Chajul, and San Juan Cotzál have cuffs, sleeves, shoulder yokes, pockets, and edges decorated with braid on a base fabric of striped or solid colored wool. Although the resemblance is not strong, antecedents of these can be found in the peasant repertoire of Cáceres in Extremadura, Navarre, and Aragón (fig. 31). This style, which swept all Europe, is known in Spain as *anguarina* (Hungarian) in honor of the Hungarian hussars who succeeded in repelling the Turks from Austria in the seventeenth century and blunting their sweep through Europe.[17]

During the 1960s and earlier many men wore locally-tailored jackets in European style but often with intriguing features. Sololá had both a *cotón* or closed jacket and a European-style open one. Both are in striped woolen fabric and both have elaborate "frogs" and decorations on back, fronts and cuffs. This town also has a white *saco* with the same decorations. The *saco* of Nebaj is made of red cotton pinstriped in black (fig. 32). It has a trim black collar and cuffs with decorative white sewing machine stitching, and similar frogs of applied tape. The jacket of Joyabaj is of red cotton with black and yellow stripes. Our example has black collar and cuffs (fig. 33). According to O'Neale, these jackets are usually distinguished by black braided designs.[18]

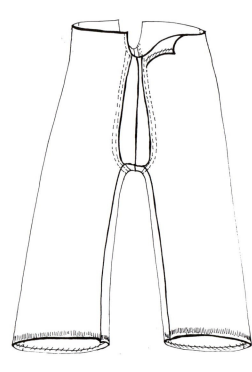

34. Traditional men's trousers composed of four backstrap-woven webs, with gusset.

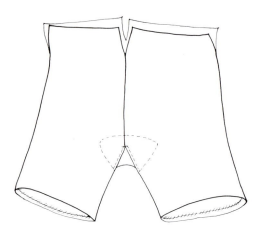

36. Traditional men's short trousers composed of two webs, halved, with gusset.

35. Todos Santos man crocheting his bags.

37. Bags from Nahualá and Sololá.

38. Todos Santos man weaving the strap for a crocheted bag.

Trousers (Pantalones). Although trousers are of Spanish derivation, they still owe something to their Guatemalan heritage when they are woven in the home on the backstrap loom. They are usually constructed of four webs sewn together, with or without a gusset (fig. 34). Alternatively, each leg would be made of one web cut in half with the cut edges hemmed (fig. 36). This is the basic shape.

The widely found simple white trousers, sometimes of rather unconventional construction, are more closely Spanish. They doubtless derive from the Spanish peasant's drawers. La Farge was probably the first to identify their source. He noted that the Ladinos in the area called them *calzoncillos* — the same term used for the Spanish drawers. Dispersed over Mexico and Guatemala, these garments are usually made of muslin *(manta)* and often wrap or tie at the waist and sometimes at the ankle. But recently, in the Guatemalan highlands, even these have more or less given way to "store bought" pants for all but a few older men.[19]

Bags (Morrales). Bags are common accessories for men, and are usually produced by them. In Aguacatán, Joyabaj, and Todos Santos they are crocheted (figs. 35,38). Sololá and Nahualá bags are knitted (fig. 37) and those from Chichicastenango are of two kinds, one knitted and the other woven. Some of the Lake villages produce bags of maguey fiber *(ixtle)* to be used as shoulderbags; the larger version of this kind is called *red* (meaning "net") and is made by a knotless netting technique in wide mesh. Such bags come in all sizes and expand to fit large burdens being carried to market. A commercial utility cloth is often used to shield and protect the burden within the *red*.

Antecedents for the capixay/cotón, the rodillera, and the sobrepantalones may be found in the northern provinces of Spain.

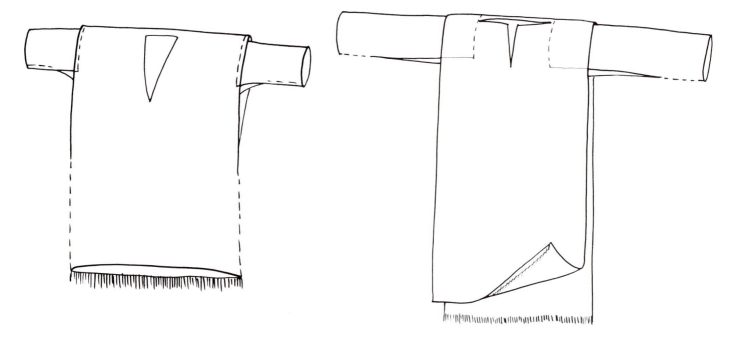

39. *"Typical" cotón.*

40. *"Typical" capixay.*

Garments with Regional Roots

In addition to the garments whose antecedents are clearly pan-Spanish, there are three unusual articles of highland men's costume for which I can find only regional prototypes — specifically from the northern provinces (map, opposite): these are the open-sleeved overgarments *(capixay, cotón),* the kilt *(rodillera),* and the split overtrousers *(sobrepantalones).* While each of these three costume elements seems to have existed in diverse parts of Spain, it is only in the north that we find a conjunction of all three. It is there, then, that we have narrowed the target to find sources for the most intriguing of the garments worn by Guatemalan highland Maya men.

Overgarments (Capixayes and Cotones)

Traditional Guatemalan overgarments are closed-front, sleeved, tunic-like garments of squarish shape that pull over the head. Characteristically made of dark wool, they are usually open (unsewn) at the sides, and are longer in the back than the front. In detail, these garments vary, but on the basis of length they seem roughly to fall into two categories — one shorter, the other longer. The shorter versions of this garment are often (but not always) termed *cotón*. The longer ones tend to be known as *capixay*. Local terminology is not consistent, however. Even within the same village, both terms may be applied to a single garment. In other cases, the same name is used generically to describe two different versions of the garment. In most towns during the 1960s, only one of the two versions was worn. Only two towns (Sololá and Santiago Atitlán) had both long and short variants. At that era the short version, which I shall call the "typical" *cotón,* was more common than the long one, or what I term the "typical" *capixay*. The latter is mentioned more in the literature, however; both were apparently once in widespread use — the full-length garment more so than the shorter one (Appendix 1a,b).

The "typical" *cotón* is of very rough wool, squarish in shape, and usually black, considerably shorter than the "typical" *capixay*, and only rarely fringed at the back (fig. 39). Often it has a V-shaped neck opening, and is machine embroidered. In the 1960s, *cotones* were still being commonly worn in several villages in the department of Huehuetenango. *Cotones* from Colotenango fit this pattern, as do those from San Mateo Ixtatán and Jacaltenango. In the literature we have found mention of twelve *cotones,* four of which were not black (Appendix 1a).[20]

The *cotones* from Chichicastenango are famous for their embroidery, which characteristically features a sun symbol with rays (fig. 250). Sol Tax, who queried Chichicastenango men in the late 1940s regarding their use of the overgarment, found that only about half of those interviewed wore the *cotón,* and that there was uncertain correlation between the age of the wearer and the quantity or nature of the embroidery on the *cotón*. The *cotón* from Sololá is unusual in both color and function. Instead of being black, like most overgarments, it is of blue-and-white striped wool. It is also worn as a sign of office by several *cofradía* officials. Alternatively, for daily wear, the men of Sololá wear a jacket which resembles the *cotón* but is open down the front. Less well known is the ceremonial overgarment from Nahualá. Although townspeople usually call it *cotón,* this garment seems more like the "typical" *capixay,* because of the way it is worn for ceremonies — so that the wearer's arms are outside the sleeves.[21]

In the 1960s, the *capixay* was worn in only a few towns, for example San Juan Atitán, Panajachel, San Antonio Aguas Calientes, and San Martín Sacatepéquez. Yet in the literature one can find mention of twenty-eight or twenty-nine. This suggests that the garment was much more widely worn in the past. Of those mentioned in the literature, all but five were actually described (Appendix 1b). On the basis of these, together with the extant examples, it is possible to list the core characteristics of the "typical" *capixay*. It is wool, usually black or natural dark, usually twilled, tunic-shaped, rectangular with a hole for the head; sleeves rectangular, each being a separate piece usually recessed under the shoulder; sleeves and sides wholly or partially unsewn; long, at least to the knees (30" or more); shorter in front than in back; and fringed at the bottom back (figs. 40,41). The wearer can put his arm through the sleeves or let them emerge from the open sides of the *capixay* while the sleeves dangle behind.[22]

41. Men from San Antonio Palopó wearing capixayes in 1894.

42. Spanish councilman from the Ansó Valley in Aragón, wearing a tabard-like garment not unlike the capixay, as shown in Arco's El Traje Popular Altoaragones (1923).

Origins of the Capixay. Many have speculated that the *capixay* stems from Spanish ecclesiastical garments. Spanish literature, however, suggests that its origin lies elsewhere. It resembles and must have derived from a garment like that worn by a *concejo* (councilman) of the Ansó Valley in Aragón. The photograph shows a tabard-like black garment with narrow pieces of cloth dangling behind the arms like unused sleeves (fig. 42). This article was also known in Navarre in the high valleys where costumes from the eighteenth century were still preserved as late as the 1940s. There, too, it was the costume of mayors *(alcaldes)*. It is described as a short, black tunic with open sleeves, and with a collar, which Guatemalan ones lack. As on many Guatemalan examples, the wearer can put his arm through the sleeves or let them emerge from the open sides of the *capixay* while the sleeves dangle behind.[23]

According to one Spanish costume authority, various shapes of overgarments were worn by humble folk throughout the Pyrenees. In the Basque Pyrenees a black hooded garment called *kapusay* was worn by shepherds. In addition, there are numerous other tabard-shaped overgarments in peasant Spain, particularly in Extremadura. In most cases they lack sleeves.[24]

The history of the Spanish garments' names as seen in the literature is revealing. The word *capisayo* appears as early as the thirteenth century and in later Spanish documents, where it is said to be an overgarment of poorer people, although it seems not to have been described. The name seems to drop out of the literature for 700 years, but the garment itself must have persisted unnoticed until it came with Spanish peasants to the New World, presumably some time around the eighteenth century. The literature of this century mentions a black cape with hood worn in the Basque provinces, and called *kapusay*, a term obviously related to *capisayo*.[25]

But other garments as well were certainly involved in the shaping of the Guatemalan *capixay* with its strange sleeves. For example, two kinds of cloaks, the *tabardo* and the *capuz* (both mentioned in the literature up until the fifteenth century), had slits for the arms to pass through, while strips of fabric dangled from the shoulders

43. *Traveling cloak, tabardo, worn by Spanish men and women, as seen in the 13th-century codices of Alfonso X el Sabio.*

44. *King wearing a capixay-like garment as seen in the 13th-century codices of Alfonso X el Sabio.*

like rudimentary sleeves. The *tabardo* was a traveling cloak worn by both men and women (figs. 43,44) and found in several areas of Spain. Another garment with adaptable sleeves was the *garnacha*, worn usually in town and found in other parts of Europe as well as Spain. A further garment, the *jornea*, also with false sleeves, may have contributed its tabard shape to the Guatemalan *capixay*. Over the course of several centuries, no doubt all these shapes and names in one way or another made their way from Spain to highland Guatemala to influence the *capixay* of San Juan Atitán and other Guatemalan towns.[26]

Kilts and Aprons (Rodilleras, Ponchitos)

The Guatemalan *rodillera* is typically a kilt of stiff, fulled woolen fabric, generally black or brown and usually checked with white, measuring from 45" to 58" long, including fringe. In the 1960s it was still worn in several towns especially in the Lake Atitlán area, Sololá, and Nahualá, but it has been found to have existed in at least twenty-four towns (Appendix 2), many of which no longer have any trace of Maya dress. From town to town the garment deviates or deviated only slightly in size and in color. While most are dark, a couple are blue and white and a group from the southern Mam of San Marcos department are all white with black pin stripes. The great majority are worn as kilts — wound around the hips in various ways. However in four towns — Tecpán, Comalapa, Patzún, and Santa Apolonia — the garment is smaller and is folded so as to fall in front like an apron (fig. 45).[27]

There is one area where the *rodillera* is not found, according to Osborne. It is what she defines as the Sacatepéquez area, consisting roughly of the departments of Sacatepéquez and northern Guatemala. Except for San Juan Sacatepéquez, with its unusual split trousers, none of the towns in that area has the three garments of special interest to us. It must be left to someone with more knowledge of movements of peoples or linguistic affiliations to explain why these garments should have been worn virtually throughout Guatemala except in that area.[28]

Origins of the Rodillera. Some believe the *rodillera* to be descended from the Prehispanic kilts of the ancient Maya. In representations I have seen, however, these did not resemble the twentieth-century *rodillera*. That garment is merely a rectangle wrapped around the hips and belted for support. The Prehispanic ones, by contrast, appear to have been triangular — formed either from a square folded diagonally, or from a shaped, rounded triangle. These tied with a knot and did not fully encase the hips. Other elaborate Prehispanic "skirts," some fringed, fell from

45. *Man from Patzún wearing an apron-type rodillera.*

46. *Early 20th-century regional costume of Huesca,*
Aragón, with a kilt akin to those worn in
the Guatemalan highlands.

the waist rather than wrapping the hips like the *rodillera*. We do not know if such garments survived up to the time of the Conquest, however. The sparse early colonial records I have found do not mention skirts or kilts. Considering the clear Spanish origins of highland overgarments and trousers, it is logical to look for Spanish antecedents to the *rodillera* as well.[29]

A long very wide sash worn by peasants in northern Spain, probably since at least the eighteenth century, wraps in much the same manner as the *rodillera* and resembles it strongly. Often soft enough to have a creased appearance when worn, it is wrapped around the waist and hips rather than around only the hips as in Guatemala. Such garments are found, for example, in Navarre and Aragón (fig. 46).[30]

I could not find published information as to the date the *rodillera* reached Guatemala. However, a most tantalizing sentence appeared in a 1858 work by Gustav von Tempsky, who spent two years in that country and one month in Santa Catarina Ixtahuacán near Nahualá. There he observed some men wearing black-and-white checked wool aprons. These, he claimed, were "shepherds, who form a class" and wore the *rodillera* as a class distinction. Shepherds no longer form a class, if they ever did, but von Tempsky at least establishes a mid-nineteenth-century date by which the *rodillera* was clearly in use.[31]

Split Overtrousers (Sobrepantalones)

Trousers per se were a pan-European concept, brought by the Spaniards and adopted very early by the Maya, as the colonial records cited earlier have shown. More challenging for the researcher are the overtrousers with a split in front or at the side. Now found only in Todos Santos for daily use (fig. 47) and in Totonicapán for ceremonial use, they were once quite widely distributed. It can be documented that they occurred in at least fifteen towns (Appendix 3). In four cases the literature does not reveal how or when they were used. In Quezaltenango they were worn for weddings, according to Osborne. In Concepción Tutuapa in the Southern Mam department of San Marcos, they were worn by old men, especially *cofradía* officials, who wore them in place of the *rodillera*. Of the remaining ten, some were certainly, and the others probably ceremonial. These constitute the most dramatic legacy from Spanish costume; but exactly where they came from, and when, remains to be discovered.[32]

Origins of the Split Overpants. Spanish paintings of the sixteenth century show quite clearly that the commoners wore trousers, in contrast to courtly males, who appear in sleek tights. Since the poor were of little interest to portrait painters, one must look at subsidiary figures in fifteenth- and sixteenth-century Spanish crucifixion scenes, landscapes, battles, and so forth. It is only here that the lower classes appear. Soldiers, boatmen, fishermen, galley slaves, executioners, gardeners, farmers, and shepherds are depicted wearing trousers — some shorter and tighter, some fuller and longer. A painting of three sixteenth-century Galician citizens shows one of them wearing *calzones* or *calzoncillos*, white pantaloons or drawers. In an even earlier reference, a pilgrim to Jerusalem describes seeing women of that area, in 1461, wearing breeches down to their feet "like sailors' breeches." Authorities are agreed that these were once the sole lower garment of the Spanish male peasant, and that, by the eighteenth century, they were covered up, when European men adopted fitted overpants.[33]

Regional studies, perhaps more pertinent, reveal that by the eighteenth century short split trousers were worn in Extremadura, Galicia, Asturias, and Aragón as well as in some areas outside northern Spain. In most cases, the split is not exaggerated as in Todos Santos. Rather, it is relatively short and located at the side of the trousers. Visible through the split and hanging below it are white *calzoncillos*.[34]

Two eighteenth-century peasants in pants and overtrousers are depicted in an 1823 publication by Cruz Cano y Olmedillo. One is a carter from Murcia in short full breeches. The other is a Galician in green overtrousers and white drawers (fig. 48). An early nineteenth-century book depicting the Spanish and Portuguese countryside also shows two men wearing pants over drawers — one a carter of Extremadura and the other a Portuguese. This is relevant because Portugal was resettled by Galicians from the north.

Placement of the Split. On the basis of current evidence, the placement of the split appears problematic. The Spanish overtrousers we know have a smallish split at the side seams. In contrast, the two extant Guatemalan examples from Todos Santos and Totonicapán are split in front. However, the apparent contradiction between

47. Boy from Todos Santos wearing black *sobrepantalones* over his trousers. The overpants, almost vestigial, are barely visible from the front.

48. 18th-century peasant from Galicia wearing side-split overtrousers, as depicted in Cruz Cano y Olmedillo (1823).

49. Men from Patzún wearing sobrepantalones split at the sides.

side splits (Spanish trousers) and front splits (Guatemalan) may be reconciled by looking at evidence from the past.

A careful scan of the literature reveals that several Guatemalan overtrousers once had side splits, like their Spanish counterparts. O'Neale's 1936 data includes two towns with side-split overpants. The first was Sololá, where "on occasion" men wore overtrousers of generally European cut except that the side seams were left unjoined all the way to a band at the bottom. Under these, and visible through the splits, were the cotton daily pants. The second was San Juan Sacatepéquez, where the man's *cofradía* costume had undertrousers and overtrousers. The latter were of black wool and open to a point 14" up the side seam; a 1930s photograph of the latter is illustrated in Ann Rowe's *A Century of Change in Guatemalan Costume*. The short white pants described by O'Neale just barely show through the split. An even more revealing photograph shows two men from the late nineteenth century dressed almost exactly like the later ones except that the overpants are ample enough to flap a little.[35]

A photograph from the Whitman Archive, taken in the 1960s in Patzún, offers evidence for a third town with split trousers (fig. 49). At first glance the men seem to be dressed in standard European men's clothes. A closer look reveals that almost all wear long pants, split up the side, over white drawers. No doubt this group is composed of members of a *cofradía* or civic group.

Chichicastenango must be counted as a fourth town with side-split trousers. These are simple trousers not intended to be worn over breeches. Yet like overpants they have a rudimentary side split which, according to Lilly Osborne, once extended to the thigh.[36]

That side-split trousers were once quite common is suggested in a late nineteenth-century description of clothing in the Lake Atitlán area. In January 1894, archaeologist Alfred P. Maudslay and his wife were in Antigua for the Feast of the Kings. Visitors from all the Lake Atitlán villages were present and "quite elaborately dressed." Mrs. Maudslay particularly noted "the short black woolen trousers which reached just below the knee, were embroidered at the seams with colored threads and left open halfway up the side to show the white cotton drawers beneath."[37]

In all, it appears that over a dozen towns wore split overtrousers at some time within the last hundred years. In addition to those already discussed, I have found illustrations or good descriptions of overtrousers in six others, including San Martín Jilotepeque, Quezaltenango, Olintepeque, San Juan Ostuncalco, Cajolá, and Tecpán. In these six villages the trousers are all cut in the front, like the still-extant pants of Todos Santos and Totonicapán. This is a peculiar configuration (fig. 50) which I believe must be a remnant of the fall-front trousers known for centuries among European sailors and probably peasants.

Fall-front trousers are said to have been adopted by the upper classes in the time of George II and lasted, at least in England, until about 1850, when they were replaced by trousers with a single opening. It is believed that the fall front originated as the medieval codpiece. The latter is easy enough to identify in paintings because upper garments left it visible, but seventeenth- and early eighteenth-century fashions usually obscure the front of the undergarment. In the late eighteenth and early nineteenth centuries the fall-front was visible, and, in England at least, was fastened on each side with two buttons. This style is quite like the Todos Santos opening, though the Guatemalan version is set diagonally rather than straight.

Trousers with a fall front occurred in northern Spain, but like their English counterparts they are difficult to identify in paintings. When visible, however, they appear quite unlike the Guatemalan and English versions. Whereas the latter have double rows of buttons, the trousers worn in several areas of Extremadura have a large flap secured with a single button.

Importance of Eighteenth-Century Immigrations

As we have seen, the origins of the *capixay*, the *rodillera*, and the split overpants suggest that the closest correspondences between Guatemalan and Spanish dress seem to lie in the peasant dress of northern Spain, particularly in Galicia, Asturias, Santandér, León, the Basque area, Navarre, Huesca (the northern province of Aragón), and Cáceres (the northern province of Extremadura). This in turn points to the importance of eighteenth-century immigrations in shaping the Guatemalan highland men's costume.[38]

It is well known that the first immigrants were mostly from the south of Spain. Records show that of the 478 Spaniards who went to Guatemala from 1568-79, only 57 (about 12%) originated in the northern provinces, for example Galicia, Asturias, León, the Basque area, Navarre, and Aragón (map, p. 40). Those reported as "southerners," however, may have actually comprised a fair number of northerners. Braudel maintains that in the sixteenth century, a substantial number of Galicians and Asturians migrated south to work either seasonally or permanently. Professor Boyd-Bowman notes that "many northern immigrants found it convenient to sail directly from Coruna or Laredo without registering with Seville after 1529 when other ports were permitted to carry traffic to the Indies."[39]

Immigration data from Spain support theories that northern Spanish influence gradually increased from the time of the Conquest to become predominant in the eighteenth century. The Spaniards, being bureaucrats, kept copious records of the passengers who embarked from Seville for the New World. Boyd-Bowman's research identifies 40,000 emigrants who left between 1493-1580. This constitutes about one fifth of the known emigrants and Boyd-Bowman identifies them by name, place of origin (kingdom, province, town) and intended destination in Latin America. Further information is given in some cases, such as marital status, social rank, and occupation.[40]

Boyd-Bowman's study concludes, "...there is considerable evidence to suggest that eventually the flood of immigrants from Andalusia and Extremadura subsided

50. Design characteristic of trousers cut in the front and worn in Todos Santos, San Martín Jilotepeque, Quezaltenango, Olintepeque, San Juan Ostuncalco, Cajolá, and Totonicapán.

somewhat in favor of increased emigration from…the North (Galicia, Asturias, Navarre, Aragón, Cataluña)." More detailed emigration figures to Chile may be relevant as they suggest what may have happened in Guatemala. A study made earlier this century ranks emigrants in numerical order for the sixteenth, seventeenth, and eighteenth centuries. The northern Spanish provinces were at the bottom of the list for the sixteenth century, higher in the seventeenth and, by the second half of the eighteenth century, the Basques were first on the list and the Navarrese third.[41]

A second reason for targeting the eighteenth century as the probable model for highland men's costume is that Spanish peasant costume solidified and stabilized during that century. Many costume authorities agree that peasant costume assumed its present appearance at that time. Therefore, even though the influences of Spanish costume on Guatemalan men's costume were felt soon after the Conquest, it seems likely that its most salient contributions and its lasting influence on highland men's *traje* can be traced to the eighteenth century.

Language Clues. Although we have used Spanish dress terminology in speaking of highland costume, all Mayan languages have their own terms for their garments. Certain garments have names that are unequivocally Maya. Others are known by terms that are clearly "Mayanized" versions of a Spanish name. This is true of almost all those male costume parts that I have designated as being of Spanish origin.[42]

A few examples illustrate the tendency for Spanish-derived men's garments to be designated by Mayanized Spanish names (Appendix 4a). The shirt, an Old World garment, is known in three different towns and language areas as *camix, kamixhj,* and *kamja*. These are all recognizable variants of *camisa,* the Spanish word for shirt. The closed jacket discussed earlier under the Spanish name *cotón* is known in three towns as *koton, cutin,* and *po't koton* (or *huipil cotón).* The European-style open jacket, or specifically a black jacket, is known in Sololá as *q'aq'achaqueta,* a compound of the Quiché Mayan word *q'aq'a,* "black," and the Spanish *chaqueta* (Appendix 5b). *Kapixaay* and, less recognizable, *xyal,* designate the *capisayo.* The man's *banda* or sash is known in San Ildefonso Ixtahuacán as *siinch,* from the Spanish *cincho,* belt.

Probably the two most interesting examples are those in which the Mayanized word does not come from the garment's name but from the textile of which it is made. In one Cakchiquel-speaking town, the split overpants so fully discussed are called *estameya,* which derives from the Spanish *estameña* or serge. Similarly the *rodillera* is called *xerka* in two Cakchiquel towns. *Xerka* is slightly altered from *xerga,* the coarsest and cheapest wool cloth exported from Spain to the New World as early as the sixteenth century.[43]

Women's garments reveal the opposite tendency (Appendix 4b). With antecedents in Prehispanic dress, they are almost all designated by Mayan terms. A couple of revealing features may be pointed out. While a man's sash or belt is known among the Northern Mam of San Ildefonso Ixtahuacán as *siinch* (a Spanish loan word), a woman's *faja* or sash of the same shape is called by the indigenous term, *b'an ky'itzb'aj.* And finally, the ambiguous hair ribbon, which could stem from either the Spanish *cinta,* or the nearly identical Maya hair ribbon, is called *xak'ap* in one Quiché town and *xo'op* in one Cakchiquel town. For this reason it seems very likely that the *cinta* descends from a Maya origin.

The Decorative Matching of Male and Female Costume

The matching of male and female costumes is an aspect of costume that seems significant although it has been hardly mentioned in the costume literature. Occurring now in only about a dozen places, it was probably once more widespread.[44]

The matching takes a variety of forms. In several towns in the Lake Atitlán area, the decorative supplementary weft patterning that occurs on the woman's huipil is mirrored on her husband's *pantalones*. Examples of this matching can be found in Santa Catarina Palopó, Santiago Atitlán, and San Lucas Tolimán (figs. 51,52). In Huehuetenango department, the Todos Santos man's everyday red-and-white striped pants match the side panels of the woman's huipil. His festive pants have weft bands of brocade like the center web of the old-style huipil. In San Juan Atitán, both the man's *camisa* and the woman's huipil have red and white stripes.

In San Martín Sacatepéquez, the sleeves of a man's long *camisa* match his wife's huipil, even when the brocading on his trousers does not match his own *camisa.* In Nahualá, the animals woven in supplemental weft on a man's *pantalones* are similar to those on his wife's huipil. A double-headed eagle worked in his sash re-

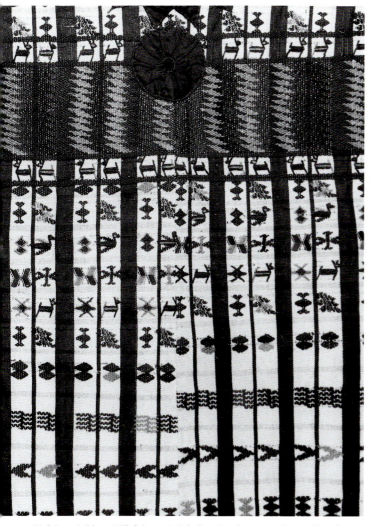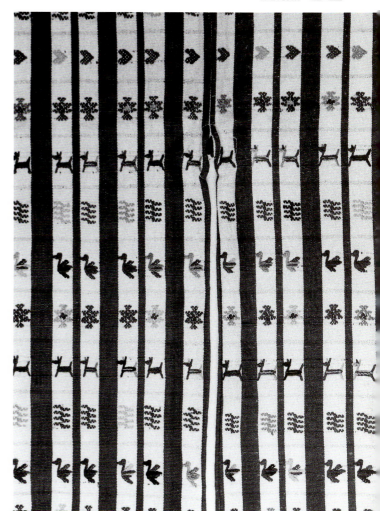

51 (above left) and 52 (above right). Details of a woman's huipil and a man's pantalones from San Lucas Tolimán show matching designs.

sembles eagles on the woman's *cofradía* huipil. The *cofradía* jacket of the San Juan Sacatepéquez man matches the woman's huipil fabric in coloring if not in the distribution of its stripes. In Santa María de Jesús, the man's fiesta shirt, tailored in European style, is made of backstrap-woven fabric that matches the woman's *tzute*. Again at Lake Atitlán, the San Antonio Palopó man's *camisa* is made from the same material as the side panels of his wife's huipil, and his sleeves usually match its central panel.

Perhaps these textiles are clues to an earlier period for which we do not have photographs and from which not too many textiles remain. While there is no proof that such matching was once more widespread, it seems fair to assume that like the overgarments, hipcloths, and split overtrousers, it might once have been quite common in Guatemala.

Conclusions

Although we may never know the exact sources of the Guatemalan highland man's *traje*, we can frame some tentative conclusions. It is clear that most of the items of male dress are descended from the costume of Spanish peasantry. Further, it appears that these influences stem chiefly from the northern part of Spain, and probably from the eighteenth century. As to why one trait persists while another vanishes without trace, we can only speculate.

Today the Maya man who still wears traditional dress is in the distinct minority. The attractive, often colorful costume has undergone changes as profound as those that befell the natives of the New World themselves. During the 1960s only about sixteen distinct men's costumes were still being regularly worn. Since about 200 women's costumes existed in the 1960s, one can see how many more men's than women's have been lost. A village-specific costume for men, with most of its parts produced on backstrap looms, is even more of a rarity today.[45]

One can assume that the men's abandonment, first of their accustomed Prehispanic costume, and then of the Maya dress that evolved after the Conquest, indicates one of two things. Either men are less conservative than women, or their more intense contact with the non-Maya world puts them under greater pressure to adapt to its customs. The loss of so many costumes leaves a gap which may be filled some day by correlation and study of all existing pieces in collections and with the possible discovery of many more labeled and dated photographs. In the meantime it is revealing to comb the literature for former patterns of garment wear.

Notes

1. Since the Maya area embraced both cool and hot climates, highlands and lowlands, no single statement made about dress will necessarily apply to all regions.

2. See Tax & Hinshaw 1969 (p. 82) on the loincloth worn in Chichicastenango. See Turok 1974 (p. 25) for her theory on the men's sash. See Morris 1984 (p. 35) for his theory.

3. Fray Matías's comments are to be found in Cordóva 1932 (pp. 254-56).

4. Re the use of the *tzute* as an marker of age, see Valladares 1957 (p. 84). Utility cloths called *sabanas*, produced on commercial and foot-powered looms, are often used by men for carrying burdens, but these are not worn.

5. For the report of 1599, see Gómez de Cervantes 1944 (pp. 135-36).

6. The drawing appears in Fuentes y Guzmán 1932 (p. 392).

7. For the seventeenth-century report of Fray Antonio, see Remesal 1932, vol. 5 (p. 588).

8. Thomas Gage's report appears in Gage 1969 (p. 219).

9. See Luján Muñoz 1978 (pp. 225-26) for an analysis of the 1678 painting.

10. Stephens's travel was published in 1842. See vol. 2 (p. 147) for his comments on Tecpán. Old Spanish garments had hoods during 15th and 16th centuries, as did the 20th-century black capes of the Basque country.

11. In Stoll's account (published in 1889), see pp. 91,165.

12. During the 17th century in the upper class, the puffed short pants developed into something that resembles women's gym bloomers of the early 20th century.

13. Boyd-Bowman 1973a is an important source of information on immigration patterns. In addition to sailors and settlers from the lower classes there were more substantial citizens on the ships and a smattering of minor nobility but they numbered only about 4.2% according to Boyd-Bowman (p. 49).

14. On the exchange of clothes between the Spaniards and the Aztecs, see Benítez 1946 (p. 25) and Díaz del Castillo 1927 (p. 83). The latter is not regarded as entirely trustworthy and little agreement is shown in translations of this incident. Some don't mention the hat, some do mention fine cambric shirts. In any case, the exchanged garments were evidently adopted by the Maya men of New Spain. The ships' manifests listed thirteen different styles of hats imported during the 16th century. Columbus, nearly 30 years before, had given and traded red caps to the natives on first contact, and even earlier than that, red caps had been popular Spanish trade objects in Africa. Confirmation of the term *sombrero* can be found in Bernis Madrazo 1956 (p. 25).

15. The *camisa* from San Juan Atitán is an exception. Its sleeve is set back under the shoulder (as on a *capixay*, discussed below). It is open under the arms, shorter in front than back, and fringed. Information on Nahualá comes from Susan Masuoka (pers. com., 1988).

16. A possible European prototype for the misunderstood Sololá collar is shown in Fisher 1983 (fig. 2).

17. Regarding the Hungarian jacket in Europe, see Ribeiro 1983 (pp. 73-74,174).

18. On the Joyabaj jacket see O'Neale 1945 (p. 268).

19. On Spanish peasant's drawers as a source for Guatemalan trousers, see La Farge & Byers 1931 (p. 34).

20. The *cotón* of Cajolá, a southern Mam town, was grey and white as was that of Santiago Atitlán at one time. That of San Andrés Sajcabajá was not only red, but made of cotton. For a picture of the San Juan Ixcoy *cotón*, see Delgado 1963 (pl. XVIII).

21. The *capixayes* mentioned but not actually described in the literature are the ones from Santa María Chiquimula, Parramos, Cobán, San Mateo Ixtatán and Jacaltenango. Sol Tax queried 88 Chichicastenango men at random about the adornment on the garment in an effort to find out whether there was a correlation between the age of the wearer and the quantity of embroidery. Of the 88 men interviewed, only 45 wore *cotones*. Of those who did, 7 wore unembroidered ones while 36 wore garments with embroidery. These latter included some with only light borders or arm bands or zigzags. Only a few carried the famous sun symbol with rays and these did not seem to point conclusively to age or youth. The men with full sun and rays were 35, 37, 45 and 50 years old (see Tax 1947, pp. 257-60). On the *cotón* of Sololá, see Mayén de Castellanos 1986 (p. 102). On the Nahualá *cotón*, see Rowe 1981 (fig. 63).

22. A few overgarments, though called *capixay* in the village or in the literature, were considerably shorter than the norm, and conformed more to what is here designated a "typical" *cotón*. The Todos Santos short closed garment with seams open under the arm is called *capixay* (La Farge & Byers 1931, p. 16). I believe its features are like those of several *cotones* from the department of Huehuetenango.

23. Those who speculate that the *capixay* stems from Spanish ecclesiastical garb include Osborne 1935 (p. 35), Deuss 1981 (p. 27), and O'Neale 1945 (p. 211), among others. The proselytizing friars wore the garments of their orders; those of the Franciscans were often ragged. Deacons or bishops dressed in a garment similar in configuration to the Maya *capixay*, known as the dalmatic, according to the 1947 *New Catholic Encyclopedia* (p. 619). Both are T-shaped, open under the arms and at the sides, and donned by slipping over the head. This ancient liturgical garment was intended for festal wear and supposed to be made of silk (Braun 1907, p. 248). Although it is unlikely that the Maya came into direct or sustained contact with liturgical garments other than those of the friars during the 16th century (the period of most intense evangelization), it is possible that city dwellers might have seen deacons or bishops wearing the dalmatic. The tabard-like garment worn by a *concejo* in Aragón is illustrated in Arco 1942 (p. 52). The version still worn in Navarre in the 1940s is mentioned in Gómez Tabanera 1950 (p. 183).

24. See Violant y Simorra 1949 (pp. 94,95,392), an authority on Spanish costume, re various overgarments worn by peasants in the Pyrenees at various times. He specifically mentions a black or dark cape worn in all the Pyrenees at the end of the 18th century.

25. See Bernis Madrazo 1956 (p. 23), on the mention of *capisayo* in the thirteenth century and in later documents. 20th-century usage is mentioned in Violant y Simorra 1949 (p. 392), and Hoyos Sancho 1954 (p. 6).

26. For the complicated problem of sleeves and shapes, see Bernis 1962 (p. 105 and *passim*), Bernis Madrazo 1956 (pp. 39-41, figs. 53,55 for example, and fig. 171 showing the *jornea*); R. Anderson 1979 (p. 110).

27. When the woolen cloth has been moistened and shrunk until felt-like it is said to be fulled. Regarding the manner of wearing *rodilleras* and *ponchitos*: As can be seen in Appendix 2, in the Cakchiquel towns where we found these items, they were worn as kilts (wrapped around the hips), except in four towns where they were worn as aprons. This would contradict Lilly Osborne's statement that "The ponchito is worn as a double apron in nearly all the Cakchiquel villages, except…in Sololá where it is worn as a kilt" (1975, p. 154).

28. See Osborne 1975 (p. 159), re the area where the *rodillera* is not found. Osborne hypothesizes that the Sacatepéquez tribe separated from the Cakchiquels about two centuries before the Spanish Conquest and the kilt evolved after that separation. I feel that it evolved after the Conquest, in the 18th century — at least four centuries after her date.

29. For the theory that the *rodillera* is descended from the Prehispanic kilt, see Gayton 1967 (p. 151).

30. On the Spanish peasant sash, see Violant y Simorra 1949 (pp. 93,285,331).

31. See Tempsky 1858 (p. 364).

32. On split overtrousers see Osborne 1975 (pp. 159, 215).

33. The painting of a 16th-century Galician in *calzoncillas* appears in Bernis 1962 (fig. 142). On the evolution of Spanish peasant drawers, see La Farge & Byers 1931 (p. 34), and Snowden 1979 (p. 141). For the pilgrim's observation, see Louis de Rochechouart, "Journal de Voyage à Jérusalem…" in *Revue de l'Orient Latin*, 1893, vol. 1 (p. 273), Paris.

34. Most Spanish split pants are relatively short, hardly longer than knee-length. In Aragón, as illustrated by Violant y Simorra 1949 (p. 331), the knee-length pants are slit up the whole side of the thigh.

35. On side-split overpants see O'Neale 1945 (pp. 191,192,269,298). See also illustrations in Mayén de Castellanos 1986 (photos 23,24,33,34). Historic illustrations of side-split pants appear in Rowe 1981 (pp. 60, 61).

36. On the side-split pants of Chichicastenango, see Osborne 1975 (p. 219).

37. For their description of 19th-century clothing in the Lake Atitlán area, see Maudslay & Maudslay 1899 (p. 29).

38. Experts include Cáceres with the north, since men from Asturias and León settled there after conquering it from the Moors (e.g. Foster 1960, pp. 29-30). In fact, even Portugal was repopulated by Galicians from the north.

39. Professor Boyd-Bowman's efforts to factor out northerners masquerading as residents of Seville are very impressive (1973b, pp. 14,15) and no doubt successful. However a paragraph in Braudel's *The Mediterranean* (1972-73, vol. 1, pp. 44-47) made me reconsider. He discussed male and female Galicians, stating they were "…found all over sixteenth century Spain…along with their Asturian neighbors…" as harvesters, miners, temporary farm workers etc. "The whole region of Old Castile was continually being crossed by immigrants from the mountains of the north who sometimes returned there." He adds that, in fact, all the European mountain areas continually sent wanderers (harvesters, unemployed artisans, vagabonds, beggars, shepherds) down to the plains, either seasonally or permanently. It is significant that the mountain areas provided soldiers. These must have pushed southward with the Moorish re-conquest of Spain and were perhaps left stranded in the south (Boyd-Bowman 1973b, p. 15). See also Braudel 1979, vol. 1.

40. The research on Spanish immigration appears in Boyd-Bowman 1973b.

41. Statistics for immigration from the northern provinces are in Boyd-Bowman 1973a (p. 93). An earlier study ranking Spanish emigrants by century is found in Foster 1960 (p. 32).

42. This theory, which has been tested only against available glossaries, seems to hold pretty well for Cakchiquel, Quiché, and one northern Mam town (San Ildefonso Ixtahuacán).

43. On the overpants called *estameya*, see Mayén de Castellanos 1986 (p. 131). On the export of *xerga* from Spain in 16th century, see Boyd-Bowman 1973b (p. 354).

44. The matching of male and female costumes was pointed out to me by co-author Caroline West. To my knowledge only Ann Rowe 1981 has commented on it, and only regarding Nahualá.

45. The exact number of men's costumes being worn in the 1960s depends upon whether one counts those towns where only one or two elements of traditional costume are worn.

CHAPTER 3

Women's Dress

Westerners are so captivated by the decorative techniques and color combinations of women's dress in the Guatemalan highlands that they often overlook another of its most remarkable aspects: the time-tested practicality and versatility of the basic clothing design itself. The Maya woman's *traje* handed down over the centuries is composed of an easy and sensible arrangement of rectangular parts as they come from the loom. The upper body covering or huipil is composed of one, two, or three rectangles sewn together, with a hole for the head (fig. 53). Utility cloths, *tzutes* and *perrajes,* come in various sizes (squarish or rectangular) and are named according to function. The skirt, *corte,* is made from a single wide panel or two narrower ones sewn together at the warp selvedges, and long enough to wrap around the body. Both the belt-like sash, *faja,* and the hair ribbon, *cinta,* are long, narrow, rectangular bands. These basic elements make up the costume of the highland Maya woman (fig. 54) and this simplicity and practicality are shared by many costumes in other times and on other continents. The toga, sari, sarong, and poncho, to name only a few, are all based upon rectangles as they come from the loom.

Cotton is the basic fiber for women's clothing, and it has served them well. For over a thousand years it has grown in the hot coastal regions of Mexico and Guatemala, and continues to be traded to highland weavers today. The practicality of cotton is well established. It washes well in cold water, retains its shape, and is durable — qualities that help it survive scrubbing on stones or in concrete tubs at the communal washing place.[1]

Other fibers are added in the weft for both aesthetic and practical reasons. Throughout the 1960s, silk decorated ceremonial garments although its cost usually precluded lavish use. Rayon was used as the main weft in at least four villages for skirts, brocade, or headties. Wool was popular for warmth. Acrylics, though not available in the 1960s, have since come into heavy use.[2]

A range of weaves from light to heavy allows the wearer to respond to the contingencies of climate as well as to her own particular needs. Dense fog can bring chill in the morning and evening to contrast with the heat of midday. Women who leave for market in the early morning chill and return later in the heat of the day also use layering to combat temperature fluctuations. Sometimes they wear two huipils or add a shawl for additional warmth. It is also not uncommon for them to wear two skirts, but this may be more to protect the underskirt than for warmth: typically, a light-weight ikat skirt covers a heavier one of an older style, which is harder to wash and dry.

Huipils

A woman may wear very few huipils over the course of her lifetime, and so each one must be practical, versatile, and durable. Closer examination reveals how this is accomplished.[3]

The huipil is constructed from one, two, or three woven lengths. If the pieces are woven on the backstrap loom, they have either three or four selvedges and we term them webs. If they are woven on the foot loom, they are selvedged on only two sides and we call them panels. The lengths are sewn together along the warp selvedges. In a two-piece huipil a slit is left unsewn along the middle of the join, allowing for the head (fig. 56). In a huipil constructed of one or three lengths, a head opening is cut into the fabric (figs. 55,57). The huipil is pulled over the head and falls to the waist or somewhere beyond. In most areas it is tucked in, but here and there it is left to hang out over the skirt.[4]

54. Woman from Palín.

53 (opposite). Huipil from Palín.

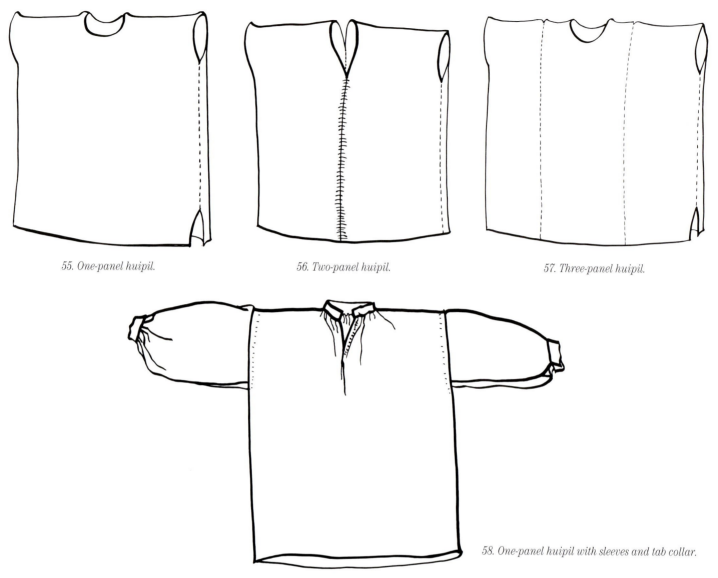

55. *One-panel huipil.*

56. *Two-panel huipil.*

57. *Three-panel huipil.*

58. *One-panel huipil with sleeves and tab collar.*

Several design features increase the practicality of the huipil. Front and back are usually identical in decoration and construction so they can be worn either way. Some huipils are also made reversible: both inside and out are embroidered with the same care, and/or the brocade is double-faced. Even when they are not reversible — that is, even when it is obvious that major brocade design areas are on a single side — they may still be worn inside out. Various reasons are given for this — some practical (to keep the colors from fading or to keep the outside clean), some ritual, some for reasons that are mysterious.[5]

The life of a worn-out huipil is extended by several methods of reconstruction. A huipil made of two lengths can be separated and reversed to distribute wear, so that the edges which were once outside are now in the center. In a three-web huipil, the two side webs may be replaced with plain fabric, leaving only the decorated center. Embellished areas around the neck, across the shoulders, or on the chest are of heavier weave and may outlast other plain sections. These decorative patches can be cut out and sewn onto other plain material, thereby gaining a second life.

Some huipils are moderately tailored and have a European appearance. Those of Sololá and Santiago Chimaltenango are blouse-like, with gathers at the nape, a tab collar, and added "set-on" sleeves (fig. 58). In a few villages the basic huipil is made to resemble a European-style blouse by the addition of a ruffled collar (fig. 59). Braid, ribbons, and ruffles are used to embellish commercial rayon brocade fabrics, as on the long huipils of San Juan Ixcoy and Soloma (fig. 60). Women from the villages of San Antonio Aguas Calientes and Magdalena Milpas Altas, near Antigua, have been known to wear a white blouse with a ruffled collar under their traditional huipil (fig. 61).[6]

59. *Huipil from Jacaltenango with ruffled collar.*

60. *Huipil from Soloma with braid, ribbons, and ruffles.*

61. *European-style blouse from Magdalena Milpas Altas.*

62.

63.

64.

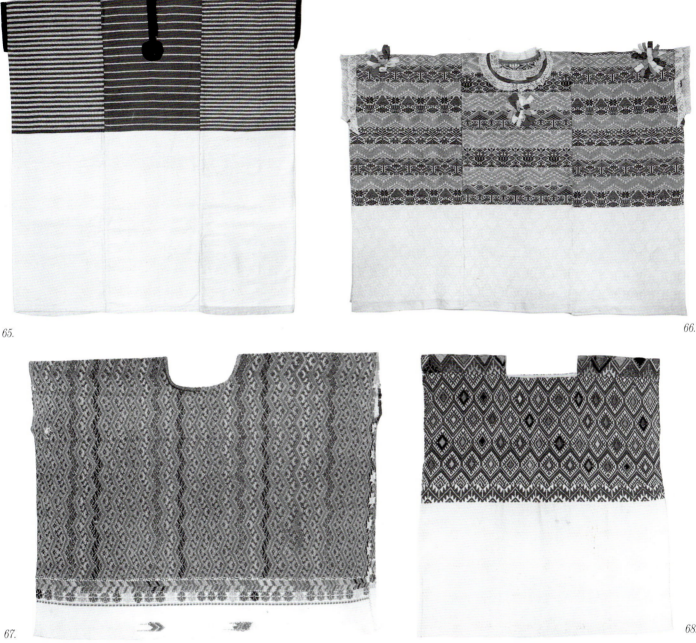

65.

66.

67.

68.

Number of Webs or Panels. Whether woven on the foot loom or the backstrap loom, huipils can be made of one, two, or three pieces. Two-piece huipils seem to be in the majority. In the Museum collection, those constructed of two pieces include all the Tzutujil huipils, most of the Cakchiquel ones, some of the Quiché ones (fig. 62), and those from Mam villages in the Quezaltenango area. Both the everyday huipils and the overhuipils of the Chimaltenango department are also made of two webs (figs. 63,64).[7]

Huipils made of three sections are scattered throughout the highlands. In Alta Verapaz, all backstrap-woven huipils are constructed of three webs. The women of Chichicastenango, Nebaj, and San Juan Cotzal, in the department of Quiché, wear three-web huipils for everyday, as do the women of the Palopós and Panajachel in the Lake Atitlán region. In many villages in the Huehuetenango and Quezaltenango areas, huipils may have two or three sections, but three are preferred for festive occasions (fig. 65). For *cofradía* wear, the huipil with three sections predominates (fig. 66).

One-web huipils are most common in the department of Baja Verapaz, where they are worn for everyday (fig. 67). Young girls throughout the highlands often wear huipils made of a single web (fig. 68).

62. *Two-web huipil from Joyabaj.*
63. *Two-web huipil from Patzicía.*
64. *Two-web huipil from Tecpán.*

65. *Three-panel huipil from Olintepeque.*
66. *Three-panel huipil from San Pedro Sacatepéquez (SM).*
67. *One-web huipil from San Miguel Chicaj.*
68. *Girl's one-web huipil from Santa María de Jesús.*

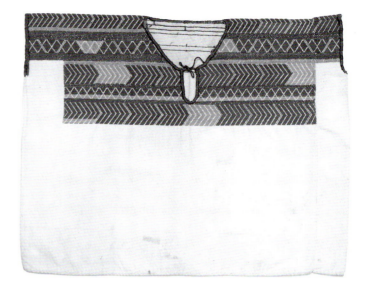

69 (above left). Two-panel huipil from Totonicapán.
70 (above right). Manta huipil from San Gaspar Ixchel.

Trade huipils produced on the foot loom are ordinarily wider than backstrap-woven ones; but with one or two vertical tucks extending over each shoulder to the waist, they are made narrower to fit smaller females (fig. 69). Commercial cloth called *manta*, made in a plain weave (one-over, one-under), is generally too narrow for a one-panel huipil, so it is widened with a supplemental strip (fig. 70).

Width and Length. The width of a huipil depends not only on the number of sections, but on the width of each section. Thus a two-web huipil may be narrower than a three-web one, but not necessarily so. Generally speaking, wide huipils, 36" (91 cm) or more, reach almost to the wrist, medium ones, 26"-36" (66-91 cm), reach to the elbow, and narrow ones, 26" (66 cm) or less, to somewhere on the upper arm. Ceremonial huipils are worn over everyday huipils and therefore tend to be more ample in length and width than those made for daily use.[8]

Huipil length from shoulder to hem varies considerably, from 14" (22 cm) as in Palín, to 44" (102 cm) as in Olintepeque. Short ones are worn outside the skirt, while medium lengths, from 22"-32" (56 cm to 81 cm), are worn tucked under the skirt. The longest everyday huipils in Guatemala are those produced on a foot loom in the villages of the Quezaltenango-Totonicapán basin. They are also worn tucked under the skirt. In the Museum collection, approximately half are in the medium range, while the long and short ones each account for about a quarter.[9]

The huipil worn in San Juan Atitán, Huehuetenango (fig. 201) is unique among backstrap-woven garments because it is the only long non-*cofradía* huipil that was worn *outside* the skirt in the 1960s. In length, width, and placement of the brocading, this huipil is the one most like those seen in the codices (fig. 71). Otherwise, long huipils worn outside the skirt are generally restricted to *cofradía* costume.

Skirts (Cortes)

Most skirts are woven on the foot-powered treadle loom. Lengths of fabric called *cortes* (lit., "cuts") are sold in the market and must be sewn together before they are suitable for wearing. The skirt fabric is often cut into two equal parts which are sewn together lengthwise at the warp selvedges (fig. 72). In a few villages a single panel is lengthened and strengthened by the addition of a strip comprised of three to four weft cuts along one side selvedge (fig. 73). In most cases, the resulting rectangle is then joined at its weft ends to form a tube. The wearer steps into the tube, folds excess length over or under depending on village custom, and then folds and wraps the excess width around her hips (fig. 74). An ample belt stabilizes the garment at the waist.

While tube skirts are most common, there are two other kinds of skirts. Sometimes the cloth is simply hemmed at the ends, wrapped several times around the body and tucked in at the ends as in Santiago Atitlán and Sacapulas (fig. 75). In certain villages, such as Quezaltenango and the villages of Alta Verapaz, women wear a hemmed skirt that is gathered on a cord, pulling in the fullness at the waist, more like a European-style skirt (fig. 76).

71. Long huipils as shown in Codex Lienzo de Tlaxcala.

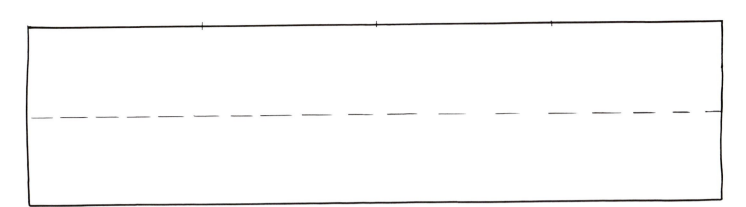

72. Two panels sewn together to form a skirt.

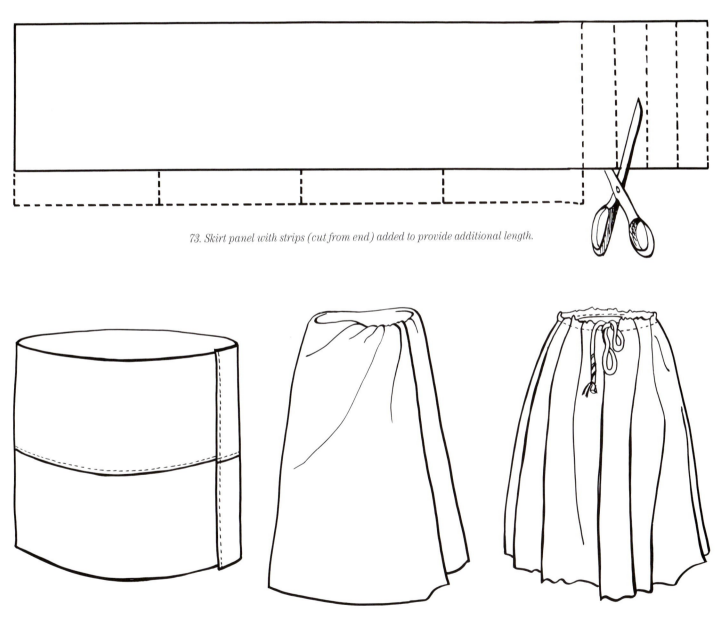

73. Skirt panel with strips (cut from end) added to provide additional length.

74. Tube skirt.   *75. Single-panel wrapped skirt.*   *76. Gathered skirt with drawstring.*

In their simplicity, skirts are as versatile as huipils and are easily adaptable to a variety of body sizes and shapes. Although the bottom border may be defined by a velvet strip, top and bottom are most often undesignated, so that either end of a skirt can be worn up. Close examination of a well-worn skirt may reveal that the skirt has been rotated, assuring an even distribution of wear. This can be done with tube skirts and wraparounds as well as with gathered skirts. Many skirts are often worn inside out as well, thanks to the nature of the flat-felled seam, which is not only strong but looks well finished on either side (fig. 77).

Sometimes the skirt panels are joined with a decorative embroidery called *randa* (fig. 78). Both the nature of the join and the way it is positioned when worn depend on village custom, the use of the skirt, and what is affordable. A woman may do it herself or pay someone else to do it. A *randa* takes a long time to execute and the finest ones are likely to be made of imported mercerized cotton *(sedalina)* or silk floss, which are expensive. A *randa* is finished on both sides, so it, too, is reversible.

The foot loom weaving of skirts has proved to be a healthy village industry for men in widely dispersed areas of the highlands and each group has produced distinctive styles traditional to their market area. The male weavers of Huehuetenango are best known for their red skirts sold to Ixil villages (fig. 79). Men of San Pedro Sacatepéquez (San Marcos) weave the golden yellow skirts of rayon and cotton with green and ikat plaid that are worn by the Mam women in that area (fig. 80). Local men in large villages like Sololá and Santiago Atitlán produce the skirt yardage appropriate for their own village. By the 1960s and early 1970s the skirt made by Rabinal weavers was no longer favored by local women, who purchased double-ikat skirts from Totonicapán. The old Rabinal style, however, was still being produced for Joyabaj and San Miguel Chicaj. The ikat skirts worn in Zunil and Almolonga are woven by local men.[10]

Only in Western Huehuetenango do women still regularly produce skirts on backstrap looms as in Prehispanic times, when there were no floor looms and women wove all the cloth for their families' needs. Women of Ixtahuacán, Colotenango, and San Rafael Petzal weave and wear similar skirts, predominantly red with indigo or black warp stripes and supplementary weft designs (fig. 81). Women of San Pedro Necta, Santiago Chimaltenango, and San Juan Atitán weave and wear a dark indigo skirt with three sets of lighter and brighter blue warp stripes.[11]

77. Flat-felled seam on a skirt from Patzicía.

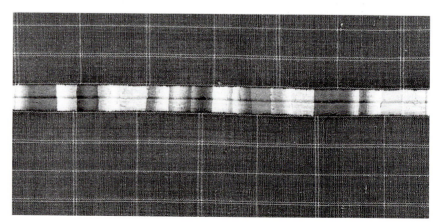

78. Panels joined with a decorative randa on a skirt from San Juan Sacatepéquez.

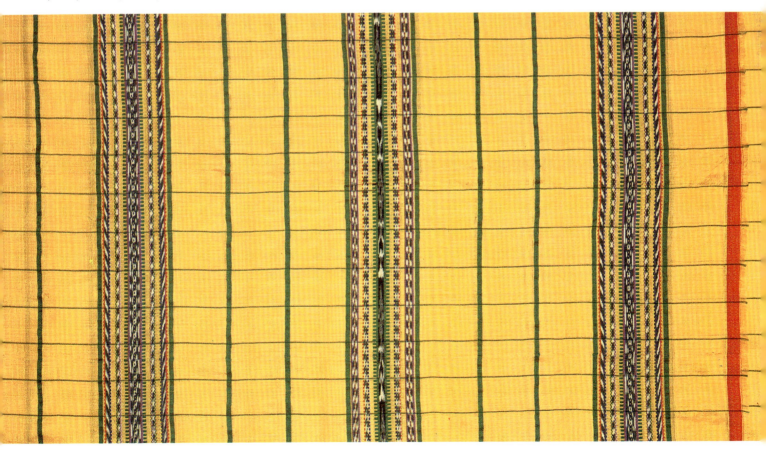

79 (above). Detail of a skirt from Soloma.

80 (below). Detail of a skirt from San Pedro Sacatepéquez (SM).

81. *Detail of a skirt from San Rafael Petzal.*

82. *Detail of a skirt from San José Nacahuil.*

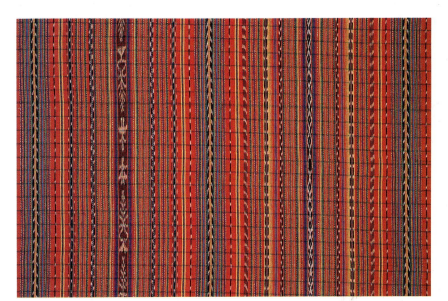

83. *Detail of an old Rabinal-style skirt.*

84. *Detail of an ikat skirt from Zunil.*

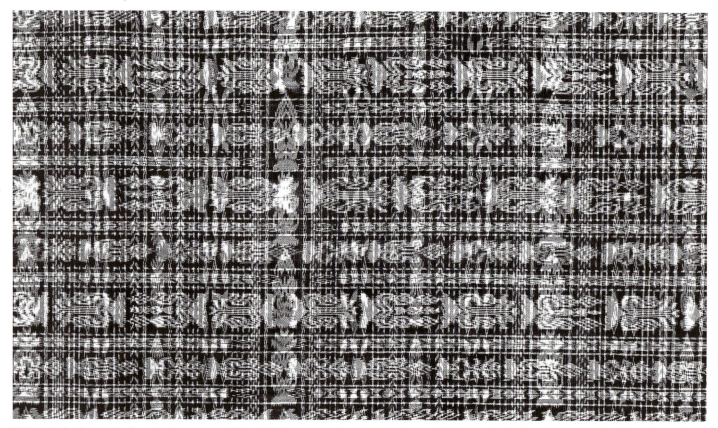

85. Detail of a double ikat from the department of Totonicapán, worn in San Andrés Xecul.

86. Boy from Salcajá untying ikat threads.

Ikat

Salcajá and its neighboring towns of Totonicapán and Quezaltenango are considered to be the real center for *jaspe,* or ikat (tie-dyed or reserve-dyed threads). Here is where the double — warp and weft — ikat skirts of dizzying patterns originate (figs. 85,87), and where the weaving workshops are concentrated. In the 1960s, ikat was growing in popularity, although it had not yet become the most common skirt choice (as it is today).

The making of *jaspe* thread is a very labor-intensive process. The threads must be measured, wrapped, and tied in the proper sequence from traditional patterns that are precisely kept in the craftsman's memory. Often it is a family operation; but the attitude is very professional. Young boys start out by sweeping, minding the dye vats, or untying the threads (fig. 86), and end up expert artisans.

The threads are dyed in vats (sometimes more than once) and then hung out to dry (fig. 89). On a clear day the whole village seems festooned with miles of dyed thread. Once they have dried, the ties must be unwrapped and removed, leaving the now indigo-and-white patterned threads to be wrapped on shuttles and thus prepared for the loom. A simple pattern of dotted lines or "bleeps," which weavers call "space-dyeing," is easy enough to create. But elaborate ikat motifs such as the tree, urn, lyre, or human figure can be tremendously complicated.

For most purposes a fuzzy effect is sufficient, but some weavers are exceptionally particular, positioning the thread as exactly as possible. For precise weft ikats, the weaver adjusts the thread at both edges of the textile, weaving the excess back into the selvedge area. The sharper designs are done mostly in San Cristóbal Totonicapán (fig. 88) and they are more expensive. An ikat skirt is more labor intensive and thus more expensive than the old-style, plain, striped or plaid weaves; on the other hand, the costly decorative *randa* that adorns most non-ikat skirts is unnecessary with jaspe. Traders with *jaspe* textiles invariably have large displays in highland markets.

Origins of Ikat. When and how ikat came to be used in highland weaving is a mystery. Ikat weaves have been unearthed in Peru and the technique could have been transmitted from there northward. Drawings from Mexican codices, however, give us no indication that it was used there in the pre-Conquest period, nor is there any evidence of its early use in Guatemala either.

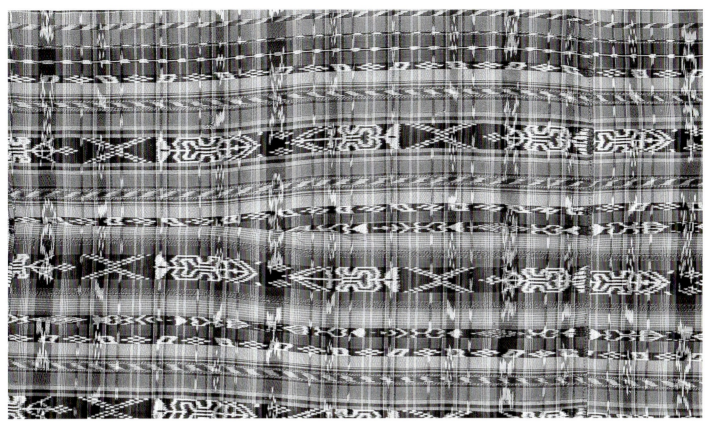

87. *Detail of a double ikat woven in Totonicapán, worn in Sacapulas.*

89. *Ikat threads, still wrapped (right), and unwrapped (left).*

88. *Detail of an ikat cloth from San Cristóbal Totonicapán.*

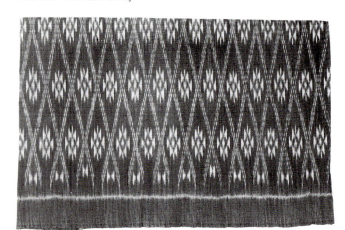

90. Ikat cloth from Eastern Thailand or Laos.

91. Ikat cloth from Totonicapán.

Merchandise lists appear to provide at least one example of late sixteenth-century export of ikat to the New World. Such imports would have been used by the Spaniards, however — not by the indigenous people. There is no evidence that this material was worn, copied, or even noticed by the highland Maya at that early date.[12]

Indigo ikat skirts woven today in Laos and eastern Thailand (fig. 90), and worn in the same manner as Guatemalan skirts, bear a marked resemblance to one of the earliest *jaspe* styles (fig. 91), pointed out to us by one of the oldest contemporary skirt weavers in Totonicapán, Pedro Velasquez. It is certainly possible that the Manila galleons could have brought examples or even practitioners of ikat weaving from the Pacific.[13]

Yet there is no sign that ikat was used by highland weavers until the late nineteenth century, and judging from available visual evidence, it was used only sparingly. A late nineteenth-century photograph shows an ikat skirt with a simple "bleep" pattern in the weft only. Double *jaspe* skirts were photographed (and labeled "…from Antigua") in the 1920s by McDougall.[14]

It was in 1861 that Salcajá installed the first foot looms for weaving ikat fabric, according to Osborne. In the 1930s, O'Neale reported that ikat skirts were making inroads into the old village-specific heavy weave *(morga)* styles and that both types were being worn in many towns. She records three different skirt styles in Santiago Atitlán: a blue-and-white plaid, a red-and-blue check, and a red with weft ikat figures and stripes. The latter was most often seen in the early 1960s. The first ikat weaves were indigo and white. Then green was added, and then other colors such as orange, cerise, and acid green were combined with *jaspe* stripes for the skirt of choice in most villages. This tendency to add color and ikat striping has accelerated since the 1970s.[15]

That the old style village-specific indigo and white plaids, stripes, checks, and plains still exist is a testimony to conservatism. In the 1960s, *cofradía* members and old women invariably preferred the old traditional styles. And in the outlying areas, there were still weavers producing the heavy *morga* weaves and dense solids seen by O'Neale in the 1930s. Many of them worked only part time at their looms (they were farmers or marimba players, for instance), so their output was irregular but available to those who could wait. Although synthetic indigo dyes had replaced the natural ones that were an item of trade for the Spaniards during the colonial period, the dyeing methods had changed little and the chemical formula was the same.[16]

Plain and simple though they are, we treasure the old indigo skirts in the Museum's collection. Indigo dyes are fugitive and new skirt fabrics are stiff with the residue of the dyeing process. Not until the cloth has been washed many times, and slapped and pounded on stones, does it lose its extra blue dye and take on a supple feel. Indigo becomes more and more lustrous with wear and washing; some of the older indigo-dyed fabrics look like molten silver (fig. 92).

92. Detail of an ikat perraje from Salcajá.

93. Detail of a tzute from Zunil.

Utility and Special Purpose Cloths

Backstrap-woven cloths with special and often multiple purposes were commonplace in the 1960s. Some were strictly utilitarian and not intended to be worn. They vary considerably in size and function and are known by a number of different names depending on language and function. The *cargador* is used for carrying a baby, and must be densely woven as its strength is vital to its function. The *servilleta* generally has a white background and is used to cover food. A *chivo* incorporates half-inch long loops of thread in the weaving and is wrapped around tortillas to keep them warm. The cloth twisted in a circle and put on the head to cushion a clay water jug or a just-purchased cooking pot is called a *yagual*. *Tzutes* are used to wrap bundles (such as firewood or clothing), cover a rolled-up loom between weaving sessions, and wrap small food items like beans, eggs, or fruit.[17]

In addition to these utilitarian functions, the *tzute* is also a remarkably versatile component of costume, most importantly as a wrap for extra warmth — sometimes worn wrapped around the shoulders with adjacent corners tied at the neck. The ample, two-web, rectangular *tzutes* of Zunil (fig. 93), Nebaj, Chajul, and Panajachel (fig. 94) are all-enveloping wraps. Those of Sololá, Santiago Sacatepéquez, and San Juan Sacatepéquez are slightly smaller and are used as wraps or *cargadores*. Small

94. Detail of a tzute from Panajachel.

tzutes are made from a single web, but larger ones are likely to be made of two sections, often joined by means of a decorative *randa*.

Used as a baby carrier, the *tzute* is tied at opposite corners over one shoulder and under the other arm, so as to cradle the baby in the folds. Folded and put on the head, it serves in almost all villages as a sunshade for women sitting in the market. For ceremonial purposes the *tzute* serves to mark status as well as to cover the head, for example in Santa Catarina Palopó and San Antonio Palopó, where red-and-white plaid *tzutes* are worn by members of the *cofradía*.

In the 1960s, backstrap-woven *tzutes*, like all backstrap textiles, were woven and decorated in keeping with village stylization and color concepts because aesthetics are an important aspect of the weaver's work no matter what utilitarian function is involved. Foot-loom-woven *tzutes* were less individualized and tended to be indigo-and-white plaids and checks, the ubiquitous style of the time; but in the Sacatepéquez region brighter color schemes were preferred.

Now commercial cloths produced on the foot loom have generally replaced backstrap-woven *tzutes* for heavy-duty utility purposes. Used, for example, to wrap around baskets filled with grains and produce that are hoisted up on top of buses or carried back and forth to village markets, utility cloths are subject to excessive wear and tear.

96. Market ladies with shawls in Santiago Atitlán.

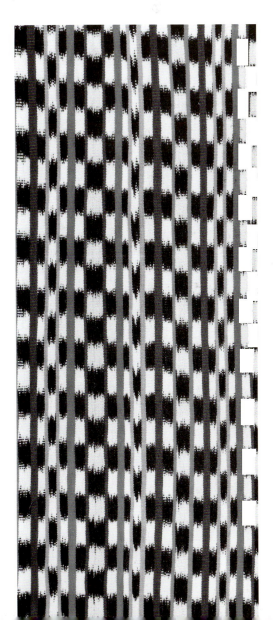

97. Simple ikat pattern of the early 1960s on a shawl from Santiago Atitlán.

Shawls (Perrajes, Tzutes, Rebozos)

In many villages the long shawl produced in quantities on foot looms, called *perraje* by Guatemalan Maya and *rebozo* by Mexicans and Guatemalan Ladinos, is gradually taking over as the wrap of choice in many villages. It is popular with tourists and Ladino women as well. The *perraje* is a long rectangle constructed of a single panel approximately thirty inches wide and six or seven feet long. Ends are fringed or knotted or both. Often large tassels are added; in the 1960s these were of wool, but since then acrylics have become more usual. The earliest *perrajes* were at first made of cotton; later, silk and wool were sometimes added. (Now they are often made of acrylic fibers, with a liberal sprinkling of cotton ikat combined with warp stripes in high intensity colors.)[18]

An all indigo-and-white ikat cotton shawl was the most popular choice of the 1960s and could be seen in villages as widely separated as Cobán and Quezaltenango (fig. 95). A lighter-weight version, sold in quantity in Guatemala City, was very inexpensive. A heavier, more opulent one with more intricate designs was sold in Antigua and Quezaltenango. Both styles were made by professional foot-loom weavers in the Quezaltenango-Salcajá-Totonicapán area and in Mazatenango. Although these have disappeared from the markets, old, beautifully faded ones are still seen occasionally on older women.

The shawl of Santiago Atitlán falls into a category of its own (figs. 97,98). Though also of one-panel construction, it is made on a backstrap loom and is narrower and a little shorter than the commercial shawl. Worn seemingly more for its decorative effect than for warmth or utility, the *perraje* is slung over one shoulder and there it stays as if by magic no matter how active the wearer is. In the 1960s it was a necessary accoutrement for all the ladies in the market (fig. 96). A *cofradía* garment of the same size and shape, and worn in the same way, is woven of brown cotton with warp stripes in mauve to resemble the ancient mollusk dye, *purpura*. Its coloring is evidence of its status. Both secular and sacred garments are selvedged on one end and hemmed on the other with thin tassels of silk or cotton fastened to the bottom corners, or the bottom is knotted and fringed. From the 1930s to the 1950s, the everyday Santiago Atitlán *perraje* was made with plain warp stripes. In the 1960s, a few ikat stripes were added (fig. 97). In the 1970s some were being made with two panels instead of one, and ikat had taken over, creating a checkered effect (fig. 98).[19]

95 (left). Detail of shawl in a style worn throughout the highlands during the 1960s.
98 (right). Complex ikat pattern on a shawl from Santiago Atitlán.

Sashes and Belts (Fajas)

The *faja* is not just a subsidiary part of the costume, it is clearly crucial as it holds up the skirt. More than that, it unifies the whole costume aesthetically, often providing the magic color or design ingredient that makes seemingly disparate parts work together. Some *fajas* are narrow, rather rigid, and belt-like, while others are wider and more flexible, like sashes. The Maya do not make such distinctions: both types are called by the name *faja*. A *faja* may be as long as seventeen and a half feet (eight or nine is the usual), and in most villages all of that length is wrapped around and then tucked in at the end to give a firm grip on the skirt. If the wearer is pregnant or old, she may use a wider sash or spread out a narrow one. This wide binding will serve as a girdle for extra support.

Women in many different villages make their own *fajas* on backstrap looms in the different stripes and brocade designs traditional to their villages (fig. 99a-i). The average is from six to eight inches in width and most are long, winding several times around the waist with the ends tucked under the band. Generally speaking, young women prefer narrow *fajas*, while older women wear them wide.

99. Backstrap-woven belts from (left to right): (a) Chajul, (b) Tecpán, (c) San Antonio Aguas Calientes, (d) San Marcos la Laguna, (e) Santa María Cauqué, (f) Santa María de Jesús, (g) Sololá, (h) Comalapa, (i) Palín.

A great number of *fajas* are woven by men using belt looms. In many villages, the *faja* has traveled the longest distance to join the costume. The women from Mixco, which has been absorbed into greater Guatemala City, used to wait for their *fajas* to be brought from Oaxaca, Mexico, by traders who came once a year in the dry season. Zunil women go to Cantel to purchase thick wool tapestry-woven *fajas* which are made in the piedmont towns of Santa Cruz Mulua and San Sebastián (Retalhuleu) and brought by traders to the highlands.

Men from the Chichicastenango area make a *faja* of black and white wool (or wool and cotton) which is sold in many villages throughout the highlands (fig. 100c). The *faja* can be worn plain or it can be used as a base for embroidery. In Chichicastenango, men embroider the women's *fajas*. One long end, enough to cover the outside wrap, is covered with either geometric designs or fanciful and colorful flowers using every possible stitch in a fine embroiderer's repertory in either cotton, silk or wool (fig. 100c). Cakchiquel women use silk and wool in many colors to embroider the belts of San Pedro Sacatepéquez (fig. 100b), Chuarrancho (fig. 100a), and San Juan Sacatepéquez near Guatemala City. Weavers say the stripe pattern serves as a guide for their many motifs, which often completely cover the belt. The *faja* of Santiago Sacatepéquez also has black-and-white stripes, is about half as wide, and ends in dangling, life-saver-like balls of multicolored yarns (fig. 101).[20]

100a-c (opposite). Belts embroidered on a black-and-white base made in Chichicastenango. Two sections of (c) are shown.

101 (below). Belt from Santiago Sacatepéquez.

Mam women from the Quezaltenango area wear a black-and-white warp-striped wool *faja* made by professional belt weavers in San Juan Ostuncalco (fig. 102d). It is wider and heavier, the white stripes are narrower than those from Chichicastenango, and the ends are twisted and tied in a tight fringe. The red wool cinch belt worn in Todos Santos and San Juan Atitán (the same style worn in Chiapas, Mexico) is made by men in San Sebastián (fig. 102a). Other woolen belts made on the foot loom are the brown-and-white striped *faja* from Aguacatán (fig. 102c) and the narrow black-and-white striped one from Almolonga (fig. 102b).

Totonicapán belt weavers make a stiff belt with maguey weft fibers and a cotton warp, used in a number of villages (fig. 103a-f). They are covered with finely brocaded designs in rows depicting hands, urns, dance figures, animals, and geometric forms. Sold to women in markets all over Guatemala, these are the belts most likely to be seen with a trade huipil and an ikat skirt, the costume for those Guatemalan women who do not weave their own clothes.

102 (above). Striped wool belts from (left to right): (a) Todos Santos, (b) Almolonga, (c) Aguacatán, (d) San Juan Ostuncalco.

103 (opposite). Fajas made in Totonicapán and used in (left to right): (a) Totonicapán, (b) San Francisco el Alto, (c) Santa Lucía Utatlán, (d) Quetzaltenango, (e) Salcajá, (f) San Antonio Aguas Calientes.

Hairties and Headwraps (Cintas)

Maya women do not cut their hair, but decorate and contain it in ways which vary from a simple binding of braids to an elaborate coiffure. To do this they use a woven band which is wound around the hair and then around the head to produce a decorative effect. This hairtie or headwrap *(cinta)* made of woven strips varies greatly in width from one-half inch, as in San Antonio Palopó, to seventeen and a half inches, as in Nebaj (fig. 104). In some villages the *cinta* is worn every day, in others only on special occasions. In certain areas women weave their own *cintas*. Elsewhere hairwraps are produced by specialists who supply a whole area with the products from their looms. By the late 1960s women in many villages had given up wearing *cintas* and instead braided wide taffeta ribbons (made up from yardage) into their hair, making fat bows at the ends or at the nape where the braids joined together.

Ixil women from Chajul and Nebaj are among those who make their own headwraps on the backstrap loom. In contrast to the ultra-wide Nebaj *cinta*, the one made in

104. Nebaj woman with an elaborate headwrap.

Chajul is narrow (fig. 105a). Nearby, the women of Aguacatán, who have largely given up making huipils and skirts, continue to weave headwraps for themselves on backstrap looms. Two to three inches wide, the Aguacatán *cinta* is known all over Guatemala for the colorful beauty of its brocaded design forms (fig. 105b). The *cintas* worn in Zunil, Almolonga, and Rabinal (fig. 105c) are woven for local use and made of cotton, with intricate and varied designs. The *cinta* with the stylized corn plant design is from San Juan Ostuncalco (fig. 105d).

105. Headwraps from (top to bottom): (a) Chajul (two sections shown), (b) Aguacatán,
(c) Rabinal (two sections shown), (d) San Juan Ostuncalco.

106.

107.

108.

Commercial *cintas* are produced in Totonicapán by men and some women, usually members of a weaving family. Stylistically reminiscent of the Zunil, Almolonga, and Rabinal *cintas*, their designs are less intricate and they are not made of cotton, but rather of rayon, usually weft-faced with multicolored rayon fibers in a tapestry weave. Some end in a long fringe with wispy balls. A section wrapped in silver thread usually indicates fiesta or ceremonial wear. Examples from the 1930s to the 1960s were often made of silk and embellished with rabbits, birds, and geometric motifs (fig. 106). The *cintas* from Totonicapán are sold all over Guatemala in tourist markets to be used as belts or hat bands. They were more popular with Maya women between the 1930s and the 1960s than they are now.

Weavers in San Sebastián, Huehuetenango, specialize in producing *cintas* for the Mam women of several Mam villages in the area. The San Sebastián hairtie material is made of red wool, measures only three-quarters of an inch wide, and is sold by the *braso* (an arm's length). The amount of *cinta* used for a headwrap varies, however, from village to village, as does the way of tying it in the hair. One *cinta* is criss-crossed over the forehead like a turban, another is wrapped and tied in a bow on the side front, a third is wrapped on itself like a halo, a fourth is tied in back, and so on.

Also of red wool, but far more unusual since it was already rare by the 1960s, is the *tupui* of Cobán (fig. 107). In the *tupui* the red wool strands are not woven or braided but simply wrapped in thread, and they end in long decorated tassels said to signify a serpent. A somewhat related type, and also of historical importance, is the black braided wool *tocoyal* with heavy tassels which is worn by the women of Santa María Chiquimula (fig. 108). Hair, considered part of the living matter of a person, might be used by a witch *(brujo)* to bring harm to that person. Therefore women would entangle their fallen-out hairs in the *tupui* or *tocoyal* to keep them from evil hands.[21]

Two *cintas* in the Museum collection offer clear evidence of the copying of motifs. The original source for both is to be found in the Chinese silk brocade ribbons used in the ceremonial headdress of women from San Pedro Sacatepéquez, in Guatemala department (fig. 109a). The narrower brocaded *cinta* from Jacaltenango (fig. 109b) copies the bird on the Chinese ribbons, even to the extent of color changes on the head and tail. A branch, a bird's nest with four eggs, and four large flowers are clearly visible in the same locations on both. A second *cinta* made in San Martin Sacatepéquez (fig. 109c) displays the same motifs and may be modeled on the Chinese pattern; but it is not as faithful to the source as the one from Jacaltenango, and may have been copied from the latter rather than directly from the Chinese example.[22]

Design Components

Color

The strongest impression one receives from a richly decorated Guatemalan costume is one of dazzling color. It may therefore come as a surprise to learn that our 1960s collection shows white to be the predominant background color of most huipils, and it is probably the white ground that contributes to the luminosity of each color. Included among these is a large subgroup of red-and-white striped huipils favored by Mam villages in Huehuetenango and several Lake Atitlán villages. Red is the second most common background color, and indigo is third. The most valued background color is the rich medium brown of *cuyuscate* or *ixcaco,* a naturally colored cotton grown locally in small plots. Because of its scarcity and the fact that it needs to be handspun since the fibers are so short, it is usually reserved for special ceremonial huipils. It was consistently used in the early 1960s as a stripe in the *camisa*-like huipils from Sololá, but no longer. The huipils of San Juan Sacatepéquez and Santo Domingo Xenacoj also often had narrow *cuyuscate* stripes.[23]

Purple is a very popular color for supplementary weft decoration, especially among the Cakchiquel people of Sacatepéquez; but it was seldom used as a background color in the 1960s and before, except when it appeared as stripes on a white background. For decoration, all bright clear saturated colors seem desirable, and half of all huipils and *tzutes* in the 1960s Museum collection have a multicolored decoration whether achieved by supplementary weft techniques or by embroidery.[24]

106. *Commercial headtie from Totonicapán.*
107. *Headtie from Cobán.*
108. *Headtie from Santa María Chiquimula.*

109 (left to right):
(a) Chinese ribbon,
(b) Cinta from Jacaltenango,
(c) Cinta from San Martín Sacatepéquez.

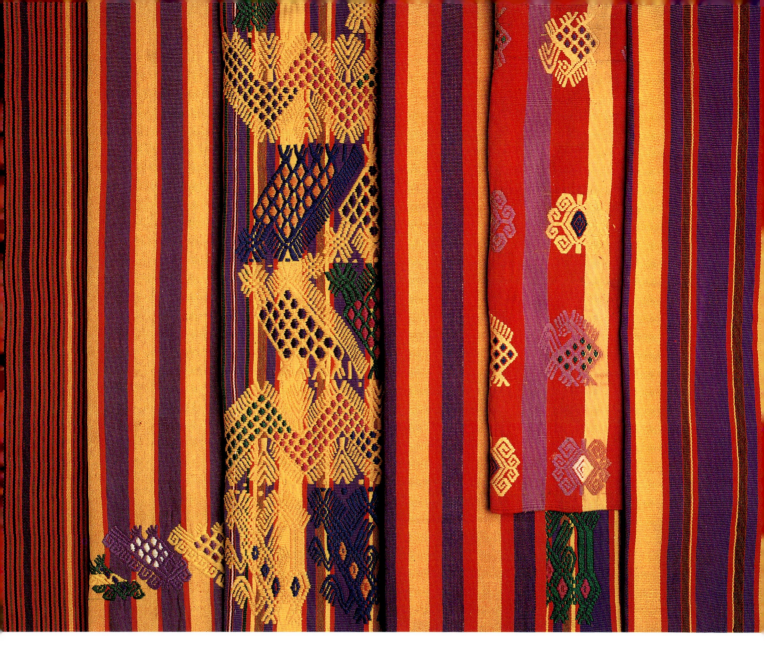

110. *Montage of textiles from San Juan Sacatepéquez.*

Stripes

While Guatemalan and Mexican huipils are similar in some ways, they differ in their use of stripes. Mexican ones rarely feature stripes in the background, except in the Mayan area of Chiapas, close to the Guatemalan border. Guatemalan huipils are remarkable for their sophisticated use of warp stripes, in color combinations ranging from subtle to boldly insistent. There are wide stripes, narrow stripes, pin stripes, saw-toothed or zipper stripes, stripes on stripes, grouped stripes, at random or in sequence, with a white ground, a dark ground, or no ground. The weaver is always in control and seems to know instinctively and exactly how much or how little will give her the effect she seeks. She is a master of composition.

The unusual color combination and the wide variety of stripes found in the textiles of San Juan Sacatepéquez (fig. 110) are especially noteworthy. They are rich and elegant — a palette of mauve, red, yellow-gold, and rich natural brown *cuyuscate*. Within this palette the variety is so great there can be no question of copying. Each solution is personal and inventive yet consistent within traditional confines.

The use of stripes or contrasting colors in the selvedge is especially interesting, for the join then provides an unexpected emphasis. This can appear at the center front and back of a two-web huipil (fig. 111), under the arms of a one-web huipil (fig. 53), and in the suspender-like stripes on a three-web huipil (fig. 112).

Warp stripe development is illustrated by two *camisa*-like huipils from Sololá. Except for its red sleeves, the one from the 1930s has a white ground lightly accented with thin stripes in red, gold, indigo, and green (fig. 113). The one from the 1960s

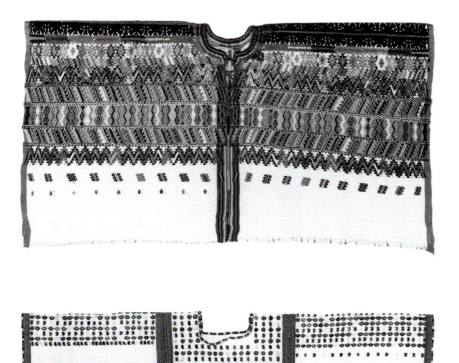

111. Huipil with selvedge stripes from San Pedro Sacatepéquez (G).

112. Huipil with selvedge stripes from Ixtahuacán.

presents a very different look: it is all stripes, ikat, and solid colors in red, blue, orange, and black (fig. 114). While the change may seem great, it was accomplished little by little over the thirty-year span. More gradual development is visible in three huipils from Todos Santos. In the 1930s huipil white predominates (fig. 115); in the 1950s, it is almost half and half (fig. 116); in the 1960s version red is the dominant color (fig. 120).

Weft stripes, less insistent in backstrap-woven huipils, sometimes combine with warp stripes for a plaid background serving as a base or grid for the more elaborate supplementary weft decoration often found in ceremonial huipils. They are sometimes difficult to see (fig. 117). In textiles woven by foot loom, however, strong weft stripes are common, for the weaver uses the weft threads to achieve variety.[25]

Weaving designs and techniques are open to individual experimentation. Some fail; others develop into a new style. Comparing huipils over a fifty-year period, it is amazing to discover how much change can occur within the boundaries of tradition. This is evident in a comparison of three huipils from Santiago Atitlán (figs. 117-119). Those of the 1930s (and up to the 1960s in *cofradía* garments) have only a faint weft stripe (fig. 117). During the early 1960s, weavers added a supplementary weft inlay, simple in execution, with running skipping weft threads (fig. 118). Before long, what had previously been a simple warp and weft stripe now became a shimmering plaid all the way to the hem with weft threads now predominating (fig. 119). This buildup of pattern upon pattern occurs in greater complexity as time goes on and as the adventurous curiosity of the weaver is challenged by new possibilities and new ideas.

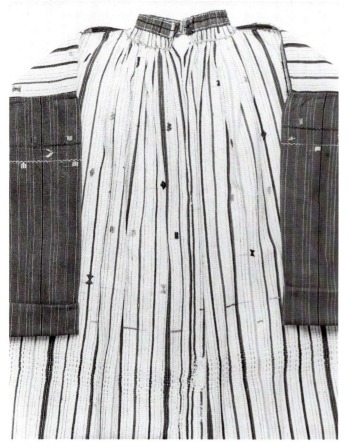

113. Sololá huipil from the 1930s.

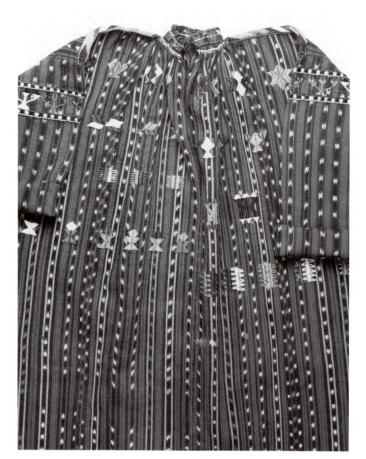

114. Sololá huipil from the 1960s.

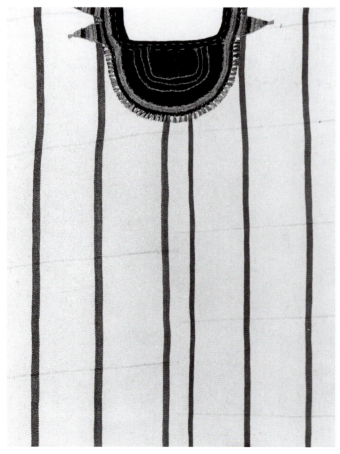

117. Santiago Atitlán huipil in style of the 1930s.

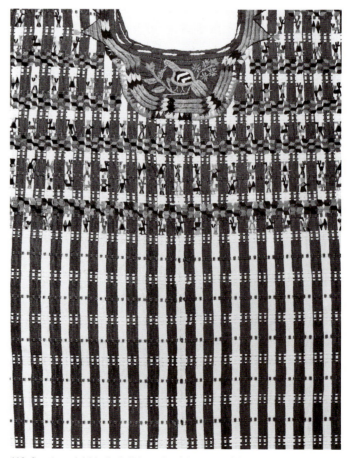

118. Santiago Atitlán huipil in style of the early 1960s.

115. Todos Santos huipil from the early 1950s.

116. Todos Santos huipil from the early 1960s.

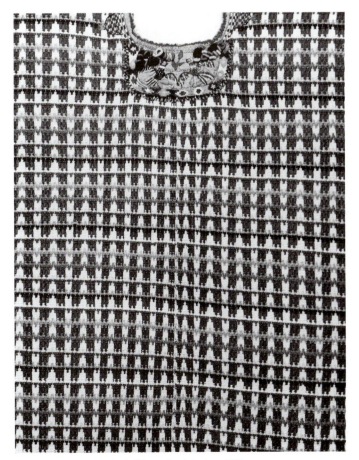

119. Santiago Atitlán huipil in style of the late 1960s.

120. Todos Santos huipil from the late 1960s.

121. Single-faced brocade on a Mixco huipil.

122. Two-faced brocade on a Totonicapán trade huipil.

123. Double-faced brocade on a tzute from San Antonio Aguas Calientes.

Brocading

The use of supplementary weft threads to float a raised pattern or design — that is, brocading — has a long tradition in Guatemala and it is a technique in which Maya weavers excel. A brocaded design can be single-faced, with a clear solid pattern on the top side and scarcely a trace showing on the reverse side (fig. 121). It can be two-faced, with a positive pattern on top and a negative one underneath (fig. 122). Or it can be double-faced, looking exactly the same top and bottom (fig. 123).

Usually a village favors one technique over the other. Sometimes, however, two techniques are used in the same garment. In San Antonio Aguas Calientes, a village famed for the quality and variety of its weaving, a number of designs (usually curvilinear) were introduced into the village from European pattern books and began to be used along with their traditional designs, which were angular. The indigenous designs are invariably single-faced, the European ones double-faced, and they are often found together on the same textile. The weavers of Comalapa, where European-style designs are commonplace, also follow this practice.

Brocaded designs can vary considerably in complexity of execution and patterning effect. Some are accomplished by means of an extra heddle stick, making a dense overlay pattern, as in San Juan Atitán and Todos Santos. Some are worked in and out of the warp threads by the use of a tapered bone pick-up tool (San Antonio Aguas Calientes). But most are worked only with the agile fingers of the weaver (hence the term finger-weaving). Some brocades are pulled taut and flat against the background (fig. 124); with the flick of a finger others are raised in loops above the textile surface creating a sumptuous effect (fig. 125), a technique especially popular with Santo Domingo Xenacoj weavers. Density is controlled by the thickness and number of the supplementary threads.

Another means by which a design is created on and in the textile is the wrapping technique called *soumak*. Again supplementary weft threads are manipulated to bring a different crispness and form by wrapping selected warps, making each float appear slightly slanted. The most outstanding example of this laborious technique is the huipil from Zacualpa with purple supplementary wefts forming a diagonal design, changing directions in every row (fig. 126). In Santa Catarina Palopó, San Lucas Tolimán, and several Mam villages in the Huehuetenango area, wrapping is used to produce small sharply outlined designs (fig. 127).

The weaver must keep count of the threads that compose each design. In a complex pattern, the count becomes more and more difficult. It would be hard even if the supplementary weft threads were continuous and all one color. Usually, however, they are discontinuous and six or more colors must be composed with the eye, remembered in the head, and then transferred to the textile by adroit manipulation of the threads. At the same time the weaver must keep the tension correct and the loom taut while she beats down on the batten to secure the firmness and stability of each row. No wonder it can take one half hour per row, up to three months for a professional weaver, and much more for a woman to weave a special huipil for herself. For a skilled weaver, these decisions are quick and sure, supported by generations of weaving skills, or as someone once said, "the endless repetition of a lesson learned."[26]

Brocading is also produced on foot looms by male weavers, but the process is more mechanical and lacks the individual look and feel of backstrap weaving. However a few male weavers in Totonicapán, Comalapa, and San Pedro (San Marcos) use the draw loom — a more intricate variety of foot loom — to produce exceptional brocaded huipils. Draw loom production is more costly, since it requires the assistance of another person, but it yields a very fine weave.

Although brocading has a long tradition in Guatemala, placement of the design area on the huipil has changed over the course of several decades. Before the 1960s, only very special garments for special people had lavish brocading. Design patterns for everyday huipils were generally small in size, spaced fairly wide apart and confined to a few set areas: a band across the shoulder, termed *mano*, and one across the chest, termed *pecho*. Silk was often used for brocading in the 1930s, especially if the garment was for ceremonial wear.[27]

124. Brocade on a faja from Sololá.

125. Brocade on a huipil from Santo Domingo Xenacoj.

126. Soumak on a huipil from Zacualpa.

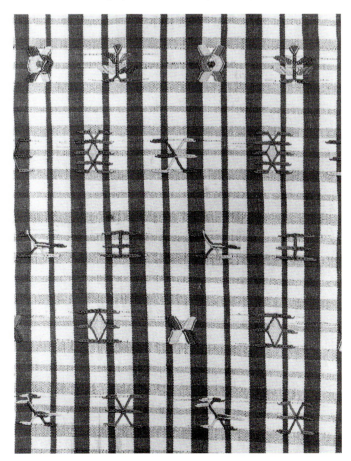

127. Soumak on pantalones from Santa Catarina Palopó.

*128. Neckline of a huipil from
San Andrés Xecul.*

*129. Neckline of a huipil from
Santa María Chiquimula.*

130. *Neckline of a huipil from Sumpango.*

131. *Neckline of a huipil from Santa Barbara.*

Between the 1930s and the 1960s, designs tended to be denser and larger in scale, covering a greater area of the garment. Motifs moved outwards from the shoulder and chest areas — first to a somewhat random placement on the textile palette, and then into clearly delineated rows. Three-panel huipils from the 1930s had little or no decorative design on their side panels. But by the 1950s the design had spread to the sides, and by the 1960s it was fuller still, often reaching to the waist in the center panel. Huipils from Todos Santos exemplify this development (figs. 115,116,120).

The same trend is visible in two-web huipils: brocading earlier confined to the shoulder area starts extending in band after band — first to the chest and then to the waist, until all the design areas meld and one can barely distinguish a *pecho* design. Upon closer look, however, the chest band usually reveals itself, signaled by a change in color or design, or by the appearance of an ancient symbolic motif in that particular position. Thus even as it changes, design remains true to the old traditions.

Embroidery and Appliqué

A significant amount of huipil decoration is accomplished by embroidery and appliqué, techniques that seem to have a long history in the highlands. Several colonial chroniclers, in their reports of native costume, mention embroidery, usually with the addition of feathers. Whether or not it was actually embroidery they saw is uncertain: it could have been brocade, since the resulting visual effects are similar. Brocade is an integral part of the weaving process as it takes form on the loom, while embroidery is added to the garment after it is off the loom.[28]

Embroidery is almost invariably used to embellish the area around the neckline. The neighboring villages of San Cristóbal and San Andrés Xecul, in Totonicapán, have a wide circle of embroidery around the neckline reaching to the shoulder and the chest (fig. 128). Wedding huipils of Cantel and Santa María Chiquimula (fig. 129) have a smaller circle of floral designs, densely compounded. The round hole cut out for the neck is often finished with buttonhole stitch embroidery, and in most villages weavers use a variety of colors complementary to the huipil rather than all one color. The handsome ceremonial huipils of Patzún have a wide embroidered yoke with a feather motif (see page 4). Those from the remote village of Santa Barbara, in the Cuchumatanes, are noted for their eccentric embroidery, and sometimes have tiny feather motifs embroidered around the neckline (fig. 131). Women of Sumpango, although they do not weave, add embroidery to the huipils backstrap-woven for them by Santo Domingo Xenacoj women (fig. 130).

132. Neckline of a huipil from San Mateo Ixtatán.

The most flamboyant use of embroidery is in the San Mateo Ixtatán huipil, with its cosmic stars or radiating sun motif (fig. 132). The decorated area extends in a circle at least to the waist and, often, a few flowers or birds are added below that. The huipil itself is made of two or three layers of cotton muslin, which give it sufficient strength to hold the heavy embroidery without tearing (and also provides additional warmth). Worn outside the skirt, the San Mateo huipil is comfortable on the body in spite of its weight.

Embroidery and appliqué are frequently combined (figs. 133-136). The densely embroidered necklines of Santiago Atitlán daily huipils are typically enhanced with appliqué in a half-moon shape at the front and back (fig. 133). Patzún daily huipils have a similar treatment. The neckline on the ceremonial huipil of Sololá features a zigzag appliqué and rosettes of silk taffeta, velvet, or even cotton, and it too is heavily embroidered (fig. 134). The necklines on huipils made in Nebaj (fig. 135), San Juan Cotzal (fig. 136), and Chichicastenango are all elaborately styled. In a few instances, appliqué appears by itself, as in the zigzag appliqué of the San Lucas Tolimán neckline.[29]

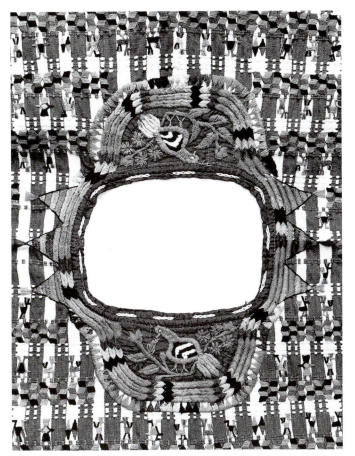

133. *Neckline of a huipil from Santiago Atitlán.*

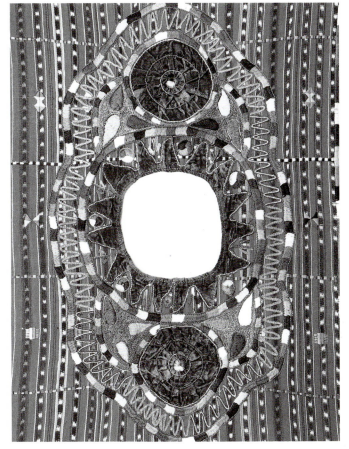

134. *Neckline of a huipil from Sololá.*

135. *Neckline of a huipil from Nebaj.*

136. *Neckline of a huipil from San Juan Cotzal.*

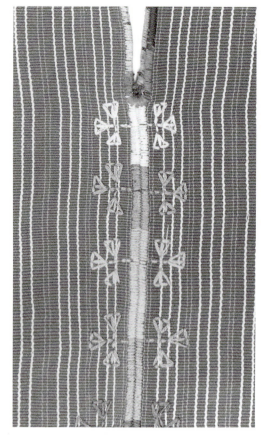

137. *Neckline randa on a huipil from San Sebastián Huehuetenango.*

138. *Decorative randa on a skirt from San Pedro Sacatepéquez.*

The *randa*, mentioned earlier, is the embroidery used to join selvedges. On center joins it usually ties in with the design and coloration of the buttonhole stitch around the neck. In a slit-neck style it appears as a continuation of the neckband (fig. 137). The *randa* is usually overcast on one side, passing under, or at least partially under the facing selvedge to reappear again at the center and then under the other side, creating an interruption or crossover at the midpoint. It can also be formed by feather stitching or other joining needle techniques. The *randa* creates a two-faced seam without overlap, in a secure and colorful way. In a simple daily garment, the *randa* may be the only decorative note (fig. 138), or may add sparkle to a multi-striped selvedge.[30]

Much attention is given to the coloring and workmanship of the *randa*, and indeed it does become a very important design element. Huipil *randas* from the 1960s are rarely more than an inch wide and usually much narrower than that. The widest and most extravagant *randas* are those of the three-panel trade huipils of Quezaltenango; they extend far beyond the join function to form flowing vines or vertical floral patterns over the chest. These are often the work of professional embroiderers, although their handiwork is rapidly being displaced by machine embroidery.

Some huipils from the Totonicapán area in the 1950s and early 1960s had ruffled collars, a trait suggesting European influence. One from San Francisco el Alto has extravagant and beautiful floral embroidery (fig. 139). A more common sort of collar, from Quezaltenango, is unruffled (fig. 140). Relatively narrow (about an inch and three-quarters), it is sewn flat around the neckline. This kind, too, is heavily embroidered — usually by professionals — with birds and flower motifs.[31]

Ribbons, braids, rickrack, and lace all find a place on Guatemalan huipils. A Swiss-type ribbon with crisp brocade daisies is often seen finishing the neckline of a Tecpán huipil. Silk brocade ribbons from China offer a surprising decorative note to several ceremonial costumes and at least one man's ceremonial shirt (from Almolonga). Lace, rickrack, and braid are sewn in circular rows on the long white acrylic brocade huipils of Soloma and San Juan Ixcoy. Colored cotton tape, some commercial and some homemade, is used on the back of muslin huipils from both Aguacatán and Sacapulas, separating decorative bands of machine-stitched flowers, birds, and animals. In the 1960s, machine stitching was so popular in these villages that if no machine was available, the women would copy the machine look by hand.

Symbolic Motifs

The distinctive designs on Guatemalan costume range from geometric patterns of an abstract nature (zigzags, diamonds, chevrons, triangles, squares) to those that are clearly representational (birds, trees, and flowers). Others (suns, rosettes) fall somewhere in between. While the symbolic theories of Carl Jung, Joseph Campbell, and Mircea Eliade, covering a wide range of societies, ancient and modern, can be substantiated in Guatemala, little has been published on motifs and their meaning in Guatemalan costume. Weavers point out that the weaving process naturally produces geometric designs. Art historians note that some of the designs appear to be copied from other cultures or simply act as fillers to tie designs together into a pleasing whole. Most interesting and pertinent, from our point of view, are the motifs common in Maya mythology. Certain ones in particular stand out: these are the feathered serpent, the world tree, the celestial bird, and the sun and moon.

139 (opposite, top). *Ruffled collar on a San Francisco el Alto huipil.*
140 (opposite, bottom). *Trade collar from Quezaltenango.*

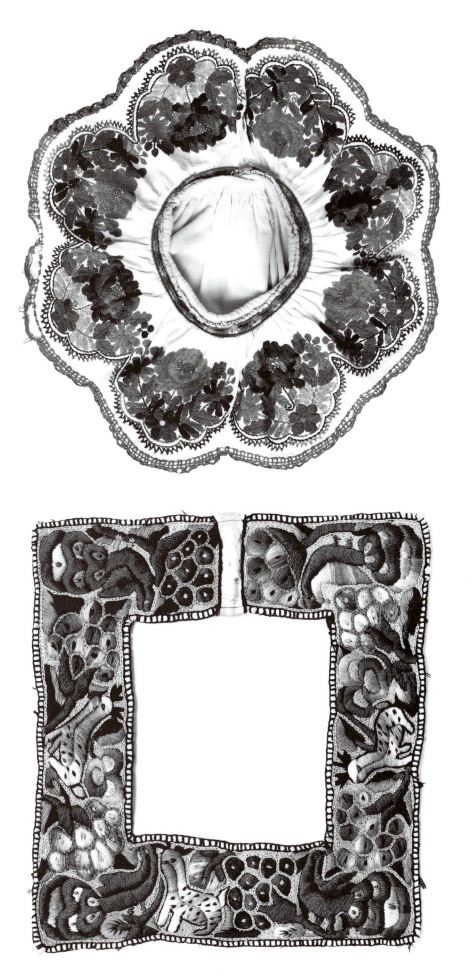

141. Diamonds on a huipil from San Martín Sacatepéquez.

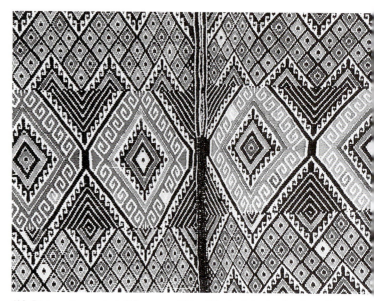

142. Diamonds on a huipil from an aldea of Santa Catarina Ixtahuacán.

143. Diamonds on a tzute from Santa María de Jesús.

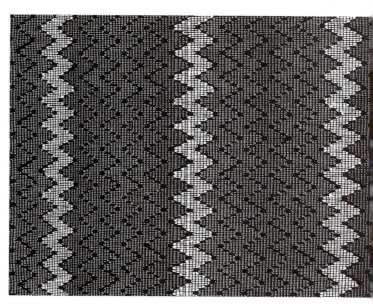

144. Vertical zigzags on fabric from Salcajá.

145. Chevrons on a huipil from San Andrés Semetabaj.

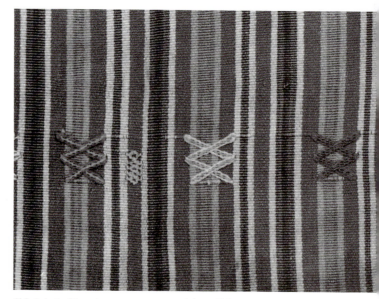

146. Interlocking chevrons on a morral from Colotenango.

Abstract Designs

Geometric forms, particularly diamonds, zigzags, and chevrons, are the most common of the abstract designs in the Museum's collection. Of these, diamonds in one form or another seem to occur most frequently (figs. 141-143). The motif may be simply decorative; however, on the basis of his research in Chiapas, Mexico, where it is also a dominant form, Walter Morris, Jr., sees the diamond as symbolizing the universe, the sky and the earth as a unit. A *Dictionary of Symbols and Imagery* from the Jung Institute library lists the diamond shape as depicting the heavenly womb, and others offer similar interpretations. Belts embroidered by Cakchiquel women of the eastern highlands as well as huipils in various areas show a diamond motif encased in a serpent motif.[32]

Vertical zigzags are almost as common as diamonds and sometimes run the entire visible length of the huipil (fig. 144). De Vries states that the zigzag "is identified with lightning and electricity; the emblem of thunder deities like Zeus." In the Maya highlands, according to Carmack, the god of lightning was the manifestation of Tojil, who also represented the sun, thunder, and storm.[33]

The chevron (one zig) is the third most common abstract design (figs. 145,146). This motif has no known Maya sources. Appearing horizontally in multiples it could indicate motion; singly it suggests an arrow. But until we can find other symbolic references we must assume it is used for aesthetic reasons.

The Feathered Serpent

Most interesting as a symbolic motif is the linear design that appears as a horizontal zigzag, usually with feather-like embellishments, extending across the full width of the huipil (fig. 147). This is the motif we have designated as the feathered serpent. Anthropologists generally acknowledge the existence of the feathered serpent as a Mesoamerican symbol; many examples exist in Maya artifacts — carved in stone or delicately painted on clay pots. J.E.S. Thompson mentions the equivalence between the rain gods of the lowlands (the Chacs) and the mountain gods of the highlands, both of which are closely associated with snakes. As depicted on monumental sculptures or on pots they appear to have feathers rather than scales. An important Maya Quiché deity was related to the Aztec feathered serpent, Quezalcoatl. Earth deities and the serpent were especially important to the Cakchiquel.[34]

On backstrap-woven huipils the feathered serpent symbol is usually found in the chest position. On foot-loom-woven huipils from the 1960s and earlier, the same serpent form generally occurs in narrow bands across the textile panels. It is not always easy to locate this motif; in fact in some cases it seems that the weaver is deliberately concealing its presence. But once the eye has picked it out it seems to be everywhere (fig. 148). It is especially noticeable on the huipils of the Cakchiquel

147 (above). Feathered serpent motifs.

148. Feathered serpent motif on a trade huipil strip from Totonicapán.

149. *"S" form on a huipil from San José Nacahuil.*

villages of Tecpán, San Juan Sacatepéquez, San Martin Jilotepeque, and San Antonio Aguas Calientes. In San Antonio Aguas Calientes this symbol is termed *arco* ("arch") and in San Juan Sacatepéquez women refer to the same form as a plant design. These modern designations may well reflect the current displacement of ancient beliefs considered to be superstitious.[35]

Another feathered serpent-like form which we call the S-curve, which can be upright or recumbent, is seen singly, in pairs, or in multiple sequences across the huipil. It is clearly evident on the huipils of San José Nacahuil (fig. 149), and the ceremonial huipil of Santa María de Jesús. A serpent symbol appearing on women's belts is said to represent the male impregnating force. On embroidered *fajas* the snake is often combined with the diamond form. Local folktales tell of the fear among women of being made pregnant by a snake.

Sun Symbols

The circle with rays, one of the most dramatic geometric motifs, probably signifies the sun. The primary importance of the sun to any agricultural society is obvious; and in Mesoamerica the sun symbol transcends all linguistic classifications. The Maya developed a solar calendar, and used a sun symbol as part of the hieroglyph that indicates the first month of the Mayan year. The main temple at Utatlán, the Quiché capital, was dedicated to the sun god Tojil (who was god of thunder and lightning as well). The Quiché conceptualized their world in terms of the sun's movements. The sun was also king of the lower worlds, where it disappeared as night fell. The color red symbolized the rising sun; white equated with the setting sun. Examples of the sun symbol are seen in figures 150 and 151.[36]

Solar symbolism also appears on the neckline decoration of huipils from Chichicastenango, Sumpango, and Todos Santos and is shown in more subtle ways elsewhere with radiating points or other emphases placed on the neckline. In the 1960s the arrangement of the brocading on a number of huipils showed a cross form; however the current trend of brocading to cover nearly the entire huipil has done away with the solar cross in many villages today. As Morris interprets it, "When a Maya woman puts on her huipil, she emerges through the neckhole symbolically in the axis of the world. The designs of the universe radiate from her head, extending over the bodice

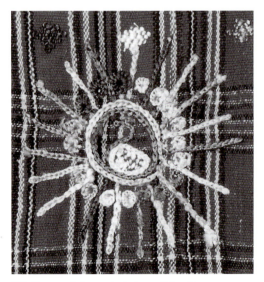

150. *Sun symbol on a tzute from Chimaltenango.*

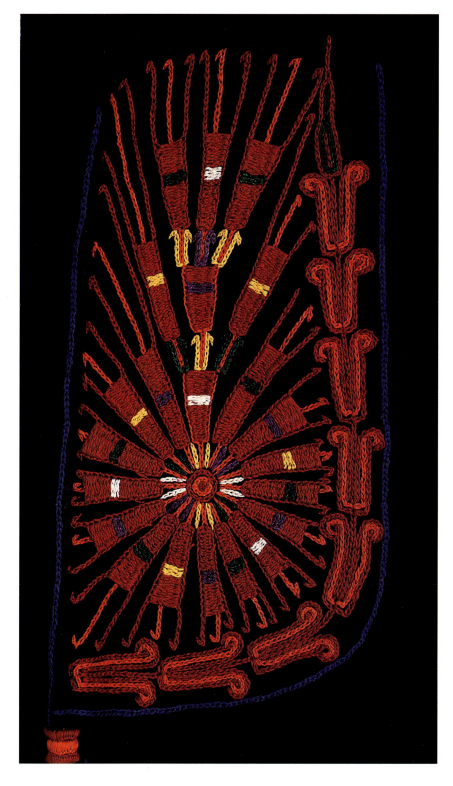

151. Sun symbol on pantalones from Chichicastenango.

and sleeves of the huipil to form an open cross with the woman in the middle." In this he seems to echo Mircea Eliade, who reminds us that archaic man conceived of the universe as expanding outward from a central point where he, himself, was. That center space was sacred; outside were evil spirits, chaos, and a kingdom of the dead from which he needed protection.[37]

In the highlands it is said that the sun represents the masculine, while the moon is symbol of the feminine — passive, fluid, fecund. The moon is believed to regulate the menses as well as the tides, and the full moon is said to ease childbirth. Standing next to the temple of the sun at Utatlán was the temple of the moon, dedicated to the moon goddess, Awilix. The moon is believed to be represented by the appliquéd rosettes found on many ceremonial huipils.[38]

152. *Birds on pantalones from Santiago Atitlán.*

153. *Birds on pantalones from Santiago Atitlán.*

154. *Birds on a huipil from Nebaj.*

155. *Birds on a tzute from Santa María de Jesús.*

156. Double eagles on a headcloth from Patzún.

Fauna and Flora

Of the figural forms seen on huipils, birds are the most obvious and numerous —
although usually of indeterminate species. Guatemala is a paradise for birds of all
kinds and descriptions. Quiché literature mentions hawks, parakeets, parrots,
crows, vultures, quail, doves, hummingbirds, bluebirds, macaws, gulls, and the most
famed bird of all, the quetzal, whose feathers decorated Mayan and Aztec royalty.
Feathers from exotic birds were significant items of long distance trade with the
Yucatán peninsula and the Aztec during the Postclassic period. The most important
month of the Mayan solar calendar was called "bird's days." The leader of the
Tzutujil tribe was called "He of the house of the bird."

In the Tzutujil village of Santiago Atitlán, a variety of fanciful birds decorate
men's pants (figs. 152,153) as well as women's huipils. Side- and front-view birds
decorate 1960s huipils and *tzutes* from Ixil villages (fig. 154) and the same kind of
squat birds are often seen on the Aguacatán hairwraps of the 1960s. Birds outlined.
in sewing machine stitches are seen on Nebaj shawls and Sacapulas huipils. The
birds that are so numerous on Cakchiquel huipils in the departments of Sacatepéquez and Guatemala and on Santa María de Jesús *tzutes* usually line up in rows in
a profile stance (fig. 155). Most of these birds' bodies are formed from multicolored
lozenges. Foot-loom-woven huipil panels also often feature birds.

A notable bird subgroup is the double-headed bird, usually defined as an eagle.
This motif, which appeared on most Chichicastenango huipils of the 1960s, and on
men's *tzutes* and knit bags of the 1950s and 1960s, is also common to many ceremonial
garments and other *cofradía* textiles. The embroidered headcloth *(paya)* from Patzún
is an unusually clear example (fig. 156). Usually these birds are so greatly abstracted
in the weaving process that they are not discernible to the casual eye (figs. 157,158).
Their probable totemic antecedents can be attributed to both European and Maya
sources. The Habsburg double eagle was the emblem of Charles V and since the
conquest of Guatemala (and Mexico) occurred under his aegis, the crest would have

157.

158.

159. *Bird-and-tree motif on a huipil from Quezaltenango.*

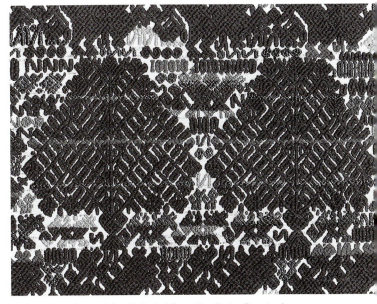

160. *Tree motif on a cofradía huipil from San Pedro Sacatepéquez.*

been used on documents at least, and possibly in other ways (for example, as battle flags). Quiché invaders were believed to have transformed themselves into eagles in order to surprise and defeat the native populations. The double-headed bird is called *cabli o c'ot* (from *c'ot*, meaning "hawk" in both Cakchiquel and Quiché). Thus the double-headed bird symbol was very useful to the indigenous Maya, who had to pretend to be Hispanicized and probably found it helpful to use this syncretism as camouflage.[40]

Birds often appear in trees. Although this motif is found in many cultures, some of the trees are in urns and look very European as indeed they may be; there is striking evidence of their derivation from European brocade designs. The birds in a tree in an urn seen on a *banda* from San Juan Ostuncalco may have European origins (fig. 161); or possibly it came via Europe from China, as did many embroidery and brocade designs and techniques.[41]

On the other hand, the bird-and-tree motif also occurs in Maya iconography. In its simplest form, Mayan cosmological order rests on the belief of a vertical axis penetrating three worlds, an underworld, a middle world, and a heavenly sphere which must be kept in balance. This world view puts humanity in the middle earthly position. More specific Mayan imagery describes a World Tree growing from a watery reptilian underworld that thrusts itself into the sky where a perching bird looks down on man at the earthly center. A bird in a tree occurs in both foot-loom-woven huipils such as the brocaded gauze wedding huipils of the Quezaltenango area (fig. 159) and in backstrap-woven huipils. It is common in Alta Verapaz and is seen in other areas as well.[42]

Trees without birds also appear on huipils — most notably the wide-branched ceiba, which is considered sacred to the Maya. A famous living example of the ceiba, in the village of Palín, is said to be over 450 years old. Designs of the ceiba appear several times on the spectacular *cofradía* huipil of San Pedro Sacatepéquez in the department of Guatemala (fig. 160). The pine tree also has special significance for some villages. Trees in urns, sometimes shaped more like bushes (but counted as trees), are found on Totonicapán belts as well as on foot-loom-woven huipils.[43]

Flowers compete with birds in popularity, and the two are often found together. This, however, seems to be a motif borrowed from European sources, since we know of no floral forms that are Maya. The most recognizable flowers of the 1960s are embroidered and appear to be borrowed from Chinese or European sources. It can be very difficult, especially in weaving, to determine if the form being presented is intended as a flower or a rosette, but we have considered most such forms to be flowers.

Animal motifs often look more mythic than real, or don't look like animals at all. If a figure was depicted with more than three legs we assumed it to be an animal, but we have since found out that the number of legs it has may be more significant than what it represents, as numbers are symbolic to the Maya. Horses appear on the men's knitted bag of Nahualá and on the old style festive huipils and *tzutes* of Nebaj but the occurrences were too few to appear significant.[44]

161. *Bird-and-tree motif on a banda from San Juan Ostuncalco.*

Opposite page:

157. *Double eagles on a tzute from Palín.*
158. *Double eagle on a banda from Nahualá.*

Notes

1. In Mexico, cotton was initially confined to the upper classes, and the lower classes wore woven bast fibers (see Anawalt 1981, pp. 29,33,70). Braudel 1981 (pp. 312-14) notes that homespun cotton, made from the least expensive local resources, was the everyday working garb the world over; and that in China, where the lower classes have always worn cotton clothing, even mandarins wore simple cotton clothes at home.

2. Silk was first imported into Mesoamerica from China by the Manila galleons. The Crown passed laws against the use of silk in New Spain, but was unable to enforce them. Wool came with the sheep imported by the Spaniards. Acrylics and rayon, of course, are 20th-century industrial imports. Warmth is one of the advantages of acrylics, which since the 1970s have completely replaced wool as a supplementary fiber. Rayon was used in Nahualá and Santa Catarina Ixtahuacán for brocade, San Pedro Sacatepéquez (SM) for skirts, and Totonicapán for headties.

3. Pancake suggests the number of huipils a woman wears over her lifetime may be as few as ten (1976, p. 4). At the end of the 19th century, Maudslay & Maudslay 1899 (p. 43) found it almost impossible to buy a huipil from a woman. They were, in fact, indignant at the overtures made, which Mrs. Maudslay found reasonable when she learned that a woman's clothing stock consisted of one huipil in the wearing and one on the loom.

4. The number of selvedges on a backstrap piece would ordinarily be four, but sometimes a backstrap-woven strip is cut from the loom, yielding a piece with only three selvedges, or a long warping is cut into two parts.

5. While most huipils are identical front and back, the one made in Nahualá is an exception, as are the blouse-like huipils of Sololá and Santiago Chimaltenango. Ixtahuacán, San Sebastian, and Sololá are examples in the Museum collection of completely reversible styles. Brides' attendants wear an inside-out huipil in San Pedro Sacatepéquez (G) and Comalapa. A woman in San Juan Sacatepéquez told Frieda Whitman that women might wear huipils inside out because they are menstruating. Osborne 1965 (p. 108) states that they wear it that way to protect it from the covetous eyes of foreigners or evil spirits. In San Pedro Sacatepéquez (G) a second huipil is folded in a triangle and worn over the shoulders. Comalapa women wear theirs over their heads and over their arms.

6. The term "tab collar" is not standard, but one of our own invention. What we call the "set-on" sleeve is often described in sewing texts as "T-shaped kimono sleeve." Re the word "brocade," Burnham suggests that it should be used only as a verb since the word is without "precise denotation." However, since the laymen will have a clear image of what is meant by "a brocade," we feel it is justified to use the word as a noun from time to time. We are grateful to Dorothy Laupa for these elucidations.

7. Of approximately 200 huipils in the Museum collection, almost half are constructed of two pieces. Huipils made of three pieces represent another quarter, as do one-piece huipils. This may be considered roughly representative of huipils in the Guatemalan highlands.

8. Half the huipils in the Museum collection are relatively wide, probably reflecting the fact that it comprises a disproportionately large number of ceremonial huipils.

9. It is worth noting that it is easier to produce extra length on commercial or foot-powered looms than on backstrap looms.

10. In the 1960s, women from Joyabaj wore the Nebaj skirt as well as the one from Rabinal. The latter was popular with tourists as well.

11. By the 1970s only a few women in Aguacatán still wove their own skirts as the same pattern was available in foot-loom-woven fabric.

12. According to coauthor Pat Altman, "*Raja jaspeada* de Granada" was listed among the woolens and garments brought from Seville to the New World for the years 1534-86 (see merchandise lists in Torre Revello 1943, vol. 23, no. 4, p. 773ff). *Raja* is a woolen textile (R. Anderson 1979, p. 175) and *jaspeado* in its present usage refers to ikat (or thread-dyed patterned cloth). The word *jaspe* is defined in current Spanish dictionaries as "mottled, marbled or spotted." In 16th-century usage it may have designated ikat fabric, although this is not certain. Ikat fabrics were dyed in Spain (Majórca) at least in the 18th century.

13. Cordry & Cordry 1968 (p. 130) suggest a source in Indonesia. We were referred to Pedro Velasquez by Roger Wolfe.

14. McDougall's photographs are published in Start 1980 (see plate II). Four photographs of women's skirts (taken by George Byron Gordon in the late nineteenth century, and now in the Peabody Museum archives) appear in Rowe 1981, pp. 43,51, 65,102. The first three show skirts with warp and weft stripes forming a plaid of white on indigo. Only one, "probably from Totonicapán" (fig. 86), has ikat.

15. See Osborne 1965, p. 46, and O'Neale 1945, p. 163, re Salcajá.

16. Fashions in America and Europe for jeans and denim goods (also requiring indigo dyes) created a price rise in indigo that brought it out of reach for most Maya customers in the 1970s. Either black was combined with a brighter blue, or black was used alone as a substitute by skirt weavers in the Guatemalan highlands. Although the foot loom weavers also began to produce trade huipils using black as one of the color components in order to go with them, black skirts were never popular. The black deteriorated into a dull and dismal grey when washed and was never really enjoyed.

17. Much of my information on *tzute* terminology and usage comes from Gwendolin Ritz (pers. com.).

18. A light-weight blue and red warp-striped *perraje* with faint ikat is in the Maudslay collection at the Victoria and Albert Museum.

19. The *cofradía* garment is always called a *tzute* rather than a *perraje* (Gwendolin Ritz, pers. com.).

20. Re the Mixco *fajas* brought by traders from Mexico, see Osborne 1975 (pp. 106-76).

21. The Museum collection contains two coral *tupuis* bought in the early 1960s.

22. A 6th-century B.C. silk embroidery found in a Chou dynasty tomb consists of a bird on a flowering tree limb executed in chain stitch (Robinson 1987, p. 68).

23. The Maudslay Collection, while small, has a number of *cuyuscate* huipils.

24. Collectors of Guatemalan textiles are often drawn to the subdued colors in old and much washed garments, but the Maya themselves prefer the bright colors. The sparing use of a vivid cerise thread caught our eye in the decoration of two sixties huipils from San Juan Atitán and Todos Santos. We thought it might be the first intrusion of acrylic thread, but on testing it discovered that it was wool. Here it was, completely and exclusively surrounded by cotton threads, but the color was new and enticing. It was the neon-brilliancy of acrylics (as well as their warmth and washability) that made them so popular in the '70s and '80s.

25. Approximately 40% of the huipils in our collection employ warp stripes for at least part of their decorative effect. Weft stripes are found in only 14%, and plaids account for only 5% of the total.

26. On the time it takes to weave a huipil, see Pancake 1976 (p. 2).

27. On the terminology of *mano* and *pecho*, see Delgado 1963 (pp. 107-8). More ceremonial garments than everyday ones have survived from the 1930s, for the former had less wear and were more likely to be treated as treasures (although it is not unknown for used ones to be sold in the village to those ascending into the ranks of *cofradía* membership). Collectors are of course attracted to the more extravagant examples of costume, and exhibitors likewise. Exhibitions of Guatemalan textiles often therefore give an exaggerated picture as to decoration.

28. Fifty-five percent of all the huipils in our collection are embroidered, and almost a quarter of them have appliqué. See Anawalt 1981 citing Duran and Sahagún on the mention of feathers in colonial chronicles (pp. 51, 52).

29. In Chichicastenango it is the men of the village who do the sewing, appliqué, and embroidery. In the 1950s, according to Bunzel 1952 (p. 61), the women did not embroider. But M. Anderson 1978 (p. 178) illustrates one in the 1970s embroidering a *randa* — so customs and habits do change.

30. This kind of decorative join appears in many parts of the world. In North Africa it is used on Berber garments. It has also been found on Prehispanic textiles from Peru (Christopher Donnan, pers. com.).

31. Patterns, printed on paper or cloth, are now available in many markets, as is the finished product, all ready to be sewn on a huipil. They are seen all over Guatemala, still mostly on trade huipils, but some backstrap weavers dress up a simple garment with them, and the cost is modest.

32. See Delgado 1963 for a thorough coverage of design motifs, including 20 pages of birds and 18 pages of animal motifs. She also catalogues 19 diamond forms — fringed, serrated, bisected, single, multiple, and so forth (pp. 210-13). For our own study, taking the huipil as the most important carrier of symbolic motif, we analyzed and counted the images on 202 huipils in the Museum's collection, so as to gain a clearer picture of the patterns of occurrence. We charted each motif in terms of the number of huipils on which it appeared, rather than the number of times it was used on a single huipil. Although the sampling cannot be considered exactly representative of highland costume in general, the results of our survey were instructive. Counting all variants, the diamond is the most prevalent, occurring on nearly 60 out of 200 huipils.

On the diamond motif see Morris 1987 (pp. 105-6); Allen 1981 (p. 3); and De Vries 1984 (p. 135). Carmack 1981 has an interesting chapter on symbols although no connections are made with textile motifs. Allen presents a convincing argument for the diamond as a birth symbol in textiles of the Middle East and the western Pacific. The myth of the union of earth and sky deities to produce a son is found in many cultures, i.e. Gaia and Ouranos (Greek), Geb and Nut (Egypt), etc. It is possible that the diamond may be symbolic of the earth and the sky as well as of the womb. Certainly, male and female forces, fertility and new life forms are suggested in many MesoAmerican creation myths. Thompson (cited by Carmack 1981, p. 36) speaks of "the sexual drama of the sky and the earth whose intercourse brings life" though he does not connect this specifically with a diamond. Possibly what we are dealing with is a case of microcosm versus macrocosm, humanity viewed as a miniature of the universe. Certainly it presents an interesting idea for further research.

33. In the Museum collection, 53 out of some 200 huipils use this form as a single or multiple design element. On zigzags, see De Vries 1984 (p. 514). Carmack 1981 (p. 201) is an excellent resource on Quiché iconography.

34. Re the equivalence between the lowland rain gods and the highland mountain gods, see J.E.S. Thompson cited in Carmack 1981. Etienne Brasseur de Bourbourg (cited in Carmack 1981, pp. 24-28) believed the connecting link was the Nahuas, who settled both Central Mexico and Guatemala. The Quiché god K'ucumatz, the feathered serpent, was known in central Mexico as Quezalcoatl. Carmack identifies the chief deity of the Quiché, Tojil Yolcuab, as Quetzalcuat, a Nahua form of Kukulcan, a major deity of the Gulf coast. Quetzalcuat was believed to be associated with clouds and water as well. The Cakchiquel's patron god was Tak'aj (or Chimalcan) a serpent and symbol of the low parts of the earth (Carmack 1981, pp. 383-4).

35. Present-day terminology in San Antonio Aguas Calientes and San Juan Sacatepéquez was pointed out to me by Gwendolin Ritz in 1987.

36. The garments depicted in Figures 116 and 117 are both male garments. However the sun symbol occurs on female garments as well. See Coggins 1985 (p. 48) on the importance of the sun in Quiché cosmology.

37. See Morris 1987 (p. 108), on the cosmic meanings of the Maya costume, echoing Mircea Eliade 1959 (p. 29).

38. The temple of the moon is discussed in Carmack 1981 (p. 201). Rodas (as cited by Wood & Osborne 1966, p. 96) suggests that appliquéd rosettes represent the moon in its four phases.

39. Included in the bird count is the fowl native to Mesoamerica, the turkey. The turkey was significant in Maya mythology, and is still used in some shamanistic sacrificial rituals. The most easily identified turkey is the sacrificed one with the broken neck.

40. I am indebted to Gwendolin Ritz for information about the Cakchiquel and Quiché terms for the double-headed bird.

41. Evidence connecting the bird-in-tree motif to European brocade design appears in Pang's contribution to the 1976 Irene Emery Roundtable on Museum Textiles (Pang 1977, pp. 388-402).

42. Coggins 1985 describes Maya cosmology; see pp. 48-49 on the vertical axis penetrating three worlds.

43. The main difference between the huipils of San Juan Sacatepéquez and San Raimundo is in the way they depict their pine trees, as Cherri Pancake pointed out to me in 1978. The variations are slight but important to the wearers.

44. The lion (upright and with a flowing mane) on the *tzutes* of Nahualá is clear; and occasionally a monkey with a long tail is discernible.

Major language groups of highland Guatemala.

CHAPTER 4

Costume and Language

Since costume and language are both manifestations of culture, it is interesting to investigate their correlation in the Guatemalan highlands. Although classifications differ, most linguists recognize approximately twenty Mayan languages in Guatemala, most of them in the highlands. Some are spoken in only a few villages (e.g. Ixil, Pocomam, and Tzutujil), while others are spread across a wide area (e.g. Quiché, Mam, Cakchiquel) and number speakers in the hundreds of thousands. The costumes in our collection represent eleven of these language areas and concentrate on those villages in which traditional (and especially backstrap-woven) costume largely survives.[1]

Do costume styles correlate with language in the highlands? The answer is complicated. Among the older language groups — Ixil, Pocomchi, and Kekchi — there appears to be a definite relationship. Mam iconography indicates consistency even in villages which are far apart, even though costume styles and weaving techniques vary. Among the Cakchiquel, costume style differs from one dialect area to the other, yet within the dialect area style tends to be consistent. The Cakchiquel were in the process of taking over new territory just prior to the Spanish Conquest, and it is logical to assume that the Conquest prevented development of a general Cakchiquel style. Among the Quiché, who are the largest and most widely scattered language group, we find no correlation between language and costume at all. In the centuries before the arrival of the Spanish colonists, the conquering Quiché spread rapidly across the highlands and this may have something to do with the lack of cohesive style. Here and there a village *traje* differs markedly from the costumes of its neighbors within an otherwise cohesive language group. In these cases costume provides a clue to a special history differentiating that village from the ones around it.

The following overview of costume and language relationships in the highlands is based primarily upon our survey of the costumes in the Fowler Museum collection.

Ixil

Ixil speakers, who numbered 46,000 in the early 1970s, are concentrated in a single area (map, left). Ixil territory, which constitutes half the department of Quiché, is bounded on the south and west by the Cuchumatán Mountains, and on the north by the foothills above the Petén rain forest. The Chamá Mountains lie to the northwest. These rugged mountain barriers separate the Ixil and provide a natural defense border.

In the Prehispanic era the area was mostly under Ixil control, as evidenced by small civic center ruins. For a time the Quiché had some command, but it "was loose and indirect, perhaps by Quiché lords who resided in Sacapulas." At the time of the Conquest, the Spaniards mounted three separate attacks against the Ixil. Resistance was fierce and many from Nebaj were taken into slavery as punishment. Dominican priests congregated settlements, but other Ixil fled from Spanish control and returned to their traditional ways. Mostly left alone, the Ixil have maintained conservative patterns in language and dress. In the late 1970s and early 1980s, however, their region was engulfed in the civil war. Numbers were forced to flee, or were placed in government-sponsored "model villages," and ultimately had to abandon traditional ways of dressing.[2]

Ixil costumes from the 1960s share enough stylistic features to form a cohesive group. Women's garments (all but skirts) are typically backstrap-woven and of fine workmanship. Surprisingly, however, their parts are joined together by machine

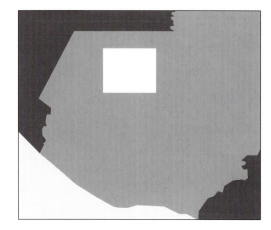

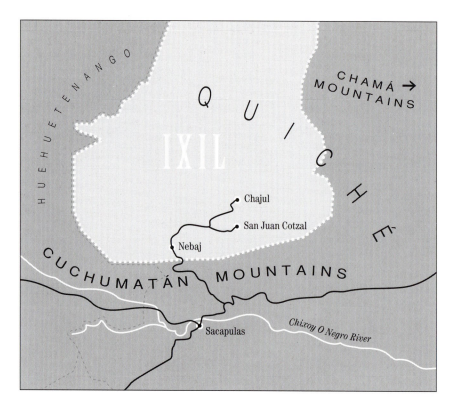

stitching, and white machine stitches are even used as a decorative touch on dark shawls. A possible reason for the acceptance of machine rather than hand sewing may be found in the typical Ixil man's jacket (fig. 32). Because it is tailored in a European style, with added on braid, the sewing machine became a village necessity at a relatively early date.

Tassels are also a common denominator in Ixil styling – on hairwraps (Nebaj and Chajul) and sashes and shawls (Chajul and Cotzal). A red skirt with narrow gold and jaspe weft stripes was characteristic of all these villages during the late 1950s or early 1960s, but by the late 1960s individual styles were preferred. Supplementary weft designs reveal a pan-Ixil iconography: triangular profile and squat-bodied frontal bird forms, the corn plant, and diamonds (many encasing double triangles) were the most common in the 1960s, although human and animal forms also existed.

Chajul, Santa María Nebaj, San Juan Cotzal *(Figure 163)*

Three Ixil towns, originally congregated by the Dominicans, lie in the department of Quiché at the end of tortuous mountain roads. Chajul people own and cultivate rich areas in the Petén lowlands. The importance of corn cultivation is reflected in legendary stories of huge corn cobs in the northern region of Ixcán, as well as in the prevalence of corn plant motifs on Ixil textiles. While the costumes of these villages differ from one another, especially in coloring, their similarities are striking.

A clear bright red is the favored background color of the Chajul daily costume. Though the huipil is simpler in execution and design than those of Nebaj or San Juan Cotzal, it does have its own drama and presence. The weaving in Chajul is especially firm and sturdy, and in order to achieve this, women usually stand at their backstrap looms rather than sit or kneel. The above-mentioned birds, corn plants, arrows and diamonds predominate in their bold style of single-faced brocade (fig. 162). Some everyday huipils are white, and a special three-web white huipil with mauve silk embroidery around the neck is worn by members of the *cofradía.* Both the sash and the hairwrap are prime examples of the skill and color sensitivity of Chajul weavers. The red skirt is woven on a foot loom by men from the Huehuetenango area. While the one pictured here is particular to Chajul, the Nebaj style skirt is also worn. White pin stripes and larger stripes of orange-red enliven the indigo shawl (folded, on mannequin's head), which is fringed at both ends with small, tightly braided tassels.

The Nebaj costume is one of the most dramatic of all Guatemalan daily costumes. Each aspect of it commands attention, from the twisted and wrapped headdress and

162. Detail of brocade on the San Juan Cotzal huipil seen in figure 163.

163. Costumes of Chajul (left), Santa María Nebaj (center), and San Juan Cotzal (right).

164. Girls in Nebaj.

the white huipil with bold purple, orange, green, and blue brocaded bird, animal, and human motifs, to the red wrapped skirt, stiff multicolored diamond brocaded sash and large striped shawl. Of all hairwraps, the one from Nebaj is by far the widest. The 1960s version, pictured here, had cotton tassels. The ones of today are much larger and made of acrylic (fig. 164). The two-panel huipil shown here is from the early 1960s. During that decade and before, both Nebaj and San Juan Cotzal huipils had four U-shaped loops of appliquéd fabric binding and/or embroidery around the neck. This quadrant reference is similar to that on a huipil in our collection from the Sacapultec-speaking village of Sacapulas, in the department of El Quiché, close to Ixil country (fig. 165). The neckline treatment retained in the Sacapulas *cofradía* garment may once have been used in its daily huipil as well, given that *cofradía* garments often preserve earlier forms. In any case, the similarity in design between the Ixil garments and the Sacapulas *cofradía* one could be the result of geographical proximity or even of historical connection. Cross-overs in styling and iconography suggest the possibility, impossible to prove, that Ixil women and the women from Sacapulas and Aguacatán, who speak Sacapultec and Aguacatec, may at one time have had a common ancestry. Fox also finds similarities in the design of their early civic centers. There is anthropological evidence that ancient clan relationships are still important. Even today, women who marry and settle out of their villages continue to wear the costume of their own natal village for the rest of their lives.[3]

The huipil of San Juan Cotzal is usually of three-web construction and all three webs are brocaded, more on the central panel than on the sides. Examples of supplementary weft in the Museum collection show both wool and cotton. The color combination is particularly striking — blue and green often with red on a white ground. The skirt shown, characteristic of the late 1960s or early 1970s, is a blue and green double ikat bought from Salcajá weavers. The sash is wide, almost the width of a shawl, and ends in multicolored wool tassels, as does the shawl. The hair ribbon is made of commercial fabric.

165. Detail of the neckline of a Sacapulas cofradía garment.

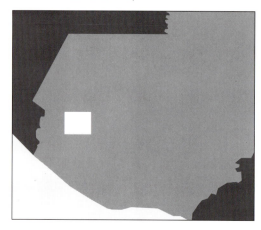

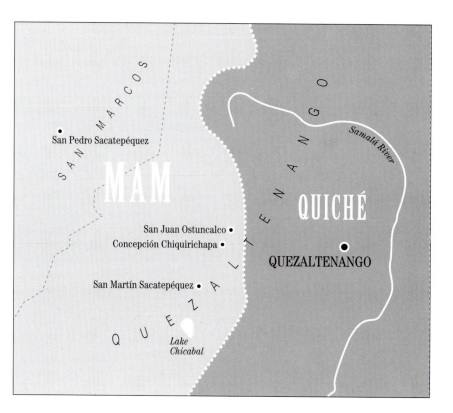

Mam

The Mam, to whom the Ixil are related by language, inhabit the northwestern highlands and are the second largest of the Maya language groups in Guatemala. In the 1970s there were 321,000 Mam in 53 pueblos speaking 15 different dialects. In the Prehispanic world their power and influence extended over a huge territory, from the Cuchumatán Mountains in the north to the Pacific lowlands in the south. The Quiché in the fourteenth century took over most of the Quezaltenango basin but left pockets of Mam, and these can be found all the way to the coast.

Mam speakers who wear traditional costume break down into three groups. The largest is situated in the Cuchumatanes, in the department of Huehuetenango, near their ancestral capital, Zaculeu. Costumes of backstrap weaving predominate here. Another group of Mam speakers inhabits the mountains south of Zacaleu in the department of San Marcos. Draw loom-woven huipils are typical of this area. In this chapter we illustrate the costumes of two villages in a Mam enclave that lies alongside Quiché territory (map, above).

San Martín Sacatepéquez and Concepción Chiquirichapa (Figure 167)

The villages of San Martín Sacatepéquez (known locally as San Martín Chile Verde) and Concepción Chiquirichapa speak a similar Mam dialect and belong to a group of Mam villages in the Quezaltenango area. San Martín Sacatepéquez has a reputation as a center for ancient Mam beliefs. Traditional rituals conducted at Lake Chicabal nearby are attended by shamans, medicine men, and others involved in supernatural practices. Particular mountains represent gods of great power and are the objects of long pilgrimages.

Huipils from both these Mam villages are backstrap-woven on a plain red ground. The construction details, weaving methods, and background coloring are the same in both villages, but strikingly different from the Quiché huipils of the nearby area, or for that matter, unlike Mam huipils in other areas.

The basic huipil, the same today as it was from the 1930s to the 1960s, consists of two webs with a split neck opening. Women here set up their looms to weave both webs with one warping. The strips are then cut in half when finished; thus one end is selvedged and the other is either hemmed or fringed. The center join is a featherstitch *randa* in either one or a combination of several colors. On all museum examples the *randa* goes only to the bottom of the brocaded area and from there the parts are joined by an overcast stitch. Huipils from both villages are medium in

166. Man from San Martín Sacatepéquez.

167. *Costumes of San Martín Sacatepéquez (left, right) and Concepción Chiquirichapa (center).*

length and width, and they are worn tucked in. The sides are usually left open, but occasionally tacked together under the armhole. The brocaded shoulder band with framed diamonds resembles those found on Mam huipils of Huehuetenango, but they are larger in scale.

The supplementary weft designs of San Martín Sacatepéquez in the 1960s were simple geometric shapes — chiefly diamonds and zigzags — in bands separated by weft floats or stripes. Although these designs were still in use as late as 1976, many have since given way to more elaborate design forms, densely brocaded almost solid to the waist, and showing influence from Quiché trade huipils. Our example from Concepción, made in the late 1960s, shows these borrowed figurative designs. They are composed mainly of paired birds and urns with trees, but in the hands of these expert weavers they have developed into a complicated mélange of design forms that are often difficult to separate and decipher. (The use of more and more colors and of variegated threads in the 1970s makes the overall design even more complex.) In contrast, the geometric styled supplementary wefts of the earlier huipil had a simpler palette — usually purple and green or purple, green, and orange. Some of the most beautiful early huipils used silk or sedalina as a supplementary fiber.[4]

Women's belts for both villages are made of stiff black wool and have five white warp stripes in cotton or wool. Twisted fringe at the ends is tucked under the belt to hold it in place. Only a few backstrap *cintas* are still woven and worn as shown. Designs and colors vary from village to village, but the size is fairly standard.

Single-panel backstrap-woven indigo shawls with groups of red warp pin stripes and wide supplementary weft bands were more often seen in the 1960s than now (fig. 168). Aprons have been worn here for many years, but the styles have changed too rapidly to pinpoint them in time. Skirts worn in both villages are woven on foot looms and made of two panels joined with a featherstitch *randa* in one or a combination of several color blocks usually copying the *randa* of the huipil. All skirts are

168. *Detail of a shawl from San Martín Sacatepéquez.*

169. Detail of a shirt sleeve from San Martín Sacatepéquez.

of indigo with lighter blue warp striations or more defined pin stripes in a regular 4-1-1-4 repeat sequence. They are sewn into a tube, turned under at the top, and then the extra width is gathered to the left and folded on the hip. Skirt lengths *(cortes)* are bought from professional weavers in San Juan Ostuncalco.

Unlike their neighbors, men and boys from San Martín Sacatepéquez continue to wear backstrap-woven costumes. Their *traje* consists of a knee-length shirt worn over calf-length pants. Both are woven on a white ground with red pin stripes. Sleeves are brocaded in the same manner (and usually in the same designs) as the women's huipil (fig. 169) and are gathered on a narrow cuff. The neckline is gathered on a narrow band like the men's *camisa* of Sololá. Pants have a drawstring at the waist and a band of brocaded designs at the leg bottoms. Brocade on the legs and sleeves are in totally different designs, more dense on the sleeves, more open on the pant legs. An extra long red *banda* with multicolored brocade on one or both ends ties around the waist twice and is knotted and falls in the back, as shown, left. The boy's costume echoes the father's.

A large red *tzute* worn on the head would have completed this costume in the 1930s; it was replaced first by a smaller *tzute*, then a bandana, and finally a straw hat (fig. 166). (Now, even *cofradía* members wear straw hats on their saint's day, rather than *tzutes*.) A *capixay* of brownish black wool would be worn when the weather is cold or when rituals are being performed at Lake Chicabal.

Pocomam

Pocomam speakers, numbering 42,000 in the 1970s, are the aboriginal remnants of the Pocomam nation that occupied the central and eastern highlands south of the Motagua River (map, below). At various times from the mid-1300s to just before the Spanish Conquest, several Pocomam settlements were taken over by Rabinal, Quiché and Cakchiquel warriors.

Although three highland Pocomam centers survive, it was impossible even in the 960s to distinguish a Pocomam style of costume; their proximity to the capital city is probably a factor. In Mixco, now a suburb of Guatemala City, Mexican and Spanish influence was evident, while most women in Chinautla, like some in Mixco, wore generic costumes made in Totonicapán. Women of Palín still wear a traditional backstrap-woven huipil, but their numbers decline with each passing year.[5]

Palín (Figure 170)

Palín clings to the cliffs south of Volcano Agua in the department of Escuintla. It is inhabited by people of the Pocomam nation, which was in the process of dismemberment by the Cakchiquel when the Spaniards arrived. They are isolated

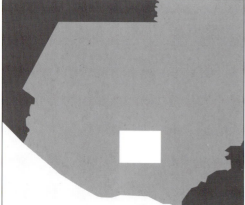

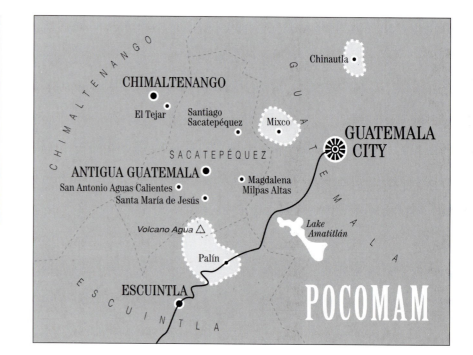

170. Costume of Palín.

from the other Pocomam speakers mentioned above, and speak different dialects. Palín is a stop on both the highway and train routes connecting Guatemala City to the Pacific port of San José, and is therefore subjected to strong Ladino influences. Today Maya represent approximately 40% of the urban population and only 11% of the rural. The percentages are arguable, however, depending on the criteria used to differentiate Maya from Ladino. Although the wearing of traditional *traje* classifies one as Maya, there are various stages in the process of its being sloughed off.[6]

Even in the early 1960s, there were three upper-garment styles: the traditional backstrap-woven huipil; a garment cut like a huipil made of white commercial cotton; and a peasant-style blouse with short sleeves in various colors of sateen or plain weave cotton. The backstrap huipil was worn by some of the older women for every day, by others for special occasions, and by relatives of the *cofrades* for *cofradía* events. The commercial cotton huipil was worn by some older women for every day, and the blouse was worn by younger women.

Palín's huipil is short, and made of a single backstrap-woven web. The one seen above was probably woven in the 1950s and is in the crepe weave that is achieved by a tight twist of its handspun fibers. In view, just below the neckline, are two sets of double eagles which could identify it as a *cofradía* huipil. A former *cofradía* member might have worn the huipil as shown here well into the 1960s. The mannequin's shoulder cloth and the one on her basket are also of the 1950s or early 1960s; small equidistant designs and rows of birds (or turkeys) predominate.

The tube skirt seen here, indigo blue with twin white pin stripes, is characteristic of the 1960s. It was woven by men in El Tejar who brought their *cortes* to the Palín market. Older women wore skirts to their ankles, younger women to below the knees. *Fajas* and *tzutes*, backstrap-woven by the women of Palín, were generally used by all Pocomam women. The *cinta* (or *tuntun*) of red wool with a dark border, was woven in another village, and no longer available in the 1960s; old ones were still being worn, as is evident in a photograph from the 1970s (fig. 171).

171. Palín woman.

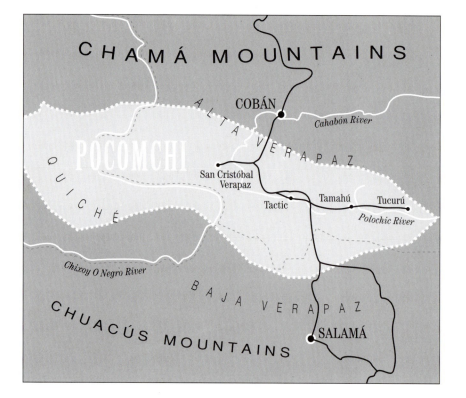

Pocomchi

The Pocomchi are concentrated to the southeast of the Kekchi, in the same department of Alta Verapaz (map, above). A splinter group from the Pocomam in the central region of Guatemala, they were pushed to this area by the invading Quiché. Sequestered in the valleys of the Polochic and Cahabón rivers, they were among the last groups to be conquered by the Spaniards.

Full red skirts were the most distinguishing feature of traditional Pocomchi dress in the 1950s and early 1960s. Pocomchi huipils, like all those from Alta Verapaz (whether Pocomchi or Kekchi) are short and woven in three strips approximately 33 inches long (one *vara*). These three webs are sewn together lengthwise and a squarish hole is cut out of the center for the head. In some huipils, this opening is hemmed; in others it is faced on the inside with matching color fabric or tape.

Tamahú and Tactic *(Figure 173)*

Tamahú and Tactic, the two Pocomchi villages considered here, share a common boundary, language, and ethnicity. In addition, they share a strong weaving tradition and regular trade relationships. Tactic has a huge market well attended by neighboring villagers. The primary source of livelihood for women is weaving, and backstrap-woven huipils are a common trade item here. Although the Pocomchi women seldom leave the region, their huipil is rapidly moving into pan-Maya status.

The red skirts shown here were once typical of both villages. Local rumor holds that this garment went into decline when a priest assigned to the area told the women that they looked like devils in their red garb. The full red skirt with black cross-barred warp and weft stripes, gathered on a cord at the waist, has been described by Osborne, O'Neale, and Delgado. O'Neale notes that some skirts have an inch-and-a-half tuck either to shorten or to decorate. Though still worn by some in the early 1960s, the red skirt was on its way out, to be replaced by skirts of *jaspe* (fig. 172).

While the red skirts have declined, the huipil styles of Tamahú and Tactic have proliferated and are now to be found in markets as far away as Quezaltenango in the opposite corner of Guatemala. Even in the 1960s, waitresses at both the Pan American Hotel in Guatemala City and the Antigua Hotel in Antigua (and possibly many other places as well) wore colored Tamahú and Tactic huipils for weekdays and white Cobán huipils for Saturday and Sundays. Being attractive, comfortable and reasonable, the costume was worn as a pan-Maya statement for the local and tourist trade.

172. Woman from Tactic.

173. Costumes of Tamahú (left) and Tactic (right).

Tamahú and Tactic huipils are very difficult to differentiate, as the same styles are worn in both villages. O'Neale writes that "some [huipils] said to come from [Tamahú] are identical to those worn and woven at Tactic." As early as 1924, a Tactic huipil was described as having "a center strip of navy, dark green, red or chrome yellow with geometric figures and zigzag bands of various colors running horizontally across the material and often a six-branched tree with a duck on top. The two strips on either side are white, often decorated with small red, yellow, or green geometric figures." This description applies to huipils described by O'Neale and Delgado, and also to the Museum's Tactic huipil bought in the late 1960s and shown here.

The vertical zigzag was only one of the popular Tamahú huipil designs of the 1960s. Deer, medallions, and bird-and-tree motifs were also used, usually as a single design element (fig. 174), in both Tamahú and Tactic. In the 1960s, the predominant motif was that of the six-branched tree with a bird (or duck) on top, and even though the design was the same, the effect varied considerably according to its treatment — thick or thin, dense or spaced. Osborne cites the heaviness of some of the brocades from here. Because of the lavish use of thread (half-inch ends are left on the underside) they are warmer but also more expensive.

The red headdress shown with the Tamahú costume was worn in this village only, but women in the village of Amatenango in Chiapas, Mexico, wear a similar turban-like wrap. As in other Alta Verapaz villages, coin silver necklaces produced locally are greatly valued as a show of status for ceremonial events.[7]

174. Bird-and-tree and medallion motifs on a Tactic huipil.

Kekchi

The Kekchi, though numerous — 209,000 in the 1970s — are geographically concentrated in the northeastern highlands (map, below). Kekchi speakers living in the department of Alta Verapaz are markedly different from their Quiché cousins, and neither group can understand the language of the other. Large populations have cultivated this tropical region from Prehispanic times, but the area appears to have been cut off from the main developments of the Classic Maya, and resistant to later Mexican influence.

The Kekchi people were protected against the harsh exploitation of Alvarado and his followers thanks to the pacifism of Bishop Las Casas and the early humane missionizing of the Dominicans who were granted control. But by the nineteenth century the church had lost control, and 1864 was marked by a Kekchi-led revolt. In 1870, Western Europeans, mainly Germans, arrived in Verapaz and dominated the area from then until the Second World War, through large-scale commercial coffee growing and export.[8]

Kekchi costume is crisp and cool, perfectly suited to the tropical climate of the Alta Verapaz area. A short white three-panel huipil is worn outside the skirt. Gauze and leno weaves produced on backstrap looms are Kekchi specialties. Though skirt material is imported from the Salcajá area, it is specially woven for this market, where it is worn like Pocomchi skirts — not folded on the hip but full, hemmed at the top, and gathered on a cord and tied around the waist.

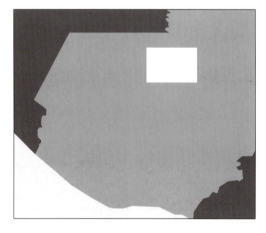

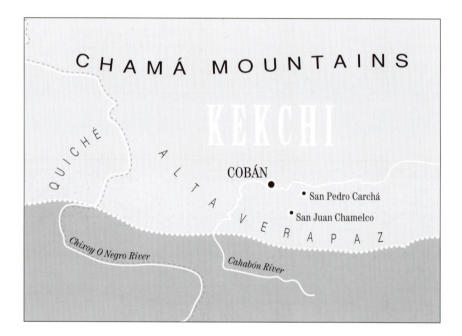

San Pedro Carchá and Cobán *(Figure 175)*

Originally settled by Kekchi who were converted under the auspices of Dominican missionaries, both San Pedro Carchá and Cobán are tucked among the folds of a long limestone plateau that begins in Chiapas and extends through the Cuchumatanes to the Caribbean Cayman Ridge. Cobán, the larger of the two, is department capital. San Pedro Carchá is noted for its ancient mask-making tradition.

A costume characteristic of San Pedro Carchá in the 1960s (seen here) included a backstrap-woven huipil, with a plain, squarish neckline faced on the underside. It was indigo with predominantly white brocading. Alternate rows of an elaborated diamond form and smaller grouped diamonds appear on all three webs. Other motifs, many of which are shared with other villages in the area (Pocomchi as well as Kekchi), can also be seen on huipils from San Pedro Carchá. Many of the huipils of the region are all white, like the one being held, which is of a gauze-like weave known as *leno*. A woman may wear either of the two kinds shown, depending on the temperature and the occasion.

The Cobán costume is from the late 1950s or early 1960s. Backstrap-woven huipils were typically three webs wide and short in length. In this example the neck opening

175. *Costumes of San Pedro Carchá (left) and Cobán (right).*

176. *Neckline embroidery on the Cobán huipil seen in figure 175.*

and armholes are embroidered with row upon row of small design elements in red, purple, green, and blue, and a serrated band of black muslin is appliquéd at the border (fig. 176). Embroidered huipils similar to the one shown here, but made of commercial material, were also sold in Cobán to women of the area (fig. 177).

Patterned gauze-like huipils have been pictured on Prehispanic sources. A similar textile, used as a shroud, was found in 1984 at Rio Azul. This cloth was carbon-dated to the fifth century A.D. — approximately 1,000 years older than any textile previously found in the Guatemalan area. Gauze huipils without the neck opening are used in many villages as veils for wedding or *cofradía* wear.[9]

Skirts from both towns are of medium-weight, indigo-dyed fabric woven on the foot loom. Fine warp and weft stripes form a plaid with a band or bands of warp ikat. The single band seen on the Cobán skirt is the older style. Skirts are full (8-11 *varas*), hemmed, and gathered at the waist. Older women wear their skirts longer than young women. Huipils are never worn tucked into the skirts. A twisted cord belt is pulled through the top casing and then wound around the skirt as well, but since huipils are never tucked in, the belts are not visible.

The Cobán hairwrap, called *tupui*, is referred to as "the coral serpent" (described earlier, p. 80), and is wound around a single braid as shown. Although Osborne reported it practically extinct, it somehow persists. A most remarkable headdress, it is probably tied to the serpent myths of the Maya.

Tzutujil

The Tzutujil speakers, 42,000 in the 1970s, live on the southern shores of Lake Atitlán, on either side of Volcano Tolimán (map, p. 118). The Tzutujil were among the early invaders of Guatemala, along with the Quiché, coming from what is now Mexico. They made shifting alliances with the Quiché and Cakchiquel, provided wives for lineage heads, and later joined the Mam and Pipil to fight the Quiché with only temporary success.

Because of their advantageous location, the Tzutujil gained control of a prestigious trade in cacao, a lowlands product so highly valued that its beans were used as money. Ultimately the Cakchiquel gained control of the southwest pass to the

177. *Cobán women in the late 1940s.*

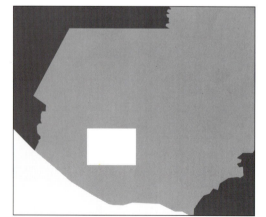

178. Men of Santiago Atitlán in traditional costume.

lowlands, cutting off Tzutujil trade in cacao and damaging their economy and status. Yet ancient pride appears to live on in their carefully executed costume traditions.

During the 1960s, men in a number of Tzutujil villages continued to wear the backstrap-woven *traje* for everyday. The matching of men's and women's garments is a phenomenon typical of several Lake Atitlán villages. Both in Santiago Atitlán and San Lucas Tolimán, for example, male and female costumes are related in color and general styling and between them they share bird and geometric motifs. Change has taken place since the 1960s, but far more so in San Lucas Tolimán than in Santiago Atitlán.[10]

Santiago Atitlán *(Figure 179)*

While evidence of an aboriginal population at Santiago Atitlán is still being unearthed, its historic written record begins in the last quarter of the sixteenth century, when work was begun on the church and two full-time priests were established there. To this day it is an important religious center, and costume is important in its

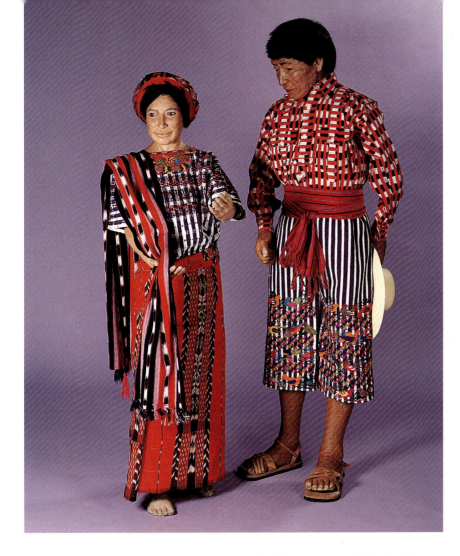

179. *Costumes of Santiago Atitlán.*

180. *The Santiago Atitlán market, run by women.*

traditions. Many of its carved saints are dressed in Maya costume. At the lavish traditional saint's day celebration, everyone turns out in *traje*. The market is run by women (fig. 180), and during the 1960s it specialized in food products and thread for weaving and embroidery.

In the costumes shown here, which are typically matched, purple and white stripes form the background pattern for both the woman's huipil and the man's pants. The huipil is of an earlier style than the pants; the birds on the huipil are sparse stick-figures while those on the pants are full-feathered multicolored birds.

The woman's skirt also relates to the man's shirt in that both use ikat patterns in indigo and white with red as a base color. Hers are more elaborate, with human figures and trees; his are simple "bleep" (space-dyed) designs. Sometimes the skirt is a tube, and sometimes it is a long single panel. In either case it is reinforced with a strip of the same fabric, approximately eight inches wide, sewn along the length of the selvedge. Women from Santiago Atitlán do not wear belts. Their skirts are wrapped around the hips, folded back at the end, and then tucked in at the waist. The elegant, halo-like headdress (fig. 181) winds around the hairbraid first and then around and around the head. The single-paneled *perraje*, worn over the shoulder, is more for effect than use.

The man's shirt is made from backstrap-woven lengths called *cortecitos*, tailored in the Western-style — patch pockets, collar, cuffs, and buttons down the front. The weaving is done by women in San Pedro la Laguna, another Tzutujil lake village. The red *banda*, striped with indigo and mauve, is knotted and fringed at the ends.

181 (below). *Detail of the cinta shown in figure 179.*

182. *Zunil woman in a Totonicopán market.*

Quiché

The Quiché are the largest Mayan language group in Guatemala. In the 1970s they numbered over 520,000 people, speaking 14 dialects, and they were scattered over 66 villages. Quiché history is one of constant conquest and assimilation of indigenous groups over a wide area of the highlands. Ancestors of the Quiché came from Mexico and their lineage-based kingdom was a confederacy designed for militaristic expansion. Quiché became a distinct language, absorbing words from Cholan, a classic Maya language, and Nahua, the language of the conquerors.[11]

The Quiché ruled a rural and scattered population from ceremonial and political centers situated on plateaus in the central highland area. The largest and most important was at Utatlán (near present-day Santa Cruz del Quiché). From there they expanded their conquest west and south into Mam territories and east and north into the Pocomam area. After the Cakchiquel, once allies, had departed to launch their own conquest state, the Quiché were forced to engage in continuous wars to protect their vastly extended kingdom. Their final defeat was by the Spaniards under Alvarado.

The Quiché conceptualized their world as extending in four directions, south (the earth), north (the sky), east (where the sun comes up), and west (where it goes down). They were also interested in pairs such as rain/sun, sky/earth, mountains/plains, sun/moon, male/female. Some of these concepts appear to be expressed in symbolic form in costume styles, but this is by no means universal.

The Museum collection has complete costumes from twenty-four Quiché villages in the departments of Quezaltenango, Totonicapán, Quiché, Sololá, and Baja Verapaz. In the 1960s, separately styled backstrap-woven huipils were still worn in only eleven of these villages; elsewhere Quiché huipils were either produced on a foot loom or made of commercial fabric. Quiché costume is highly variable: there is really no discernible set of Quiché costume traits. Where two villages have a dress style in common, it is probably more attributable to shared geography, trading patterns, and so forth, than to shared language. The villages illustrated here are ones in which backstrap weaving was still being done in the 1960s (map, below).

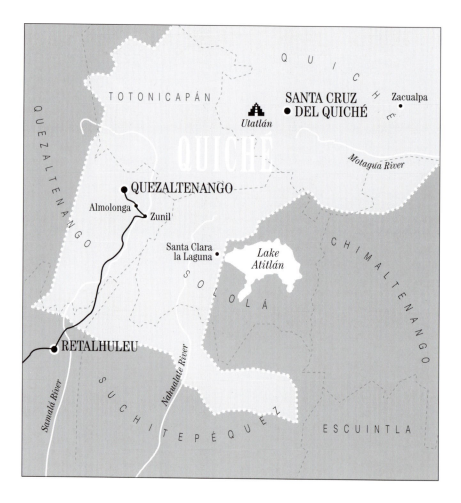

183. Costumes of Zunil (left) and Almolonga (right).

184. Detail of an Almolonga foot-loom-woven strip, made for a child's huipil.

Zunil and Almolonga (Figure 183)

Zunil and Almolonga are neighbors in the Quezaltenango trade area, sharing a history that dates back to the Conquest. They both speak the same Quiché dialect. The setting for Almolonga is a long narrow valley of volcanic spring-fed earth ideal for truck farming. Almolonga women are active traders in their busy local market and in the larger regional market at Quezaltenango. A major Quiché settlement in the pre-Conquest period, Zunil occupied a shelf 400 meters above the gorge cut by the Samalá River, near the summit of Zunil mountain. Present-day Zunil is ten kilometers north on the sloping lower region along the Samalá River, and on the main road from Quezaltenango to the Pacific lowlands. Men from Zunil use the slopes along the river bed to grow wheat, tomatoes, and a few other vegetables. They also produce rope and net bags from maguey fiber. Women in both villages still wear costumes from their own backstrap looms and from the foot looms of local men weavers who produce *cortes, cintas* and huipil strips.

The Almolonga huipil is intricate and solidly brocaded above the waist. The most common design of the 1960s was a vertical zigzag in maroon, purple and orange-gold (figs. 184,185). The background warp is a fine red and white stripe and extends under the skirt to hip length. Each of the two webs is backstrap-woven separately; but to avoid the tedious join and filling-in process involved in making a textile with four selvedges, one end is cut from the loom and hemmed.[12]

The skirt seen above is one of several styles worn in the last three generations. The oldest style, completely shunned by the young women, is plain indigo, but to this day it is worn proudly by a few old women. By the mid-1960s the ikat styles had begun to predominate. The change from plain to such intricate skirts appeared to take place in an unusually short space of time. Patterns were conceived and executed with

185. Detail of an Almolonga huipil, woven on the backstrap loom.

great technical skill. In its use of ikat, the Almolonga skirt resembles the Zunil skirt, but it is worn longer, and with two folds facing center front rather than folding once on the hip as in Zunil.

The *faja* for Almolonga has a simple black-and-white warp stripe made in either cotton or wool (or a combination) by professional belt weavers in San Juan Ostuncalco. It is usually not visible as the skirt top turns down and covers it. The locally-made Totonicapán-style headwrap is cotton, rather than rayon.

Zunil's huipil is one of the simplest backstrap-woven huipils in Guatemala, depending solely on color and a contrast of stripes for its decorative effect. In the 1960s, wide warp bands of purple or magenta were set off by narrow warp stripes in yellow, green and orange and faint weft stripes in purple and mauve. The background was blue-grey or white. It was made of two webs joined in the center by a featherstitched *randa*, but the *randa* has grown more decorative and elaborate over the years.

The woman's shawl is unusually large, and resembles in size the Maya man's mantle of pre-Conquest times. In the 1960s it was commonly found in red or purple with white and indigo ikat warp stripes, widely spaced, as seen here. It is made of two backstrap-woven webs joined with a multicolored decorative *randa*. One end is selvedged; the other terminates in knotted fringe. It is worn with a selvedged edge over the shoulders. The *randa* runs horizontally, and the fringe end hangs vertically. On cold mornings two corners would be tied together in front, wrapping its wearer in a straight column.

The headwrap made in Zunil is of tapestry weave, like that of Totonicapán, but in cotton. The unique stiff Zunil *faja* is woven in the piedmont especially for Zunil women, and sold in the market in Cantel. In the 1960s (as in the 1930s) it was made of brown wool with bright red decorative tapestry woven stripes, triangles or zigzags in black, cerise, yellow, blue, and green. Now it comes in several other colors but is woven the same way. Zunil's distinctive skirt is particularly intricate in its ikat patterns or brocade designs. There are several versions, all worn short, and all sewn into tubes. They are produced by male foot-loom weavers in the village. A small striped cloth in typical village colors is used as a basket cover or rolled and twisted and put on the head to steady a basket or jug of water.

Zacualpa (Figure 187)

Zacualpa lies in the northern part of a valley of the Sierra de Chuacús, in the department of El Quiché. Site of a Late Classic settlement, it was again constituted after the Conquest when Dominican friars gathered together a number of outlying villages for the sake of the Spanish *encomienda* of Don Fernando Ruiz de Contreras, Secretary of Consejo de los Indios of his Majesty. Nowadays most of the Maya live in the rural areas, where they cultivate subsistence crops of corn and beans, squash, chiles, and tomatoes. Non-agricultural resources are limited, so trade in outlying markets is essential. Local trade is dominated by Ladinos.

Zacualpa's costume stands apart from all others. Supplementary weft decoration, subtle and elegant in effect, is accomplished by *soumak,* a time-consuming wrap technique more often reserved for small motifs than for the overall herringbone-like bands that cover the shoulders and part of the front and back of the Zacualpa huipil. This particular use of *soumak* has been unique to Zacualpa for as far back as records and examples exist. In fact the Zacualpa huipil does not resemble any other huipils in the department of El Quiché. It does not even share styles with its neighboring village of Joyabaj, which speaks the same Quiché dialect.[13]

The Zacualpa skirt is cleverly decorated with several rows of richly colored tape — blue, red, green, purple, bright pink, and pale lavender — which are fastened to the cloth by rows of running stitches in the same or similar colors. The tapes are applied on both sides of the join, but on opposite sides of the cloth, so that when the tape appears above the join, the running stitches appear below it, or vice versa if the skirt is reversed. No other skirt in Guatemala uses this reversible double-duty decorative technique.

The Zacualpa woman's *tzute,* usually worn on the head, is triangular, which necessitates cutting and restitching the rectangular backstrap-woven web. It is the only triangular *tzute* known to us in Guatemala. A larger *tzute* of traditional rectangular shape is used to carry the baby (as seen here).

186. Detail of a cinta from Zunil, also seen in figure 183, left.

187. *Costume of Zacualpa.*

188. *Costume of Santa Clara la Laguna.*

Santa Clara la Laguna *(Figure 188)*

By name and map location, Santa Clara la Laguna appears to be a lake village, but it is a two-hour climb up a steep escarpment from the lake. Established in the fifteenth century by order of Quiché overlords, the town's whole purpose was to prevent the encroachment of Tzutujil people into Quiché territory. Its settlers came from Santa Catarina Ixtahuacán, a Quiché village to the north, near what is now Nahualá. Its new neighbors in the village of Santa María de Jesús (now named Santa María Visitación) were Tzutujil, sent from San Juan la Laguna to keep the Quiché from moving into Tzutujil territory. As enemies, the two villages had little occasion for cultural exchange.[14]

Santa Clara's costume differs as much from those of other Quiché villages as from those of its Tzutujil and Cakchiquel neighbors around Lake Atitlán. In an area where red-and-white striped huipils predominate, the one worn in Santa Clara is plain indigo blue. In an area where skirts are produced on the foot loom, this one is backstrap-woven, matching the huipil. In fact it is unique, the only matching skirt and huipil in the Museum's Guatemalan collection. In an area where weavers revel in brocade and *soumak s*upplementary weft patterns, the Santa Clara huipil and skirt have only a simple *randa* and neck edging in magenta thread. The use of the magenta is reminiscent of Santa Clara's origins in Santa Catarina: magenta was a favored decorative color on early Santa Catarina Ixtahuacán huipils.

Cakchiquel

Cakchiquel speakers can be found in four departments, spanning a wide area of the central highlands. In number they rank third after Quiché and Mam. In the 1970s there were 271,000 Cakchiquels in 48 pueblos speaking 12 dialects.

From the fourteenth century until the middle of the fifteenth, Cakchiquel tribes served as warriors for the constantly expanding Quiché state. According to the *Annals of the Cakchiquels*, when the great Quiché leader Q'uik'ab was overthrown by his sons, he advised the Cakchiquels to abandon their Quiché homeland and set up their own state. They selected a site in the northwest corner of the Chimaltenango plateau overlooking rolling tableland where corn, the vital crop, could be grown in abundance. The capital, called Iximche, consisted of a fortified complex of palaces, temples, ball courts, and great plazas. Although this was a militaristic state, a majority of the population engaged in farming, only taking part in the political and social life of the community on feast and holy days of the Maya calendar. The various indigenous people absorbed into the Cakchiquel nation may have influenced the evolution of Cakchiquel costume styles. Whatever the case, in the 1960s Cakchiquel dress varied considerably from area to area.

From the Museum's collection, it appears that stylistic variations correlate with dialect areas, which in turn often correspond, albeit roughly, with department divisions. Thus in the department of Sololá we see a preponderance of warp-striped huipils and indigo skirts, often with white weft stripes. Both huipils and skirts are comparatively light weight, and huipils are narrow in width. Motifs tend to be small and favor geometric forms or stick-figured animals, birds, or insects. *Fajas* are backstrap-woven in warp stripes, and are often brocaded.

Cakchiquel costume from the department of Guatemala shows a marked preference for the color purple (including mauve), dense amounts of it being used in brocading or in warp stripes. Motifs are large and bold, with animals, birds, trees, zigzags, and S-curves predominating. Ceremonial huipils tend to be wide and some are left unsewn at the sides. Plaid *morga* skirts are common; usually the ceremonial skirt is of heavier weight and a bolder plaid. The most common *faja* is of multicolored wool, elaborately embroidered on a black and white warp-striped band.

Cakchiquel costumes from the department of Chimaltenango share a number of stylistic traits not found in other Cakchiquel villages. We have chosen to illustrate the costumes of Comalapa, Tecpán, and Santa Apolonia, whose dialects are closely related (map, below). All are notable for their use of an overhuipil *(sobre-huipil)* as well as an everyday underhuipil. Both garments are made of two webs joined at the center and sides without a *randa*, but the overhuipil is longer, considerably wider and of a heavier weave.

Huipils from the department of Sacatepéquez show little cohesion, some relating to Chimaltenango styles, others relating to Guatemala, or Sololá; dialects in this department are similarly diverse.[15]

189. *Detail of a folk painting by an anonymous Comalapa artist.*

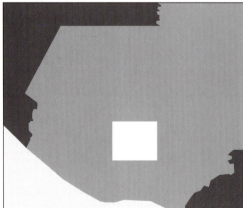

190 (above). Costumes of Comalapa.

191 (right). Detail of the banda
shown in figure 190, left.

Comalapa (Figure 190)

Comalapa is situated at the base of a mountaintop archaeological site called
Chij-Xot. It is famous for its folkpainting tradition; some painters have had exhibitions
in Europe. The two huipils (over and under) of the Comalapa *traje* share the same
general design, but the overhuipil has more elaborate brocading extending all the
way to the bottom. A wide band of red across the shoulders (called *creya*) and bands
of multicolored motifs separated by groups of weft stripes, called "separators,"
distinguished this 1960s design.

The overhuipils are worn for ceremonial functions, such as weddings, *cofradías*,
and fiestas, as well as for more practical purposes upon occasion. Although the
sewn-up sides leave openings for the arms, these are seldom used: the huipil is
thrown over the shoulders and arms like a cape and hangs loose over the skirt in the
Prehispanic manner. The underhuipil is worn tucked into the skirt, which is in turn
wrapped with a backstrap-woven sash.

The Comalapa huipil was strongly influenced by foreign design sources. European
double-faced brocade patterns were introduced at an early date and continue to
displace indigenous forms. A San Martín Jilotepeque huipil style has also emerged
as a popular choice for Comalapa women. At the present time, foot-loom-woven
huipils are rapidly replacing backstrap-woven huipils for everyday wear. In spite of
the construction similarities, there is considerable variety in color and design forms,
and more and more changes take place as the years go by.

During the early 1960s and before, old-fashioned heavy *morga* skirts were seen
in the village; but for daily wear, double-ikat skirts from Salcajá were customary.
Local men, having learned to weave the popular ikat skirts, now supply village
needs. Huipils of a fine quality are produced by men on draw looms and sold to
women in surrounding villages as well as to local women and tourists. A thriving
weaving cooperative established in the 1960s produces items for export, such as
bags, coin purses, and wallets.

The men's costume worn in the 1960s, and still worn for *cofradía* occasions,
features a dark blue wool jacket with a set-in back belt and flap-based buttonhole,
a bright blue tailored shirt, the traditional Comalapa *banda*, an apron (*ponchito*)
of black and white checked wool, and tailored white cotton pants. The straw hat is
of the style worn in many villages during the late 1960s and 1970s.[16]

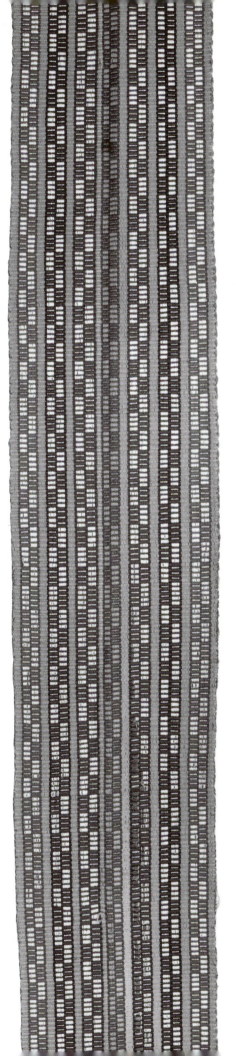

192. *Costumes of Tecpán (left) and Santa Apolonia (right).*

193. *Underhuipil from Tecpán.*

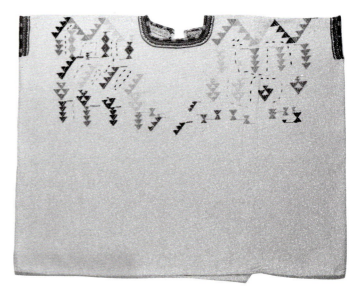

194. *Underhuipil from Santa Apolonia.*

Tecpán and Santa Apolonia *(Figure 192)*

Tecpán, the village nearest the Iximche ruins, was the first temporary Spanish capital established by Alvarado in Guatemala. Today it is an important Cakchiquel market town in a rich farming area producing alfalfa and wheat as well as corn and beans. Saw mills and flour mills are run by Ladinos. Santa Apolonia, a historic supplier of pottery and lime, is now a very poor village and most women wear foot-loom-woven huipils and skirts bought from Totonicapán traders. Men here produce utility baskets that are sold in local markets.

Unlike the matched huipils of Comalapa, the under- and overhuipils of Tecpán and Santa Apolonia differ altogether in design and coloring. Their overhuipils, however, are very much alike. Both are woven of natural brown cotton and display widely-spaced red warp stripes interspersed with pin stripes in yellow or gold. The underhuipil of Santa Apolonia is made of *manta*, its embroidery carefully executed to look like brocade (fig. 194); the underhuipil from Tecpán is skillfully and lavishly brocaded (fig. 193). The Tecpán skirt is especially handsome — a bold plaid in indigo and white in the heavy *morga* weave. The Santa Apolonia skirt, in the style of Comalapa, has warp stripes only. Backstrap-woven *fajas* are worn in both villages. Tecpán's is embellished at one end with bands of brocaded motifs.

Pan-Maya Acculturation in Cakchiquel Costume

Except among the Quiché, where commonalities are rare, connections between costume stylization and language groups appear quite evident. In the Museum collection, costumes that looked very much alike usually turned out to be from villages that shared a language. Among Cakchiquel villages, dialect differences were usually mirrored by costume differences. Working on this principle we were surprised by the striking similarity of style in the huipils of San Antonio Aguas Calientes (fig. 195) and San Martín Jilotepeque (fig. 196). These villages, while both Cakchiquel, spoke very different dialects and were separated geographically (map, below). The similarity of their huipil was so remarkable we felt the need to investigate these two villages more thoroughly and found that a multi-cultural history probably accounted for these unexpected similarities of style. Huipils from these villages may well illustrate the earliest examples of pan-Maya acculturation after the Conquest.

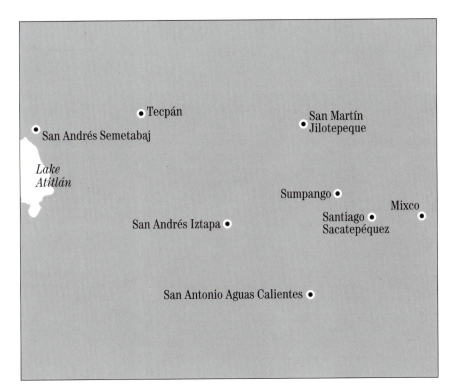

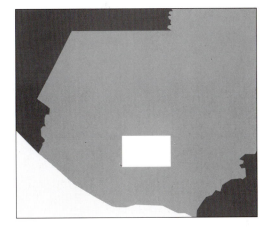

195.

196.

The 1960s huipils shown at left (figs. 195, 196), like most of the huipils from these two villages, have multiple bands of geometric brocading — some just to the waist, others to the garment edge — and an emphatic placement of horizontal zigzags (which we read as the feathered serpent), usually across the chest. They also resemble trade huipils, which are characteristically adorned with multiple weft rows of geometric motifs.

This is interesting because the people of the two villages do not seem to be related. The people of San Antonio Aguas Calientes and their neighbors in nearby villages and *aldeas* are all classified as part of a single dialect group whose origins could not be traced to any Prehispanic grouping. San Martín Jilotepeque's location, near two archaeological sites, suggests both Pocomam and Akahal origins, but its huipils show no similarity to the ones from those villages with which it is grouped linguistically.

The story of San Antonio's beginnings, as told by anthropologist Sheldon Annis, provides a clue to the mystery. San Antonio began as a colony of slaves taken by Alvarado as he fought his way from Mexico City to Guatemala. Their heterogeneous origins are suggested in a letter to the Spanish Audencia Real in 1567. Included were Quiché from Utatlán, Tzutujil from Santiago Atitlán, Kekchi from Alta Verapaz, Chontales from Tabasco or Oaxaca in southern Mexico, and Pipil from the Pacific coast of Guatemala. Annis suggests that the leveling of this population by disease and death probably hastened a pan-Maya acculturation process.

San Martín Jilotepeque, located at the nexus of a number of different tribal groups, has similar origins. It was, like San Antonio, one of the first villages in Guatemala to be organized economically and politically in the Spanish style, even though there were many protests and riots. In 1800, according to a *padre* cited in Gall, San Martín Jilotepeque was populated with great numbers of Spaniards, Africans, and about four thousand Maya, and the growing and processing of sugar cane was the major economic base. Murdo MacLeod argues that slavery, largely ignored in Guatemala history, had a great impact on social patterns in Guatemala, as did the Spanish-instituted sugar industry. Armies of Maya were recruited to work in the sugar harvest, and sugar mills were known to use slaves. Thus like San Antonio Aguas Calientes, San Martín Jilotepeque has as its base a heterogeneous population leveled by disease and death and unified by slave status. According to Osborne, the use of trade huipils — especially those of San Pedro (SM), Quezaltenango, and San Martín Jilotepeque — is a sign that the village was populated by Maya from various parts of the country. Like most trade huipils, the general characteristics of the huipils of these two Cakchiquel villages seem to reflect a process of acculturation.

Two backstrap-woven huipils purchased in the early 1980s illustrate how pan-Maya acculturation has accelerated (figs. 197, 198). The daily huipil shown above at right is from Tecpán, but this same style is now being worn in San Andrés Semetabaj as well. The huipil shown below at right was made in San Martín Jilotepeque, but this style is now also worn in Sumpango, Mixco, and San Andrés Itzapa. Both have multiple bands of geometric brocading covering all areas of the huipil above the waist. Both are of medium width and length. The most recognizable symbolic motif is the one we call feathered serpent (although weavers may not use that term). The Tecpán-Semetabaj style uses the flag motif found in the San Antonio Aguas Calientes huipil of the 1960s (second and fourth rows); it also uses the stairway to heaven or stair-step motif (fifth row) seen on Santiago Sacatepéquez huipils of the 1960s. The feathered serpent, clearly visible across the chest of the Tecpán-Semetabaj huipil, occurs less importantly but in the same location on the one worn in San Martín, Sumpango, and San Andrés Itzapa. Almost all the bands of design elements can be traced to other huipils. Chevrons, zigzags, and grid patterns are represented on all, and appear to be the common denominators in a process of style mixing that is occurring more and more as communication between villages increases.[17]

197. Huipil in the Tecpán style, worn in San Andrés Sematabaj, collected in the 1980s.

198. Huipil in the style of San Martín Jilotepeque worn in Sumpango, Mixco, and San Andrés Ixtapa, collected in the 1980s.

195. Huipil from San Antonio Aguas Calientes.
196. Huipil from San Martín Jilotepeque.

Notes

1. **Costume and Language**. For language data and population figures throughout this chapter I rely on Kaufman 1976. For those who read Spanish, Terga and Robles 1977 provide information on early settlement patterns. Gall's Spanish 4-volume geographic dictionary (1976-83), organized alphabetically by township, is also an excellent resource, although since much of the historic material is based on the reports of Catholic friars to the crown, one must be wary of some biases. I am grateful to Fresia Brenes Dunlap for consulting these sources on my behalf.

The major Maya families are: Mamean (including Mam, Ixil, Aguacatec); Quichéan (including two branches, an earlier and indigenous one comprising Pocomam, Pocomchi, Kekchi, and a later one influenced by Toltec invasions from Mexico, including Cakchiquel, Quiché, Sacapultec, Uspantec, and Kanjobalan (including Chuj, Kanjobal, and Jacaltec). Minor language families, which add several other languages to the list, are not considered here at all. It was the late William Swezey who pointed out that our division of Cakchiquel costume types looked very similar to the latest linguistic breakdown of Cakchiquel dialects (pers. com. 1983).

2. **Ixil**. See Fox 1978 (p. 91) on Ixil ruins. See Lovell 1985 (pp. 51-52) on the nature of Quiché rule and reaction to Dominican rule. See Sperlich & Sperlich 1980 (p. 75) on red skirts. The number of Ixil speakers has decreased considerably as a result of the civil war. Anderson and Garlock (1988) deal with the impact of the civil war on highland Maya communities.

3. **Chajul, Santa María Nebaj, San Juan Cotzal**. The two-panel Nebaj huipil was replaced in the '70s by a simpler three-panel huipil which took less time and skill to produce. In the '80s, many wear a daily *manta* huipil with different neckline decoration. In the Miss Universe pageant of 1975, "Miss Guatemala" (a Ladino) wore a Nebaj costume and won first prize in the costume selections. On Chajul weaving, see M. Anderson 1978 (p. 93). For possible historical connections between the Ixil and the people of Sacapulas and Aguacatán see Brinton 1953 (p. 77). See also Fox 1978, who cites the *Popul Vuh* re abductions (p. 281) and makes observations on early civic centers (p. 112). On the possible significance of women retaining their natal costume even when they marry exogamously, see coauthor Pat Altman's Note 28 in Chapter 1.

4. **San Martín Sacatepéquez and Concepción Chiquirichapa**. Other Mam villages in the group are San Juan Ostuncalco, Cajolá, Sigula, and Palestina. The brocaded shoulder band with squared designs resembles not only that found on Mam huipils in Huehuetenango, but also, curiously, the one seen on the huipils of Cakchiquel-speaking Santa María de Jesús. On supplementary weft designs of San Martín Sacatepéquez, see Sperlich & Sperlich 1980 (p. 138), and Rowe 1981 (p. 114). Rowe reports their use in Concepción as early as the '30s. Concepción weavers would appear to be the initiators of change as they were the first to enlarge their color palette with clear bright pastels and to incorporate new motifs into their *cintas* and their huipils.

5. **Pocomam**. Pocomam is also spelled Pokomam, Pocoman, or Pokoman. For history of the Pocomam prior to the Spanish Conquest I relied on John W. Fox 1978, who cites several native documents. Fox suggests that the conquered Pocomam communities were incorporated as peasants into those of their conquerors. See Fox 1978, pp. 229, 255, 261, and 279. The people of Ayampuc in the department of Scatepequez have Pocomam antecedents, but now speak Cakchiquel. Kaufman 1976, our source on language lists three other villages that speak Pocomam, but they are not in the highland region and do not wear an indigenous *traje*.

6. **Palín**. Maynard's study of Palín (1963) provides insight into the role of women, the changing costume, and the process of Ladinoization. Comparative census figures from the 18th century illustrate the progress of Ladinoization. The population of Palín in 1769 numbered 974 Maya and only 128 Ladinos. The 1950 town census lists 2581 Maya as 48% of the total population. Maynard's study of the roles of Maya and Ladino women helps us understand why Maya women might prefer to stay Maya. Maya marriages offer women more of a partnership both from the standpoint of economics and security. Maya women are expected to contribute to their families income as the wages paid Maya men are seldom sufficient to support a family. Women usually take over the role of marketing surplus produce raised by their husbands, or they may market eggs or chickens or even pigs they have raised themselves. Alternatively, they may weave extra textiles and sell them. They may embroider or sew, do household chores for upper class Ladinos, or act as midwives or even spiritualists. These roles gives them a freedom of movement and social life outside as well as providing money to spend on household needs. Whatever the job, contributing to the earning process gives them greater security and status in the marriage relationship.

7. **Tamahú and Tactic**. Two Guatemalan informants, Gwendolin Ritz and Ana Cayaz, tell of an early Tactic skirt that had weft stripes only. The skirts shown here were purchased from the shop in the Ixchel Museum in Guatemala City, and are modern copies of the old fabrics. By 1977 when we made a door to door search to buy a 1960s-style red skirt in Tactic, we found only a ragged and patched example owned by an old woman. All the women we saw except for the one were wearing Salcajá type *cortes* in indigo and white or with red combined with indigo and white, still

gathered in their traditional fashion. Osborne 1935, O'Neale 1945, and Delgado 1963 all describe the full red skirt; see in particular O'Neale, p. 301.

In 1980 we saw a group of young village women from Olintepeque wearing typical Tactic huipils, which were for sale in Guatemala City and Antigua as well. The 1924 description, the earliest on record, is by Popenoe, cited in Delgado 1963 (pp. 270-71). Of Tamahú Popenoe writes, "The huipil made here bears a strong resemblance to that of Tactic but it is nevertheless distinguishable...by the presence of a much branched cross which has in the center a spot of different color from that of the branches." Osborne 1965 (p. 152) describes the Tamahú huipil and headdress. See Morris 1987 (p. 208) on the wrapped turban of Amatenango in Chiapas, which is similar to the headdress of Tamahú.

8. **Kekchi**. On the history of this area in the early colonial era see King 1974 (pp. 16, 25 passim). Las Casas, an activist for peaceable conquest, persuaded Charles V to give his Dominican priests control over this area. Arriving in May 1544, they instituted a practice of learning and teaching in the local language and established the first successful Spanish-style villages *(reducciones)* with the founding of Cobán, San Juan Chamelco, and San Pedro Carchá. By 1547 most of the area had become Christianized, and Charles V renamed the land Verapaz, "true peace." The Germans, who did not bring women, formed semi-legal marriage relationships with the Kekchi women. Their trade arrangements bypassed Guatemala City; cargoes went by way of Lake Izabal to Port Livingston on the Caribbean, and then on to the Atlantic and European coffee markets. During World War II, the Germans were expelled by the Guatemalan government.

Quiché women in Quezaltenango also wear their skirts in the manner described for the Kekchi.

9. **San Pedro Carchá**. See Delgado 1963 (p. 265) on San Pedro Carchá motifs and on the *tupui*. Not many women were still weaving in this village in the '70s, though M. Anderson 1978 (p. 99) reports talking with a skilled weaver who employed many different designs, plant, animal and human forms, and geometric shapes. This woman was also familiar with gauze weaving techniques.

Our Cobán costume is one of the first Guatemalan costumes purchased for the UCLA collection by (then) Chancellor Murphy and his wife. On Cobán costume see O'Neale 1945 (p. 122) and Osborne 1965, who wrote that "all white of fine texture was the rule for all self-respecting matrons, but now many huipils with middle sections of colored material are worn" (p. 106). In the '70s the favored embroidery locally was garlands of roses, and then other flowers became desirable; however, a simple version of the old style continued to be made and sold in the Guatemala City market as it was popular with the tourist trade.

The 5th-century A.D. gauze huipil is illustrated in the April 1986 issue of *National Geographic*.

10. **Tzutujil**. Orellana 1984 was my primary source of information on the Tzutujil. The Quiché, Cakchiquel, and Tzutujil languages and cultures were related. All believed that the day of an individual's birth, as set forth in their 260-day calendar, also determined one's fate, alter ego *(nagual)*, and personality. Ceremonies included fasting, ritual purification, sacrifice, confession, drinking to become intoxicated, dancing, and abstinence from sex. In return, people asked for long life, health, children and sustenance. This belief system continues today in the rituals practiced by shaman guides. Many disasters befell the Tzutujil and contributed to the weakened state of the indigenous peoples at the time of the Conquest. The plague began in 1521, believed to have been brought by Mexican traders who had been in touch with the Spaniards in Mexico. Repeated epidemics and famine reduced the pre-Hispanic population of Chiya, the Tzutujil capital. By 1528 the Spaniards were in control and began exacting tribute from the natives. Tzutujil lords and commoners were made to serve as gold miners, warriors, and burden carriers. A few Maya *caciques* were allowed to continue as overlords as long as the tribute that they collected satisfied the greedy demands of the absentee Spanish *hidalgos* who usually lived in splendor in more comfortable areas. Providing sufficient tribute to keep duplicate overlords in luxury goods reduced the Tzutujil population at the lake even further.

11. **Quiché**. For historical background on the Quiché, see Carmack 1981, pp. 3,50, 54,204,205 passim, and p. 77 citing Villacorta 1962. Nahua words that have carried over into Quiché pertain to military and ritual matters — fortified towns, domination or power, receiving tribute, sacrificial victims and political offices and symbols. Cholan terms carried over in Quiché are mostly names of plants and animals. Native people spoke a form of Quiché which was assimilated and changed by the incoming warlords.

12. **Zunil and Almolonga**. In the '70s, we counted seven different geometric styles of huipils being worn in the market place — chevrons, diamonds, horizontal and vertical zigzags, large and small, alone or in combinations. The latest style were huge multicolored diamonds executed in neon-bright acrylic threads. Most predominant colors were maroon, purple and orange, some faded into pinks or roses with mauve and pale orange. Webs were sewn together with a simple randa; most were left plain at the neck and arm holes but others were bound with velvet ribbon. Perhaps foot-loom weavers from Totonicapán married into the community (as they

did in many other villages) and used their previously acquired skills in making *cortes* for the local trade creating their own ikat style. Regarding the Zunil shawl, at one time it was said that red was for single women and that married women wore purple (O'Neale 1945, p. 306). Several other colors are worn at the present time.

13. **Zacualpa**. Many Zacualpa natives have moved permanently to the piedmont area of San Antonio Suchitepéquez where they are said to live with more abundance. The huipil of neighboring Joyabaj has embroidery around the neck; its skirt is foot-loom-woven, with a red ground, like that of Nebaj or Rabinal.

14. **Santa Clara la Laguna**. Orellana's 1984 publication, which explains the early history of Santa Clara, solved the puzzle of this atypical Lake *traje*. Susan Turner's photographs from the '70s and '80s show the skirt randa worn at the back.

15. **Cakchiquel**. According to Kaufman, the people of Tecpán and Santa Apolonia speak the same dialect, along with Patzicía; very closely related is the dialect spoken in Comalapa (and also in Patzún). To our knowledge, there have been no anthropological studies published relating specifically to the Cakchiquel. Such a study is overdue and would inevitably clear up some of the anomalies.

16. **Comalapa**. Regarding Comalapa, I have relied on Linda Asturias de Barrios, whose thorough coverage of Comalapa textiles and costume was published in 1985 (see pp. 36, 40, 5, passim). According to Asturias de Barrios there seem to be no strict injunctions against wearing the overhuipil for more practical purposes later. She notes, however, that "The *sobre huipil* is about to become extinct. When the old women who use it today die, it will disappear from the feminine wardrobe, but it could possibly survive in the *cofradías*." She cites the popularity of the San Martín Jilotepeque style (p. 36). Since the disastrous earthquake of 1976, weaving as a trade has taken precedence over weaving just for the family's needs. All villages of Chimaltenango department suffered severe property damage, and many lives were lost.

17. **Pan-Maya Acculturation**. I found Fox 1978 to be particularly interesting for his study of Prehispanic sites, which because of its focus on design forms and style, had relevance to my investigations. Fox says that Jilotepeque Viejo was the principal Akahal community at Spanish contact from which San Martín Jilotepeque was formed (p. 203). He also points out a dichotomy in plaza patterns and architectural styles at Jilotepeque Viejo which suggest strong intra-community differences — possibly a regional capital of allied social groups or autonomous socio-political divisions within the elite community (p. 208). Kaufman groups San Martín Jilotepeque linguistically with the Cakchiquel speakers in San Juan Sacatepéquez, San Raimundo, Ayampuc, and Chuarrancho. Gall (*op. cit.*, chap. 4, note 1) cites padre Domingo Juaros on San Martín Jilotepeque.

See Annis 1987 (pp. 13-17) on San Antonio's beginnings. See Gall 1976-83 on early San Martín Jilotepeque. See MacLeod 1983 (pp. 197, 208) on slavery. See Osborne 1965 (p. 147), on trade huipils.

For information on the Tecpán-San Andrés Semetabaj style and the San Martín Jilotepeque diffusion I thank Axel Orlando García.

199. Family in San Antonio Palopó.

Costume and Geography

T he Guatemalan highland landscape has been characterized as "a land of ravines and gorges, dissected by mountains with limited plateaus and the open level space of the Quezaltenango basin." The inequitable distribution of this land has resulted in widely contrasting cultures and costumes.[1]

Geography has an impact on costume. Certainly clothing responds to climate; clearly, too, the materials used in the making of clothes depend upon local availability. Perhaps less obvious is the influence of topography on the degree of continuity or change in costume. Certain areas by virtue of their relative inaccessibility become locked into traditional patterns and exhibit steadfast continuity in their costume stylizations.

Villages in the Cuchumatán Mountains and the Lake Atitlán area demonstrate conservatism in costume stylization. In both regions, the local people not only cling to backstrap weaving, but also show a preference for red-and-white upper-body garments and indigo skirts. This reflects an earlier time when the natural dyes, cochineal red and indigo blue, were used. Huipils from the earliest collection we have seen, dating from the turn of the century, showed a prevalence of cochineal on white. Another example of continuity is expressed in the number of men from both regions who continue to wear backstrap woven garments, some of which match women's garments in coloring and weaving details.[2]

Other areas with more inviting topography encourage trade, communication, and settlers. New concepts introduced by outsiders bring change in living patterns that are reflected in costume changes. The topography of the Quezaltenango-Totonicapán basin favors interaction with the larger world; there, geography encourages change. This densely populated Quezaltenango area offers almost ideal conditions for human settlement. The land is rich and naturally irrigated by meandering streams. Communication lines are enabled by easy access and major trade routes pass through it. Flourishing markets create a constant flux of locals and outsiders. The commingling of different peoples and ideas is consistently reflected in costumes of the area. Fabrics are made on commercial looms or foot-powered treadle looms — in other words, by post-Conquest techniques. Costumes generally show the influence of Spanish and Mexican styles. Geographic accessibility has apparently influenced costume in other highland areas as well — for instance, along the Negro River basin, at the central highland crossroads at Utatlán, and across the border between Huehuetenango and the Mexican state of Chiapas.

200. *The Cuchumatán Mountains.*

The Cuchumatán Mountains

The Cuchumatanes, a part of the Andean cordillera, are the highest mountains in Central America, with peaks that rise to over 3,650 meters (approximately 12,000 feet). The diversity of altitudes, with high peaks, plateaux, and deep ravines, creates a corresponding diversity in temperature and agricultural possibilities. Three climate zones — cold, temperate, and hot — enable a variety of market products that make the region self-sufficient except in cotton, which has to be imported from the coastal lowlands.

This forbidding landscape has sequestered local traditions by minimizing outside influence. Foot trails have served the people well, but there were no roads through this area until the Pan American highway was built in the 1950s. Even as late as the 1960s, vehicular access was limited. Historically, the Quiché conquered the Mam and their capital at Zaculeu, but left them under only minor supervision because the area presented more problems than assets. The Mam here had broken away from their Quiché overlords by the time the Spaniards arrived. Spanish interest in the Cuchumatanes area was never very great, as it was a long distance from the comforts of the capital. Practices initiated by the Spaniards were gradually abandoned, and Prehispanic rituals were revived and continue to be followed to this day. Native shamans *(chimanes)* still mediate between the individual, the community, and the supernatural world. Ancient ritual and ceremony accompany the agricultural cycle, especially in the planting of corn, the most sacred crop of the Maya.

Market trading has contributed to cohesiveness between the Mam villages dotting the area (map, below). A number of crops are grown in small plots in the mountains. Tomatoes, onions, and a variety of fruits are village specialties traded in local markets. Pitch pine for lighting fires, lime, lye, and copal incense are available locally. Palm fiber hats and woolen cloth are specialty products in several villages. A family's land is usually too meager in size to sustain them in work and food so most Maya men seek part-time employment as wage laborers on the coffee, cotton, and sugar plantations of the Pacific coast.

Women are the main preservers of Maya culture in the Cuchumatanes. It is they who stay by the hearth, rear the children, speak only the local dialect, and continue to produce the indigenous costume on their backstrap looms. Women in this group of Mam villages come closer than any other women in Guatemala to providing all the clothing for their families. In most villages they even continue to weave their own skirts on backstrap looms, a practice abandoned in other areas after dependency on the foot loom became widespread. Some women in Todos Santos, San Juan Atitán, and San Sebastián continue the tedious practice of hand-spinning the threads for their huipils, rather than using commercially prepared thread.[3]

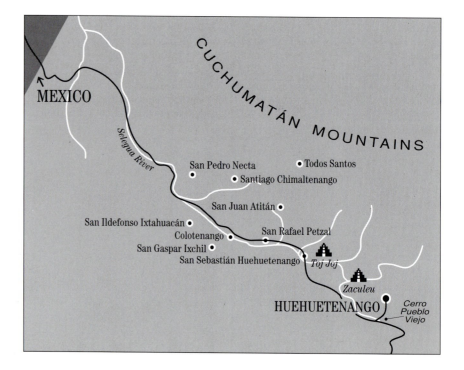

San Juan Atitán *(Figure 201)*

San Juan Atitán is truly an isolated village. It can be reached only by a perilous jeep trail (if the road is dry) or by several hours' climb on foot (fig. 202). Earthquakes have plagued it ever since 1692, when the church and a number of other buildings were destroyed. Two hundred years later on the same day — Saint Geronimo's Day, September 30th — the earth opened, and again in 1970 seismic action caused damage to public buildings and houses. The village is an impressive sight on market day — hundreds of villagers dressed in starkly simple red-and-white costumes, against a somber backdrop of dark green pine and spruce.

San Juan Atitán women, who seldom travel outside the village, wear long huipils (right) that closely resemble those pictured in the Prehispanic codices. In other places, long huipils are mostly produced on the foot loom and worn tucked in. This one, by contrast, is backstrap-woven and worn outside the skirt. Sometimes it is gathered up in the back and tucked into the *faja* leaving a draped swag in front (as seen here); sometimes it falls free over the skirt. The chest decoration has undoubtedly been elaborated over the years but it is still a simple decorative statement incorporating the squared or triangular motifs so often found in Mam weaving. As in Todos Santos, this density is accomplished with a compound weave using an extra heddle stick. In contrast with the background fabric, which is white with widely spaced, inch-wide red stripes, a heavy black thread is used to join the seams of the huipil (and the hems of the men's white pantlegs, as well). The backstrap-woven skirt, worn folded on the hip, is indigo blue, with three groups of four warp-stripes in bright blue.

The men of San Juan Atitán wear a red-and-white *traje* topped with a dark wool *capixay* (left). The man's shirt (fig. 203), hardly visible under the *capixay*, is like a narrow huipil to which a collar and sewn-on sleeves have been added. Its body is a wide, single web of white handspun cotton, with red stripes, similar to the huipil. A separate warping and weaving has yielded the red sleeves and collar, which are accented with orange, green, and white pin-stripes, as well as several zipper-like stripes called *saayin*. The collar is distinctive for its long ends (seen dangling over

202. People in the mountainous terrain of San Juan Atitán.

203. Man's shirt from San Juan Atitán.

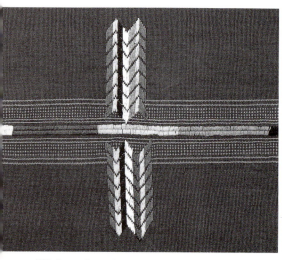

204. Brocade on the tzute shown in figure 201, right.

the top of the *capixay);* these ends are doubled and often have a small slit left unsewn on the neck side so that a few coins or a *milagro* can be hidden away inside. The sleeves show a band of multicolored brocade, near the elbow, and end in a strange squared tab sewn on at the wrist; this, which serves no real function, is possibly a misconceived cuff.

Men as well as women can be seen wearing *tzutes* on their heads in San Juan. As shown here, the man's is folded cornerwise and tied behind the head with its loose ends hanging down in back. San Juan *tzutes* are characteristically squarish with a red ground. Though most are undecorated except for a *randa,* some have a rectangular patch of brocade at their center (fig. 204).

Straw hats for men and women are plaited and sewn together by local men. The hat is worn alone in hot weather, and over the *tzute* when it is cold. The brown wool *capixay,* abandoned in many villages but still worn here, is described in Chapter 2. The *banda,* worn as shown over the *capixay,* is backstrap-woven by San Juan women. San Sebastián weavers provide the red wool *cinta* worn by the women. San Juan men crochet their own bags *(morrales),* and local cobblers make high-cuffed sandals for them and for the men of Todos Santos.[4]

Todos Santos *(Figure 205)*

Todos Santos was isolated like San Juan Atitán until a road was built in the early seventies. Mountains rise to 3,500 meters and are covered with pine forests. Potatoes and apples are a product of these high altitudes, and sheep are raised primarily for their wool that is sold to weavers from Momostenango. Lumbering is also a source of livelihood. As in San Juan and throughout the Cuchumatanes, men often seek seasonal labor on the lowland cotton or coffee plantations to supplement their income, and sometimes bring home raw cotton for their wives to spin into thread.

The Todos Santos huipil of the 1960s (right) shows little change from that of the 1930s except that there is considerably more brocading to cover the red-and-white-striped ground. The huipil is always three webs and has a white ruffled collar; in the 1930s it was loose, but here it is sewn down and zigzagged with bright blue rickrack and pink braid. Multicolor brocading in geometric patterns once decorated only the chest area but by the 1960s, as seen here, has filled all visible areas with design.

Unlike the women of San Juan, Todos Santos women do not weave their own skirts and utility cloths, although they do produce lengths of backstrap-woven cotton (seen in the basket) to wrap their babies. They purchase their skirt lengths from professional men weavers and have done so for a long time, according to photographic evidence from the thirties. Often they use an extra length of the same indigo fabric with bright blue weft stripes for a *tzute.* Their red wool *fajas,* like those worn in San Juan, are made by San Sebastián men weavers.

Todos Santos women weave *pantalones, camisas,* and *bandas* for their menfolk as well as their own huipils and children's clothes. Bold red-and-white stripes are typical of the everyday pants style. The subtler *camisa,* made of handspun cotton,

205. Costumes of Todos Santos.

combines black, bright blue, gold, and red pin-stripes; selvedges are decorated with a denser pattern. The tailoring represents a more Western adaptation with set-on sleeves that are slightly recessed and a "proper" cuff. The one pictured is made to go over the head and shows how the decorative selvedges add emphasis to the center join. The *banda* is of darker, multi-colored warp stripes worn knotted at the side front. Barely visible are the buttoned-on, split-leg overpants described and sketched in Chapter Two. Todos Santos is the only village where they are still worn for everyday; in other villages where they exist at all, they are worn only for important ceremonial occasions. The straw hats seen here — worn by men and women — represent styles from the early and late 1960s or early 1970s.

Men's wool jackets and *capixayes* (not shown here) are produced in Santa Eulalia and Soloma, further north. A rope bag (known as *red*), like the one seen under the mannequin, is also made there.[5]

San Pedro Necta and Santiago Chimaltenango *(Figure 206)*

San Pedro Necta and Santiago Chimaltenango are neighboring villages. Politically joined by governmental edict for a period of ten years in the late 1930s and 1940s, they are now independent. San Pedro Necta is dominated by its Ladino population, whereas Santiago Chimaltenango is run by Mam people, whose values exert a controlling influence.

San Pedro Necta, lying in one of the low pockets of the Cuchumatanes range, has a temperate climate very unlike that of their high altitude neighbors. Its main trading crop is fruit — oranges and lemons, bananas, mangoes, and peaches. Coffee, meat, and lime are also traded for maize and other products. Maize was the main crop in Santiago Chimaltenango until the 1960s, when coffee cultivation began to supplant it as a cash crop for those whose land was suitable. Because of the scarcity of arable land, homes here are crowded into the town center rather than being scattered throughout the countryside, in *aldeas,* as is usually the case.

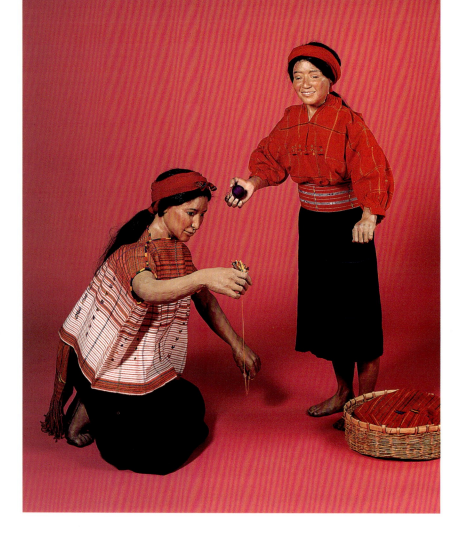

206. Costumes of San Pedro Necta (left) and Santiago Chimaltenango (right).

207. Woman from Santiago Chimaltenango.

Women of both villages still produce all of their own costumes on their backstrap looms. The skirts of Santiago Chimaltenango and San Pedro Necta are alike: both are of plain indigo with two widely spaced warp stripes of lighter blue running horizontally around the body. Their width is skimpier than most, but there is enough to fold over the right hip; the length comes to the calf.

It is in the upper garments that the two villages differ. San Pedro Necta women wear a huipil that is unique in Guatemala (left), made of one backstrap-woven web, but with the warp turned horizontally instead of vertically. It is short and worn outside the skirt. A decorative and exceptionally well-made padded *randa* in blocks of various colors provides the joins at the under-arm side seam and circles one armhole, continues across the shoulders and around the neck, and borders the opposite cut-out armhole. Red and white stripes predominate but other primary colors are intermixed both in the stripes and in the *soumak* designs arranged vertically in rows. Stripes are more concentrated in the top half than in the bottom. (Since the 1970s, the trend has been towards ever more stripes, colors, and *soumak* designs). The backstrap-woven sash (dangling below the huipil, left) is worn tied around the waist with the fringed ends hanging down in back — a style more common to men than to women.

The Santiago Chimaltenango huipil is remarkable for its sleeves, which are semi-long and cuffed (right). The only other sleeved backstrap-woven huipil is the one worn in Sololá. Both are constructed like a man's *camisa*. Our example is a brilliant red with fine warp and weft stripes of gold, green, and blue; others are made with white stripes. The chest area is decorated with three rows of small *soumak* motifs, including the squared diamonds typical of the Mam (these have increased in number, type, and size since the 1960s).

The women of Santiago Chimaltenango produce their own sashes. The one shown here, red with black and white warp stripes, is one of two styles; the other is shown in a field photo from the 1970s (fig. 206). Here and in San Pedro Necta, red woolen hairwraps are bought from weavers in San Sebastián. Although the same kind of *cintas* are worn in both villages, they are wrapped differently. San Pedro Necta women tie them in front while Santiago Chimaltenango women tie them in back or on top.[6]

208. Costumes of San Rafael Petzal (left), Ixtahuacán (foreground), and Colotenango (right).

San Rafael Petzal, Ixtahuacán, and Colotenango *(Figure 208)*

Costumes of these three villages are so similar it is natural to think of them as related. Ixtahuacán is believed to pre-date the Conquest, while Colotenango is thought to have been established by the Spaniards who gathered together scattered families for a Spanish style village. Two of its *aldeas* were taken to form the town-ship of San Rafael Petzal, which was later annexed back to Colotenango along with San Gaspar Ixchil. All three villages produce fruit (oranges and lemons), legumes, chile peppers, cane sugar, peanuts, and coffee. Twine bags and tiles for roofing are made in Colotenango. Ixtahuacán's specialty is copal incense and pitch pine. The regional market at Huehuetenango provides those products not available in local markets and other basics such as salt and matches. Everyone grows corn and beans to meet family needs, but half the males must supplement their income by working seasonally on the coastal plantations. Men may also earn extra income as *chimanes*, or as musicians, and women may work as midwives.

Early in this century these villages were beset by a series of disasters, from a volcanic eruption in 1902 to a smallpox epidemic, famine in the wake of a Chiapas uprising, more seismic activity, and flu — part of the worldwide epidemic of 1918. Although the laws forcing Maya to work on coastal coffee and sugar plantations were abolished in 1934, new ordinances sent most of them to work on the highways. Ladinos were put in charge of municipal affairs and took over Mam land.

The opening of the Pan American highway through this region ushered in a new era of commerce, allowing their lumber and mining products to reach a market; and the outside world began to find its way in. This change in economic status may well be reflected in the decoration added to their costume. In the 1930s local garments were reported to be without decoration.

The backstrap-woven skirts of these three villages are extraordinary. Red and indigo or red and black warp-striped, with supplementary weft decoration, they represent the most complex patterning of any daily skirt in Guatemala. A *saayin* (zipper-like stripe) in a sharp combination of green and yellow is seen on both skirts

209. *Weaver in Colotenango.*

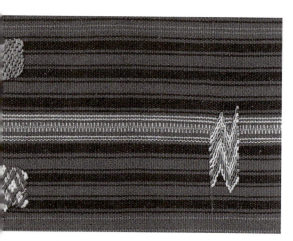

210. *Detail of saayin stripe on a skirt from Colotenango.*

and huipils. In the 1960s the *saayin* was unique to the Cuchumatanes region (fig. 210). The corn plant motif appears on three of the five Museum skirts from this area. Skirt colors differ from village to village; Ixtahuacán uses a more yellow-red than either Colotenango or San Rafael Petzal.

Backstrap huipils with red and white warp-striped backgrounds are common to all three villages, even up to the present. Fiesta or special occasion huipils are usually made of three webs. Two-webbed huipils are also worn and are sometimes decorated to imitate three webs (fig. 211). The wide band of satin stitch embroidery around the neckline of the Ixtahuacán huipil, seen on the kneeling figure, distinguishes it from the others. This Ixtahuacán huipil is completely reversible, perfectly finished on both sides. An added embroidery motif (called *pajaro*) crosses the red selvedged join at regularly spaced intervals, but it is possible that this is a later addition to the original huipil. The child's costume copies the adult one, except that the neckline is simpler, and the skirt unadorned. Huipils from the 1960s have banded designs across the shoulders and chest (the *mano* and *pecho* placement common to many huipils), but these are so often integrated into the total design that they are apt to be over-looked. It is probable here, as elsewhere, that at an earlier period they were the only design elements.

There appear to be many crossovers between the huipils of Colotenango and San Rafael Petzal. These may be detailed but neither our efforts nor those of other investigators have been able to pinpoint them. Possibly they are known only to the local inhabitants. Mejía de Rodas mentions that costumes from *aldeas* at higher elevations tend to be more densely woven or have double-faced brocade, but this probably reflects considerations of warmth rather than identity.

Men wear commercial white manta pants and shirts, but they retain their backstrap-woven bandas and tzutes. In Colotenango the sashes of men and women are indistinguishable. Women also carry the same woven bag as men, a surprising inroad into what is normally considered men's costume.[7]

211. *Two-webbed huipil decorated to imitate three webs.*

212. Costumes of San Sebastián Huehuetenango.

San Sebastián Huehuetenango *(Figure 212)*

San Sebastián is thought to have been a large Mam population center in the Pre-hispanic period, and ruins of the old town (called Toj Joj) are visible to the north of the present one. In 1891 it had to move to higher ground when the village was destroyed by flooding from the Selegua River. The present village is divided into an upper and lower level. In addition to subsistence farming, men engage in limestone and lead mining, lumbering, and the manufacture of rope, while women produce pottery.

All elements of the woman's costume pictured here are part of a complete *traje* purchased from a single owner. The huipil is made of two webs, in split-neck style. Embroidered star forms are scattered at random in the chest area on a red-and-white-striped warp. The skirt, also backstrap-woven, is sewn into a tube, with a join so skillfully executed that it appears seamless. Both top and bottom selvedges are buttonhole-stitched in blocks of color matching the *randa* joining the two lengths. The same *randa* joins the two huipil webs — all in all, an incredible amount of work, beautifully executed. Young girls or less skillful weavers substitute a white muslin huipil for the backstrap-woven one.

The red wool *cinta* of San Sebastián calls for twelve arm lengths and is worn wrapped around the head a number of times crisscrossing in front like a turban. It is produced by local men who use a simple loom combining features of both the backstrap and treadle loom to make hairwraps for the women in a number of nearby villages. Women will usually add a few embroidery stitches, pompoms or *milagros* at the ends to personalize their own. The red sash is of a stiff durable ribbed cotton weave and has a few embroidered designs in multicolor threads across the warp striping. The utility cloth seen here was used as a basket cover. It is white muslin with scattered motifs, a *randa* and two selvedged edges embroidered in cotton and wool.

Women weavers produce woolen *rodilleras* for the menfolk of San Sebastián — an unusual circumstance since in other villages most wool is fabricated by men. The brown and white checked *rodillera* shown here is characteristic. Ordinarily men wear cotton *manta* and white *manta* pants; a red belt and a handsome backstrap-woven *tzute* complete the costume.[8]

213. Lake Atitlán.

Lake Atitlán

Lake Atitlán lies about halfway between Guatemala's two largest cities, Guatemala City and Quezaltenango. This would appear to be in a central position for trade routes and communication, but the map can be deceiving. Lake Atitlán itself is the result of ancient earth forces, and the land that surrounds it has been continually twisted and upturned by volcanic action and earthquakes over the centuries. Because of the many abrupt altitude changes that occur in this landscape, the main intercity route, the Pan American highway, bypasses the lake. Boulder-filled valleys and steep escarpments thwart land travel around the lake and restrict access from the outside. Intervillage communication is sustained by daily mail boats which set forth in the morning, before the onset of winds called *zocomil*, which often make lake water treacherous in the afternoon.

During the 1960s, five of the villages discussed here were accessible only by foot trails: Santa Catarina Palopó, San Antonio Palopó. San Juan la Laguna, Santa Cruz la Laguna, and San Marcos la Laguna. (Roads have since been extended to the first three). Panajachel and Sololá, less isolated than the other Lake Atitlán villages, were nevertheless part of this same cohesive group. Lake villages had (and still have) a special symbiotic relationship with Sololá, which is the seat of the regional market. Most of the smaller villages, unable to sustain a local market, depend on the one in Sololá. While Sololá has prospered fulfilling this function, it is also dependent on these villages for its livelihood.

The costumes worn in this area reveal conservative attitudes and represent a cohesive group. Of the only thirteen villages where Guatemalan men still wore backstrap-woven garments in the 1960s, eight were in the lake area. Women in most lake villages wore backstrap-woven huipils and other garments, as they still do today, although their skirts were woven on the foot loom. In several lake villages, the colors, stripes, and motifs on men's garments (usually pants) match those on women's (usually huipils). This kind of matching may have originated as a marriage custom; in any case, from the standpoint of the weaver it seems a logical plan. Among the most isolated villages red-and-white stripes seem to prevail, as in the Cuchumatanes.[9]

Sololá (Figure 214)

Situated on the highest inhabited ridge above Lake Atitlán, Sololá is the political center of the department of Sololá, and the indigenous market center for all Lake villages. It was from here that the Cakchiquel ruler Jun Ik' of the Xahil lineage began the *Annals of the Cakchiquels*, which Brinton, its translator, has characterized as "one of the most important in aboriginal American literature."

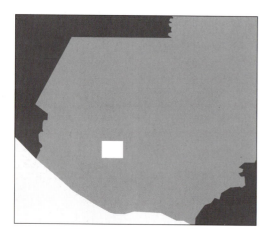

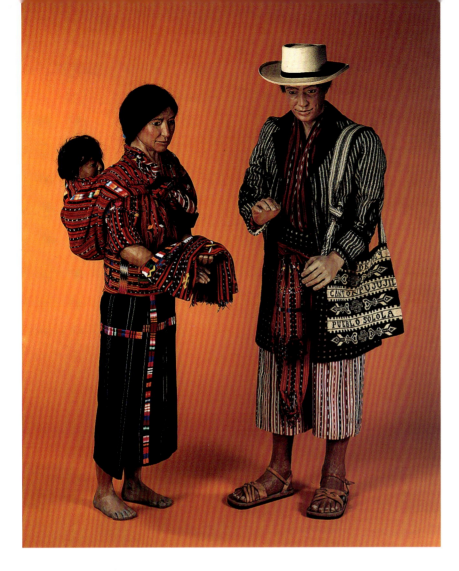

214. Costumes of Sololá.

In spite of its seeming modernity and the large number of Ladino residents who hold most of the governmental jobs, Sololá is a very traditional village and was even more so in the 1960s when there were fewer tourists. On market and fiesta days it is crowded and full of activity; other days it is quiet. *Solotecos* adhere to ancient customs and still wear the backstrap-woven costume (fig. 215). Sololá *cofradía* garments are elaborately designed and decorated, including all-enveloping huipils trimmed with rich fabrics and embroidery, *sacos* with a corn design at the bottom, black high-crowned hats with imported silk ribbon bands, and elaborate dance costumes in satin and velvet, with gold and silver braid and fringe. The 1960s daily costume, shown here, has its own grandeur. Rich reds and greens combine opulently with orange, *cuyuscate*, and ikat to create a sumptuous effect.

The men's costume of Sololá is particularly noteworthy. Tailored jackets are distinctive, elaborately trimmed with braid; some are white, but the striped style is preferred by local people. The *pantalones* and *camisa* are well fashioned, too. The fabric of the pants and shirt do not match; however they are alike in the structure of the striped elements and differ only in the amounts of color and ikat chosen (as seen here). Four webs are used in the making of the men's pants, as is true in all Lake villages where backstrap pants are still worn. Most *pantalones* have a set-in gusset at the crotch; others are sewn without a gusset. They are held up by means of a long wide sash with warp-striping on a red ground and rows and rows of weft-brocaded motifs, providing a decorative note. In size, color, and design it matches the woman's *faja*.

The Sololá kilt *(rodillera)*, made in Nahualá, is wrapped around the man's waist and secured by a leather belt which is then covered by a turned-down flap of the textile. Made of wool, it provides warmth and protection for the pants and for the lower part of the body in the daily physical chores. The bag *(morral)* seen here would typically be the product of the wearer's own skill as a knitter. Men often knit as they walk the trails. The one shown has the date it was made, the name of the owner and maker, and the canton and village where he lives.

215. People from Sololá.

In the 1960s, Sololá men and women wore nearly identical upper body garments. Both have carefully constructed tab collars and sewn-on sleeves. The only difference in the styling of the man's and woman's tops is in the sleeve treatment. Men's *camisas* have vestigial cuffs — a short section gathered on a narrow band that makes no pretense of encircling the arm. Women's sleeves end in a straight selvedge, and are rolled up on the arm. Two long webs form the body, and two smaller webs form the sleeve. Fabric needed for the collar and sleeve binding is cut from the sleeve portion. The 1960s huipil has from four to six rows of small multicolored geometric patterns brocaded front and back, as seen here, giving a jewel-like sparkle to the garment. A narrow band of double-faced brocade crosses the shoulders and goes around the sleeve a couple of inches below its join to the shoulder.

There is more ikat in Sololá than in other lake villages. Two early huipils in our collection have either no ikat or very little, indicating that its use here is a fairly recent innovation. It is not difficult to imagine that the garment of an earlier time was predominantly red and white. A *tzute* in our collection dating from the 1930s also lacks ikat, has considerably more white and *cuyuscate*, and is altogether a much simpler and yet very elegant textile. The large two-panel ikat-striped *tzute* shown here as a baby carrier is in the traditional village stripe of the 1960s and has wide indigo stripes near the outer selvedges. This large size is usually undecorated except for the *randa*.

The woman's skirt, locally woven on a foot loom, is in the typical Sololá style. Of medium-weight fabric combining indigo and white thread, it has groups of vertical white weft stripes every three inches; little importance is given to lining up the stripes on the two panels. Most skirts are embellished with a finely executed *randa* at the join (as shown here). The *randa* is double-faced, so that the skirt can be worn either side out with equal effect. Garments were handsewn throughout the 1960s.

Small *tzutes* such as the one seen at left are used to carry personal belongings or purchases from the market. This one is brocaded randomly with the multicolor geometric motifs at which the Sololá women are so adept. *Tzutes* of this size were also used around the crown of men's straw hats during the 1960s, a practice seldom followed anymore except by certain *cofradía* officers, the *regidores*.[10]

Santa Catarina Palopó *(Figure 217)*

Santa Catarina is located in an area formerly called Upper Tolimán, a name deriving from certain lake grasses used to make mats and tumplines. The land in Santa Catarina is rocky and unsuitable for farming; and over the years, government interventions have made it difficult for the men to find steady employment through the use of the lake's resources; thus for economic reasons Santa Catarina women were impelled to sell their textiles at an earlier period than other women weavers. Catering to the tourist trade has produced the uneven workmanship found here: the

216. Santa Catarina Palopó women.

217. Costumes of Santa Catarina Palopó.

textiles they wore were usually of better quality than those they sold. Santa Catarina and its neighbors, San Antonio and Panajachel, are the only Cakchiquel villages to have a three-web huipil for daily use; and all are notable as well for the decorative matching of men's and women's costumes.[11]

The woman's huipil seen here is characteristic of the late 1960s, with its decorative *soumak* designs, small but precise bird and animal forms over the center and side portions of the three-web huipil. The central web is wider and redder; the side webs, more sparsely decorated, are in simple red-and-white stripes. (Now, in contrast, the design area is brocaded in wide bands to the waist, and all three webs are heavily embellished with acrylic threads.)

The skirt worn by Santa Catarina women is the same style worn in several lake villages, and is produced on a foot loom by weavers from as far away as Olintepeque who make this medium-weight indigo skirt cloth with widely spaced groups of thick and thin white stripes for this market. There may be other weavers who produce this type skirt as well.

Santa Catarina women weave small *tzutes* to cover their baskets or to wrap around a man's straw hat. In the 1960s they also made the small single-web cloths like the one seen here on the mannequin's head. A special large *tzute* with a white ground and both warp and weft stripes in red signifies status and is only worn for ceremonial *cofradía* occasions.

The old-style man's costume includes red and white calf-length *pantalones* and a red and white *camisa* with white banding at the sleeves and neckline. Nowadays Santa Catarina men are more apt to wear an ikat shirt of the type made in San Pedro la Laguna. Both the man and the woman wear wide red sashes with bright blue warp stripes, woven locally. The woman's is usually decorated with supplementary weft bands of multicolor zigzags (at least on one end) while the man's is plain.

218. People of Santa Catarina Palopó.

219. *Costumes of San Antonio Palopó.*

220. *Onion sellers in San Antonio Palopó.*

San Antonio Palopó *(Figure 219)*

San Antonio Palopó is above the lake and in the 1960s was accessible only by climbing up from the mail boat dock or down from the narrow dirt road at Godinez. Its people maintain themselves by farming terraced plots of corn and beans, and anise and onions which they trade in Sololá. The costume of men and women (fig. 199) has not changed since the 1930s and before, and the weaving is of excellent quality.

The San Antonio three-web huipil is undecorated except for a contrasting pattern of stripes in the central and side portions: red predominates in the former, white in the latter. In the 1930s and 1940s the color contrast between these areas was greater, but it has become less so with time. The special feature of San Antonio weaving is in the clarity of the thread, and in the fineness of the thread count. The huipil is long, coming almost to the knees, and is tucked under the wraparound tube skirt. The woman's skirt is plain indigo sewn by hand without a decorative join.

The man's camisa is long, falling to the knees, and it too is tucked in. Its body and sleeves reverse the color contrast seen in the woman's huipil. It has a banded collar, much like that of Sololá, but it is wider, stands higher, and is embroidered. The man's *pantalones* are striped, like his shirt, and when he stands they are too short to be visible under his *rodillera*.

Panajachel *(Figure 221)*

While Panajachel's Ladino population catered to tourists and Guatemalan vacationers, the Cakchiquel people were protective of their culture in the early 1960s and tended to keep to themselves, staying on one side of the river that dissects the town. Mostly agriculturalists, they made use of the rich soil of the river delta to raise vegetables (fig. 223), which are planted in raised beds called tablons in a method dating back to the classic Maya. Panajachel women have traditionally done much of the gardening, and many do not weave for themselves, but instead buy their huipils from local professional women backstrap weavers.

221. Costumes of Panajachel.

222 (below). Detail of the huipil shown in figure 221.

223. Market in Panajachel.

Again we see the three-web huipil with undecorated side-panels, red with either white or *cuyuscate* stripes, and the central web with weft brocade bands of repeated or alternating motifs in purple (as seen here) or green. The skirt fabric is made in Sololá; its *randa* is of purple silk interspersed with white.

The men's backstrap-woven pants are striped like the huipil. They survive as *cofradía* costumes, but were seldom worn otherwise in Panajachel, even during the 1960s. During the early 1960s the *capixay*, as shown here, was worn only for ceremonial occasions. Nowadays most local Cakchiquel men are indistinguishable from Ladinos in their dress except that they tend to wear sandals rather than shoes.[12]

Santa Cruz la Laguna, San Marcos la Laguna, and San Juan la Laguna *(Figure 224)*

The Cakchiquel-speaking villages of Santa Cruz and San Marcos la Laguna and the Tzutujil-speaking village of San Juan, all located on the south side of the lake, are the most conservative of the Lake villages and the most isolated from the outside world. Great blocks of stone upended in volcanic action give a steep pitch to the meager land area around Santa Cruz and San Marcos. During the rainy season these cliffs serve as waterways; in 1950, most of Santa Cruz was washed into the lake. It is only by digging holes into the rock and filling them with soil that the people maintain corn, beans, and marketable fruit crops — plums, oranges, and limes; the men also produce and sell rope from the henequin plants that grow wild in the area. San Juan is slightly more prosperous. In addition to growing corn and beans, men from San Juan cultivate coffee and produce wicker baskets and rush mats from reeds gathered from the shallows of the lake. Its people still practice their ancient traditions, offering their prayers to gods and spirits of the earth and the air, and honoring their *cofradía* obligations.

The conservatism of all three villages is manifest in their costumes. All three huipils are narrow in width, medium in length, and depend on warp-striping and

*224. Costumes of Santa Cruz la Laguna (left),
San Marcos la Laguna (center),
and San Juan la Laguna (right).*

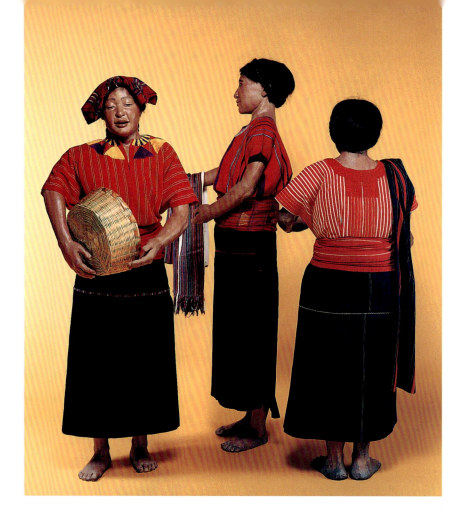

225. Huipil neckline, Santa Cruz la Laguna.

226. Huipil neckline, San Marcos la Laguna.

227. Huipil neckline, San Juan la Laguna.

modest embroidery for embellishment. Santa Cruz women continue to wear the costume illustrated by O'Neale in the late 1930s. Their huipil is distinguished by its neckline, which is embroidered in rays of purple and yellow-gold (fig. 225). On the body of the huipil, faint orange warp stripes, barely visible against the red ground, create an illuminating effect. Santa Cruz women buy fabric for their plain indigo skirts from Nahualá; some, like our example, are joined with the typical Nahualá-style *randa*.

The San Marcos huipil, center, has a red ground accented by wide white and purple warp stripes. In place of rays, its round neckline is bound and embroidered with turquoise silk thread (fig. 226); the use of silk suggests that it may have been a *cofradía* huipil. The simplicity of the costume is dramatized by a beautifully executed but understated belt. The plain indigo skirt is joined by feather stitching in the same colors that decorate the belt.

The costume of San Juan la Laguna is ultra conservative, as evidenced by the basic red-and-white stripe of the early 1960s-style huipil. Since the late 1960s women have added more colors in warp stripes (blue, green, etc.), but there is no change in design or embroidery techniques used to decorate the neckline (fig. 227). San Juan's skirt is also indigo with clusters of white weft stripes (like the one from Santa Catarina, seen in figure 217) and a white featherstitched *randa*. The old-style San Juan *tzute* used for daily wear is indigo with white stripes; those with *cuyuscate* stripes on indigo are for *cofradía* wear.[13]

Quezaltenango - Totonicapán Basin

Few areas in the highlands are as productive as here, where a deep soil layer replenished by volcanic matter, as well as two rivers (the Samalá River to the west and the Nahualate River to the east) cut natural passageways from the highlands into the lowlands, facilitating trade and irrigating crops (map, opposite). Disparate climates producing different crops form the basis for a continuous exchange of goods between the highlands and the coastal lowlands. Four huge markets — Quezaltenango, Totonicapán, San Francisco el Alto, and Momostenango — serve the trade area and beyond.

The Quezaltenango-Totonicapán basin has seen centuries of trade, migration, and warfare. All have contributed to change. In the Prehispanic period, prior to Quiché expansion, the area was heavily populated by Mam people. In the fourteenth century it fell to the Quiché warlords; then in the sixteenth century it was taken by the Spanish conquistadors under the leadership of Pedro de Alvarado, who was aided by Mexican auxiliaries. As a result of war and disease brought by the invaders, by the mid-sixteenth century the local Maya population, which had been dense, was decimated by half. Some survivors were forced to migrate to other areas. There was a considerable degree of acculturation to Spanish ways, and many of the inhabitants learned to speak Spanish.

New technologies introduced by the Spaniards made a decisive impact on the textiles and costumes of the Quezaltenango area. Most significant was the foot loom, introduced into this area soon after the Conquest. Considerably larger and faster than the backstrap loom, it could produce material that was wider and longer. Many different huipil designs could be made with one warping of the loom just by varying the color and/or pattern in the weft. It was here as well that the first textile mill was built in 1885 at Cantel for large scale commercial production of cotton thread and cotton yardage. In addition to finer weave muslins and sateens, the mill produced plain white manta, a sturdy one-over one-under weave, used for men's pants and shirts as well as women's huipils.[14]

In all of Guatemala the Quezaltenango-Totonicapán area is the acknowledged center for the production of foot-loom weaving. In the 1960s, many huipils and skirts produced here for the local trade were village-specific — designed for a particular village in its own colors and styles. More general patterns suitable for a wide range of non-weaving villages were distributed by itinerant traders to all parts of Guatemala. Other textile specialties — sashes and headwraps — were widely sold throughout Guatemala. Woolen textile production in Momostenango was enabled by the introduction of sheep and the technology of wool processing initiated by the Spaniards.

To the casual observer, probably the most striking evidence of costume influence appears in the realm of style. Costume adornment often copies the fashionable details of eighteenth-century Spanish dress: ruffled collars and cuffs, elaborate embroideries, full gathered skirts, and the use of silk (or rayon which is referred to as silk).

Quezaltenango *(Figure 228)*

Despite earthquakes, floods, and fires, Guatemala's second city, Quezaltenango, has never ceased to exert its influence as the western Guatemalan trade link to the Pacific coastal lowlands and to Mexico. Although the urban population is now largely Ladino, Maya culture is manifest here in the large number of women who wear traditional costumes, and Quiché have reached important and influential positions in the community. Until it burned in the 1960s there was a textile market on the city's central plaza. A huge market ten or twelve blocks from the center of town now handles local textile products and caters to other local needs.

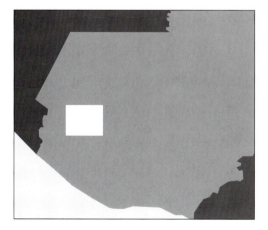

228. Costumes of Quezaltenango.

229 (below). Detail of the fiesta huipil from Quezaltenango shown in figure 228, right.

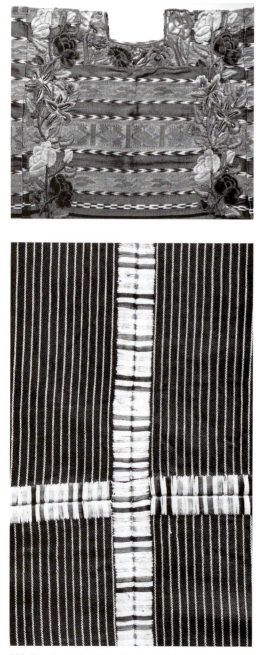

230. Randa on the Quezaltenango skirt shown in figure 228, right.

Two examples of fine weaving, produced locally by male foot-loom weavers are shown in figure 228. The everyday huipil of Quezaltenango (left) is of cotton brocade; the fiesta huipil (right) incorporates silk with cotton. Noteworthy also are the extravagant *randa* joins in red, yellow and mauve on the huipil and the skirt and the embroidered collars and floral pattern on the huipils. This is the contribution of the women, sometimes done by professionals, sometimes by the wearers themselves. Both huipils are of three panels and extend under the skirt to the hip or knees although the under-portions are plain white weave rather than brocaded. The skirts (one double ikat and the other weft-striped) are made from eight to eleven *varas* of fabric. With a cotton cord passed through the casing at the top, the skirt is gathered into folds around the waist; the narrow belt on top is a finishing touch. The multihued shawl *(perraje)*, typical of those woven in the area, is worn on all occasions. The hairwrap made in Totonicapán is saved for special events.

Olintepeque, Momostenango, and Santa María Chiquimula *(Figure 231)*

In the costumes of these three villages there is a stylistic similarity that cannot be overlooked. Momostenango and Santa María Chiquimula, neighbors in a mountainous area bordering the basin, have a symbiotic economic relationship based on sheep's wool. Woolen goods from Momostenango are sold in large quantities in all the area markets and as far away as El Salvador and Honduras. To make these trade goods, Momostenango obtains much of its wool from sheep-herders of Santa María Chiquimula. The latter is also a supplier of copal, lime, and cooking pottery for the area. Olintepeque, some 25 kilometers away, lies just north of Quezaltenango in a peaceful stream-fed valley on the old road to Huehuetenango. Though geographically at a distance from the first two villages, its costume suggests a relationship. Perhaps the original settlers of Olintepeque migrated there from the Momostenango-Chiquimula area. Perhaps their historic battles against the Spaniards drew them together. We don't know.

During at least part of the 1960s the huipils of these three villages were foot-loom-woven in cotton and clearly related in style. Women in Momostenango and Olintepeque

231. Costumes of Olintepeque (left), Momostenango (center), and Santa María Chiquimula (right).

wore both two- and three-panel huipils, all long, coming under the skirt to the knees; the three-panel ones, seen here, were more costly and therefore more desirable.

Men in Olintepeque produce weft-striped panels for both the two- and three-panel styles worn there. The three-panel one, shown here, has more red than white in the wider central panel, and more white than red in the narrower side panels. The indigo, red, and white striped panels for the two-panel huipil are the same. Weavers here also produce plain indigo medium-weight fabric skirt lengths which are sold here and in Chiquimula, Almolonga, and as far away as Sololá, where they are sold to women from San Antonio Palopó, and other Lake villages.

In the 1960s the huipils of Chiquimula were all two-paneled and a little shorter. The one pictured here has warp stripes of indigo and white on a red ground; its two panels are joined at the center with a purple and orange silk floss *randa*, and the same threads embroider the neckline and the *tzute* (fig. 232).

The Momostenango huipil, made of the same heavy weave as that of Olintepeque, has weft stripes in indigo and red. It is also bound at the neckline in black velvet ribbon. Although this particular huipil does not have white stripes, many of the other two- and three-panel styles here do incorporate white striping along with the red and indigo, and all are woven on a white ground fabric. The weaving is done in Momostenango.

Skirts from all three villages are indigo dyed, foot loom woven, and worn long. Momostenango's skirt has warp and weft stripes in light blue or white; Olintepeque's and Santa María Chiquimula's are plain indigo, and gathered with fullness in the front. Chiquimula, unlike the other two villages, has its trademark purple and orange silk joins on skirt and utility cloth alike.

The Chiquimula headwrap is of braided black wool with heavy tassels, and is unique to that village, but similar to ancient Maya examples depicted in clay. The Momostenango headwrap, woven in the fiesta style, is made in Totonicapán, as is the belt. The necklaces of silver and coral are worn only for special events.[15]

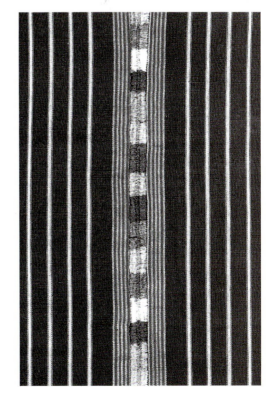

232. Embroidery on the tzute from Santa María Chiquimula shown in figure 231, right.

233. *Embroidering frame in use in San Cristóbal Totonicapán.*

234. *Costumes of San Cristóbal Totonicapán (left), San Francisco el Alto (center), and San Andrés Xecul (right).*

San Cristóbal Totonicapán, San Francisco el Alto, and San Andrés Xecul
(Figure 234)

The clear similarities between the costumes of these three villages suggest common origins. All three may derive their unique styling from Mexico. Osborne speculates that these prime villages were given by Alvarado to his Mexican cohorts in payment for their services and loyalty, and asserts that immigrations of Mexican tribes before and after the Conquest were reflected in certain details of the indigenous costume. The huipils of San Cristóbal and San Andrés are long, full in cut, and of plain commercial sateen or manta. Tlaxcalan huipils from Mexico show the same shape but not the embroidered yoke. The embroidery on all three seems to indicate Spanish influence, though Spain, Mexico, and Guatemala might all have been influenced by Chinese embroidery brought to Mesoamerica during the colonial period on the Manila galleons.

The ideas and techniques to be found in these three villages (all in the department of Totonicapán) are innovative, in contrast to those of more isolated communities. Here, a woman does not weave her own *traje*; all huipils are made of commercial materials, either imported or produced at the Cantel mill near Quetzaltenango. They are embroidered locally, in a European style — that is, with floral patterns taken from European designs. The collar *(gola)* and sleeve are not an indigenous legacy, nor is smocking. While skirt fabrics are handwoven, they are made on foot looms imported by the Spaniards and frequently incorporate ikat, which probably was not introduced until the nineteenth century.

The Friday market at San Francisco el Alto, located on a bluff overlooking the Quetzaltenango-Totonicapán basin, is one of the liveliest markets in Guatemala, as itinerant traders buy here traveling great distances to sell their goods. A wide list of textile items are sold here: wool blankets from Momostenango, skirt lengths from Salcaja, and Totonicapán headwraps, sashes, skirts, and huipils.

The huipil of San Francisco el Alto shows definite Spanish influence in its gathered collar (*gola*) and gathered, set-on sleeves. It was probably made earlier than the 1960s, but could still have been worn then for special occasions. The other two huipils represent a modification of the embroidered collar, which in these later examples becomes an embroidered yoke.

Huipils of San Cristóbal Totonicapán and San Andrés Xecul are so similar that outsiders usually confuse them. Both are made of commercial cotton (of plain weave or sateen) in white or a variety of pastel colors. Both are long, worn under the skirt to the knees. Both have necklines encircled with a wide yoke of embroidery in multicolored threads. The embroidered designs of San Andrés are animals and birds in organized circles row after row with scallops or points; those of San Cristóbal Totonicapán are usually flowers, as are those of San Francisco el Alto. Embroiderers use a large square frame of wood (fig. 233), very much like the kind used by Chinese embroiderers. During the 1960s all of this embroidery was done by hand. The commercial fabric is wide. To take up the extra width so that the garment will not fall too low on the arms, a mock smocking stitch is usually employed over the shoulders and down the sides. Vertical tucks serve the same purpose.

San Cristóbal men are very fine foot loom weavers of ikat, and produce most of the skirts for their own village and for San Andrés. Women from San Francisco are more likely to purchase their skirt lengths from Salcajá weavers who produce them in larger quantities on bigger looms, and sell them in the Friday market in San Francisco. The quality may not be as high as in San Cristóbal Totonicapán, but the cost is lower and the choice is wide. The skirts are often as colorful as the huipils. Skirts of the 1960s were woven with weft stripes in assorted colors combined with ikat stripes (fig. 235). Double ikat weaves were also common. As skirts began to be more colorful, so did *perrajes*. The main difference between the two is that the latter are usually warp-striped and skirts are weft-striped. Accompanying the San Cristóbal costume is a *perraje* made of cotton with wool tassels. The one shown with the San Andrés *traje* is made of silk and cotton.

Sashes for all three villages are made by professional weavers in Totonicapán and combine maguey fibers with cotton for extra stiffness. These, too, are in many colors with traditional motifs of hands, urns, birds, animals and geometric patterns (fig. 103). During the 1960s the women of these villages also wore hairwraps made in Totonicapán (fig. 236), at least for festive occasions. Rayon taffeta ribbons are now preferred.[16]

235 (above). Detail of ikat skirt from San Cristóbal Totonicapán.
236 (right). Detail of cinta from San Cristóbal Totonicapán.

237. Costumes of San Pedro Sacatepéquez (SM) (left), Totonicapán (center), and Santa Lucía Utatlán (right).

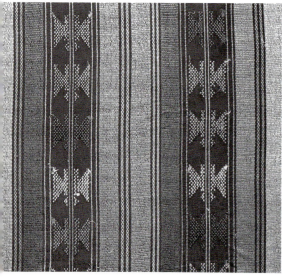

238. Detail of the skirt from Santa Lucía Utatlán shown in figure 237.

San Pedro Sacatepéquez (SM), Totonicapán, and Santa Lucía Utatlán
(Figure 237)

Both San Pedro Sacatepéquez (SM) and Totonicapán are departmental capitals (the former Mam, the latter Quiché) with thriving agriculture and craft industries and flourishing markets serving large populations. The foot-loom weaving of skirt lengths and huipils is an important industry in both places. Totonicapán also produces sashes, hairwraps, and shawls that are sold all over Guatemala, and its prosperity is evident in the extravagant and beautiful clothes worn locally for special occasions. Santa Lucía Utatlán is a small Quiché farming village in the mountains southeast of Totonicapán. We include it here because its festive costume relates so strongly to those of San Pedro and Totonicapán, despite its geographical distance from them. The costumes of all three show Spanish influence in styling, especially in festive, *cofradía*, and wedding dress. While none of these towns is directly situated on a major trade route, their proximity to and trade associations with towns along the trade route have brought new ideas, new styles, and new customs. They, like the others, have experienced the disruptions of local peoples along with the immigration of the new.

Spanish influence in San Pedro goes back to its early collaboration with Alvarado. This collaboration was the choice of the *cacique*, and for his cooperation, according to Spanish documents, he was rewarded with "special privileges." (Ruling heads of other small tribal groups made other choices). Until 1935, anyone here not wearing native dress was legally considered Ladino. By this law all Maya men in this area would be classified Ladino today, since they have abandoned their *traje*. But women of the area still conserve a distinct costume although they no longer weave it themselves. Some of the finest examples of draw-loom weaving, as on the San Pedro *cofradía* huipil (left) are to be found here. The yellow-gold rayon skirt with green and ikat warp and weft plaid is unique to this area.

In Totonicapán the local people who had fought against the Spaniards were banished to peripheral lands, while the more productive lands were given to the Mexican followers of Alvarado who settled there. Quiché ways are still very strong in the countryside, but the city of Totonicapán is highly Hispanicized. This appears evident in the white ceremonial huipil (middle), whose styling details are copied from Spanish women's dress. While the changes have not been great, the addition of lace or net sleeves and wide collars creates a very different effect to a basic huipil.

The Totonicapán huipil shown here is woven in plain open weave with "laid-in" designs. Two types of machine-made lace are used for the full flounces that form the wide double collar and cuffs. The fabric is similar to that of a white wedding huipil from Quezaltenango, also in the Museum's collection, which is worn with the round neckline pulled over the forehead and under the chin, framing the face.

The wedding huipil of Santa Lucía Utatlán is one of the most beautiful Spanish-influenced costumes in Guatemala, indicating prosperity as well as social grace and status. The material for the huipil is specially made in Totonicapán, and the elaborate cotton and rayon skirt, woven on a foot loom, is imported from Suchitepéquez in the piedmont region (fig. 238).

Ceremonial garments often call for a special headcovering *(tzute* or *tapado)* like that seen with the costume of San Pedro Sacatapéquez. While the concept of headcovering is probably an indigenous one (utility cloths are used for everyday), the importance of covering the head in church was undoubtedly reinforced by Spanish clergy.[17]

Other Areas of Cultural Interaction

Throughout the highlands are other routes well trod by travelers and traders. Some follow river valleys such as the Rio Negro basin, which connects Aguacatán and Sacapulas, tying them together in a symbiotic relationship. Another, overland, threads its way through the mountains of the central highlands, crossing at Utatlán, the former Quiché capitol, near present-day Santa Cruz del Quiché. Geographic location determines relationships between villages and can influence costume in the process. High in the northwest corner of Huehuetenango, for example, San Mateo Ixtatán maintains trade relationships with villages in the Mexican state of Chiapas, and its costume reflects a Mexican orientation.

Certain villages, although not on long-distance routes, participate in a trade network in which one village provides traje for another. The women of San Pedro la Laguna, for example, make backstrap shirts that are sold throughout the lake area. On a smaller scale, costume may be shaped by the neighborly trade between nearby villages, as in the non-weaving village of Sumpango, where clothing items are provided by the weavers in nearby Santo Domingo Xenacoj.

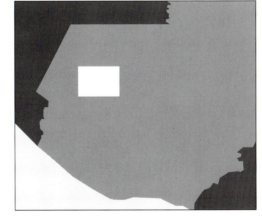

Sacapulas and Aguacatán (Figure 239)

The villages of Sacapulas and Aguacatán are both situated at the foot of the Cuchumatanes range where many small streams branch into a larger river system. Residents of Aguacatán live in the department of Huehuetenango and speak Aguacatec, a Mam dialect. Aguacatán is one of three important centers of garden

239. Costumes of Sacapulas and Aguacatán.

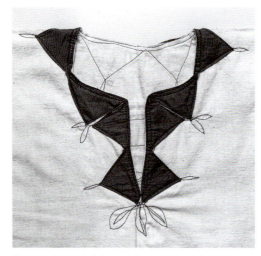

240. Machine stitching on the neckline of the Sacapulas huipil shown at right.

241. Aguacatán woman.

cultivation in the highlands. Its name derives from the local avocado (*aguacate*) trees. It was settled from a number of hamlets, and some groups here continue to preserve their autochthonous identities.

Sacapulas residents live in the department of El Quiché and speak Sacapulteca, a dialect of Quiché. Their town was valuable to the Quiché for its products (copper, small fish and, especially, salt) and for its location as a crossroads along the Rio Negro Basin, with roads from Sacapulas leading west to Aguacatán and Huehuetenango, and north to Nebaj and Ixil country.

Although they do not share the same department nor even the same language, these two villages have had easy access to one another by virtue of geography. Both were conquered by the Central Quiché in the Prehispanic period, and both were strong enough to expel their conquerors in the early sixteenth century, before the arrival of the Spaniards. They also share possible connections with Ixil culture. Hints of this appear in dress, as suggested by the design motifs and appliqué pattern of an early backstrap-woven Sacapulas *cofradía* huipil from the Museum's collection (fig. 165).

It is curious that both towns gave up backstrap-woven huipils early, and yet continued to produce hairwraps on the backstrap loom. The earliest known example of an Aguacatán huipil, as described in Gall, is made from a white commercial fabric with a band of red embroidery around the neckline; it is very much like one from the 1930s described by O'Neale, and one in the Museum's collection bought from an elderly woman in the late 1970s.

In the 1960s, the huipil styles of Aguacatán and Sacapulas were remarkably similar; both were made of commercial muslin and decorated with stitching made on the sewing machine. These machine-sewn motifs are banded in rows separated by tucks and colored ribbons or tape. In Aguacatán these were located front and back. In Sacapulas they were usually only on the back which then terminated in scallops, faced in contrasting color to match the neckline appliqué. We have no record of when or by what route the sewing machine arrived in Guatemala but its wide use in these two villages suggest a fascination with its possibilities beyond the practical. The Sacapulas muslin huipil of the 1960s seems quite unrelated to the beautiful tapestry-woven silk and cotton one of the 1930s, but the machine stitching at the front of its neckline does imitate a leaf pattern on the older one (fig. 240).

The skirt from Aguacatán shown here is backstrap-woven. Foot-loom-woven ones have been produced for at least twenty years and are certainly predominant today. The skirts of Sacapulas are multicolored weft stripes with ikat and are a trade item from the Quezaltenango region. Our example is sewn into a tube, which is then wrapped around the hips and tucked in at the waist. This is a slight stylistic change from an earlier Sacapulas skirt style, which was not sewn into a tube, but wrapped around, with one corner tucked in at the waist.

The backstrap-woven hairwraps made and worn by Aguacatán women appear related to Ixil weaving techniques and motifs with their big tassels and angular birds and geometric forms (fig. 241). Women from Sacapulas also wear a backstrap-woven *cinta* with large tassels that fall over one eye in a very provocative fashion. Neither shawl nor *tzute* seems to be worn in either village, probably the result of the hot climate here.[18]

Santa Cruz del Quiché *(Figure 242)*

Santa Cruz del Quiché lies at the crossroads of several major land routes. One is a main south-north route from Lake Atitlán through Los Encuentros, Chichicastenango, to Santa Cruz del Quiché and Ixil country. Another is a main west-east road from Totonicapán through San Antonio, Santa Cruz del Quiché and Chinique to points east. The third is an important route from Santa Cruz and Chichicastenango through Patzite and on to Totonicapán. Santa Cruz was settled after the old Quiché capital of Utatlán had fallen to the Spanish conquistadors, and the Santa Cruz *encomienda* was given to one of Alvarado's captains. Other lands to the east were taken over by Spaniards for cattle and farming ranchos. By the mid-eighteenth century it was estimated that half of the area had been taken over by the would-be *hidalgos* from Spain.

Costume of the 1960s reflects the influence of cross-cultural trade in its fabric, styling, and trim. The huipil shown here is of commercial muslin made in the Cantel mill; it is tailored in a European style, gathered on a yoke, with long sleeves which are set-on and gusseted; imported binding is used as decoration. Foreign influence is also apparent in another style of huipil from Santa Cruz, made of a commercial lavender brocaded rayon with ruffled sleeve flounces and a square neckline.

The wraparound skirt is made of double-ikat, probably from Salcajá. It is folded on one hip and held in place by a commercial belt from Totonicapán. A length of foot-loom weaving from San Cristóbal Totonicapán is used as a shawl.[19]

242. *Costume of Santa Cruz del Quiché.*

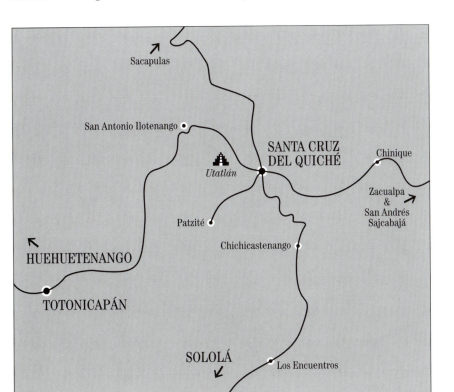

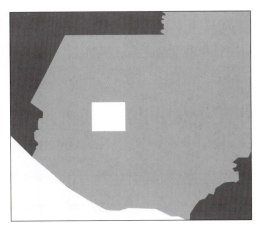

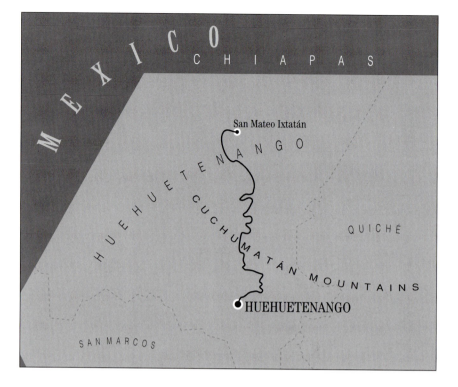

243. Costume of San Mateo Ixtatán.

San Mateo Ixtatán *(Figure 243)*

The markedly different huipil from San Mateo mirrors the geographic and linguistic apartness of the area and probably shows Mexican influence. At the fringes of highland Guatemala, San Mateo Ixtatán is close to the Mexican state of Chiapas. Chuj, the local language of San Mateo, is related to Tzeltal-Tzotzil of Chiapas and incorporates many Tzeltal-Tzotzil loan words. Salt, the major export product of the Prehispanic period has made San Mateo Ixtatán an important township in this remote northeast corner of the department of Huehuetenango.

It is difficult to locate any stylistic antecedents to the San Mateo Ixtatán huipil. The earliest known style, dating approximately to the turn of the century, was formed from white commercial cotton fabric in double thickness. This was modestly embroidered around the neckline and along the chest where the two background strips of fabric are joined. As early as the 1930s, its embellished area had expanded to reach its current cape-like proportions. The density of the satin stitch embroidery is remarkable. In the example shown here, most stitches are composed of ten threads, and this together with the base fabric makes for a heavy garment.

The design arrangement shown here is typical of San Mateo huipils. Vibrant star motifs appear in motion. While stars are used elsewhere as embroidery motifs (for example on the huipils of Joyabaj and early Cobán), none can compare with the bold extravagance found in San Mateo. The *corte* is weft-striped and foot-loom-woven by professional men weavers in the Huehuetenango area. The ubiquitous Totonicapán skirt fabric also manages to get to this area as well. Headscarves like the one seen here are made of a commercial rayon or acrylic brocade in bright colors and are shown tied at the nape. An earlier style, as photographed in the 1930s, was a square of white cotton folded triangularly and tied either on the forehead or under the chin.[20]

San Pedro la Laguna *(Figure 246)*

It is trade with other lake villages that fuels the highly entrepreneurial women of this predominantly Protestant village. Women from San Pedro don't go to the fields to help their husbands or fetch firewood or carry burdens long distances; it is their weaving that contributes to the family economy. Skilled backstrap weavers, they make fabric not for their own consumption but rather for the men of several lake villages, including their own. Excellence of weaving is widely admired, and there is considerable scope for innovation and individual expression within a stylistic pattern, affording the individual weaver aesthetic and creative gratification as well as cash income.

The trade in woven cloth is part of a pattern of special industriousness typical of the people of San Pedro, who are notably open to new ideas. Though they own some

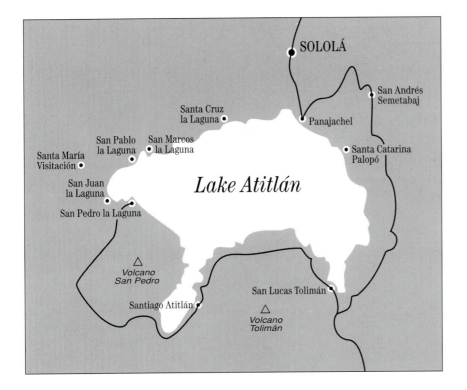

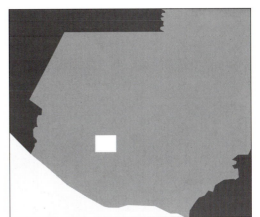

of the best agricultural land on the lake, they are by no means just milpa farmers. They prefer the cash crops, coffee and avocados. It is the San Pedro men who are most skillful in making and handling dugout canoes. Locals run a factory producing hand knotted woolen rugs and wall hangings with Mayan glyph designs that are popular trade items.

The warp-striped fabric the women produce (usually with *jaspe*) is woven in lengths called *cortecitos,* which are more expensive than material made on foot-powered or commercial looms, but also more distinctive. Shirts made of this fabric are tailored

244. Men and boys in San Pedro la Laguna.

246 (right). Costumes of San Pedro la Laguna.

245. Girls in San Pedro la Laguna.

in Western style with collars, cuffs, and buttons down the front, and represent a satisfying middle ground for the Maya man who must deal in the world beyond the village without abandoning his Maya identity.

The San Pedro man's shirt gives a plaid effect but is an adroit manipulation of ikat blue-dyed warp threads, as are the stripes on his red backstrap woven *banda*. His white pants are streaked with indigo-dyed ikat threads. These garments are all woven by women, but men embroider the decorative bands and figures on their pants.

San Pedro women's white blouses are sometimes backstrap-woven as shown, and sometimes made of commercial fabric. They are put together just like a huipil but a wide gathered collar and ruffled sleeves are added. The collar is attached at the neckline with colored binding and the cuffs are set off with triangular appliqués and lace. The skirt is a fine example of double ikat weaving for which the women here must have a special appreciation since they are so adept at working with these tie-dyed patterns. The stiff sash is made in Totonicapán, as is the skirt.[21]

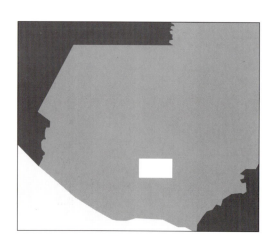

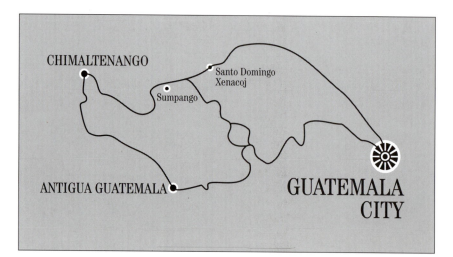

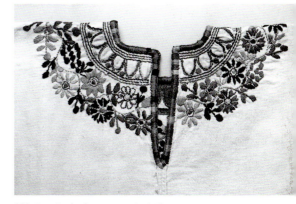

247. Costumes of Santo Domingo Xenacoj (left) and Sumpango (right).

248. Detail of a Sumpango huipil.

Santo Domingo Xenacoj and Sumpango *(Figure 247)*

Neighborly trade affects the costume in these two villages, which speak the same Cakchiquel dialect. Sumpango women do not weave, but obtain their huipils from the talented women weavers of Santo Domingo Xenacoj. Their particular specialty is in a heavy double twist woven fabric with warp striping which commands attention and respect even without further decoration. For their own wear they usually add a narrow stripe of expensive, handspun brown cotton or *cuyuscate*. This sets their weaving apart from that of other villages who gave up using *cuyuscate* early. The brocading is also remarkable. The frequent use of picked-pile brocade is especially noteworthy here as it is used in everyday huipils as well as ceremonial ones. By this technique, an extra flick of the finger on the thread creates a raised design sticking up from the base fabric, giving it a more opulent look than plain flat brocading. Since the background weave is heavy and ribbed, this extra bulk in the design provides a stylistic balance and even a small amount of decoration provides visual impact.

The striping on the Sumpango huipil is slightly more elaborate but the weave and the background color are the same. To the basic huipils obtained from Santo Domingo Xenacoj weavers, Sumpango women add the traditional floral and sun motif embroidery at the neckline themselves. They also wear an underhuipil of white manta with embroidered flowers at the neckline (fig. 248). This huipil is worn tucked in, unlike the overhuipil which hangs loose over the skirt, as pictured.

The Santa Domingo *corte* is shadow-striped and of a medium-weight *morga* weave made by men foot loom weavers in the area and traded in this village and Santiago Sacatepéquez. The joins both for the huipil and the *corte* are more elaborate here than in other villages though their designs of joined arrows and "jars" *(jarros)* have caught on and are currently seen in a number of widely dispersed villages. The skirt of Sumpango is lighter in weight and solid indigo with a crisscross multicolored *randa*. Women of both villages wear Totonicapán-style hairwraps for special occasions.

The sashes Santo Domingo women make for themselves are in plain weave with spaced weft stripes in purple and gold, as shown. Both the sashes for Sumpango women (not visible here) and the belts for Sumpango men are dark blue with multicolored spaced stripes and some are further elaborated with supplementary weft brocading. They are also made in Santo Domingo Xenacoj.[22]

Notes

1. *Costume and Geography*. McBryde 1947 (p. 6) is the source for this characterization of the Guatemalan landscape.

2. *Costume in Isolated Areas*. According to McBryde 1947 (p. 66), cochineal was virtually the sole source for red dye until as late as 1920. At the time of McBryde's visit in 1939, 95% of all yarn dyed for skirts was indigo (p. 63). The turn-of-the-century huipils were in a privately owned collection shown to us by Sam Bright of Dallas, Texas.

3. *The Cuchumatanes*. The highway that skirted the Selegua River was washed out repeatedly by devastating floods. As late as 1964, that section of the highway between the Mexican border and Huehuetenango was called *"el tapon,"* the bottleneck. Lovell 1985 provides a sensitive portrait of the Cuchumatanes region. On the revival of Prehispanic rituals there, see pp. 84-87; on corn planting rituals, see p. 34. The *chimane*, by his knowledge of the ancient aboriginal Maya calendar and an understanding of "good" and "evil" days for intervention and prayer, intercedes in marital difficulties, matters pertaining to childbirth, and illnesses brought on by imbalance to natural forces. The saying of prayers and the burning of candles and incense is necessary for the proper germination of the seed. Harvest is accompanied by the offering of the blood of a sacrificed rooster to the spirit of the corn field. If prayers are not offered, the corn crop may not have sufficient rainfall or may be attacked by frost. Community well-being is entrusted to shaman guides. On market trading in the Cuchumatanes, see Lovell 1985 (pp. 22,25,29).

This area, so rich in regional costume, was the one area not covered by O'Neale 1945 in her study of Guatemalan Maya costume in the 1930s. Delgado's dissertation research (1963) included costumes of this area, but wider coverage on the weaving of several towns in this area wasn't available until Sperlich & Sperlich's 1980 publication, based on research in the 1970s.

4. *San Juan Atitán*. The Prehispanic style is shown in *El Lienzo de Tlaxcala* (Chavero 1979 [1892], p. 24). See Sperlich & Sperlich 1980 (pp. 111,115) on the use of a compound weave and an extra heddle stick to create density on the chest decoration in San Juan Atitán.

5. *Todos Santos*. See Sperlich & Sperlich 1980 (p. 3) re Todos Santos men bringing home raw cotton for wives to spin. In the seventies and eighties the huipil collar disappeared and emphasis was placed on a squared yoke. The 1935 photo of Todos Santos women appears in Rowe 1981 (p. 123).

6. *San Pedro Necta and Santiago Chimaltenango*. Santiago Chimaltenango is well described by anthropologists Wagley (1941,1949) and Watanabe (1981). According to Wagley it was a traumatic period for Santiago Chimaltenango to have to go to another rival village to register births and deaths, pay taxes and vote, and take care of other judicial and municipal matters. Watanabe notes that many aspects of the traditional religion have fallen into disuse. A political system is replacing the civil-religious hierarchy and it is possible for a Maya to be elected to office if he speaks and writes Spanish and has some technological education. Thus Chimaltenango men are now able to rise to positions of prominence in the village by the electoral process, but without giving up Maya values and cultural patterns. Maya culture places great value on work. Money has no value in itself. Riches are not a prerequisite for respect, and poverty does not imply incompetence or failure. The purpose of work is to provide for one's family and have an inheritance to give to one's children (Watanabe 1981, pp. 20-24). More income can be had from less land with coffee and some Chimaltecos have even been able to buy land for growing coffee in La Democracia (Watanabe 1981, p. 25). Wagley (1941, p. 73) calculated that in 1937 the average size land holding necessary to feed a family was 120 *cuerdos*, and 79% of Chimaltecos had this. Now, according to Watanabe, the average land holding is 38.1 *cuerdos*. Migratory labor must make up the difference. In 1978, according to Wagley, 64% of the men went to *fincas* on the coast for anywhere from two to six months. Fortunately, the coffee harvest does not conflict with their own agricultural cycle.

7. *Ixtahuacán, Colotenango, and San Rafael Petzal*. All three villages are in the vicinity of a ceremonial center with a pyramid and plaza, excavated north of Colotenango, and called Pueblo Viejo. Ixtahuacán is also known as San Ildefonso Ixtahuacán. See Gall 1976-83 on its pre-Conquest history. On the early history of Colotenango, and on garments in the early part of the twentieth century, see Mejía de Rodas et al. 1987, pp. 13-14. San Rafael and Ixtahuacán are listed by Kaufman 1975 (p. 54) as sharing the same Mam dialect; the dialect of Colotenango has only a few small differences.

Mejía de Rodas et al. give a thorough description of the striping techniques along with their Mam names, and also illustrate some of the innovations of the 1980s: larger and larger design patterns and punch machine flowers replacing the traditional brocade and *soumak* pattern of red squares with rhomboids inside called *sweg*. On the costume of the 1950s see Delgado 1963 (p. 302). In 1978 at a Sunday service we attended in Colotenango, the priest gave a sermon in which he encouraged the congregation to continue to wear the *traje indigena* and to value their ethnic identity. He himself wore a wide red *banda* diagonally across his chest and tied at the hip.

According to John Watanabe (pers. com., 1986), the elaborate *cofradías* of the central highlands never seem to have developed in the Cuchumatán area, and no huipils are ever identified as being for *cofradía* use.

Delgado, who was in this area in the 1950s, points out that skirts at that time were without supplementary weft decoration, and huipil backgrounds had more white than red.

An atypical huipil with a plain white ground, brocaded but not embroidered around the neckline, can also be found in Ixtahuacán.

8. *San Sebastián (Huehuetenango)*. On the ruins of the old town see Glassman 1978 (p. 202). On costume in San Sebastián 30 years ago, see Sperlich & Sperlich 1980 (p. 5). They also reported seeing women stand at their backstrap looms when making lengths of skirt fabric (p. 47). Elderly women and men from outlying hamlets of San Sebastián sometimes wear wool garments. We saw several wool *camisas* in the San Sebastián market. Thirty or forty years ago, most of the people in the village wore wool, and wool blankets are still produced by women on backstrap looms.

9. *Lake Atitlán*. A marketing interrelationship comparable to that of the Lake Atitlán villages is described by Braudel 1982 (pp. 161-6), writing about French villages during the Middle Ages. This reference was suggested by Howard West. Re backstrap-woven men's garments, we know of only four Guatemalan highland villages outside the lake area where men still wear backstrap-woven pants, shirts, and sashes: San Juan Atitán, Todos Santos, and San Sebastian in the Cuchumatanes, and San Martin Sacatepéquez near Quezaltenango.

10. *Sololá*. On the *Annals of the Cakchiquels* see Brinton 1895. Though the king and his son died of the plague in 1521, other members of the Xahil royal lineage continued to dominate the politics of Sololá serving as mayors of the village established by the Spaniards in 1547.

By the late 1970s all backstrap weaving for both men's and women's costumes became more and more embellished; the supplementary weft fiber was then high intensity acrylic and lurex rather than cotton, and new simpler methods of achieving a *randa* effect were employed. (These new methods of handling *randa*s and new styles in metallic-looking fibers have changed them considerably in the '70s and '80s.) My information on the use of *tzutes* by the *regidores* comes from Gwendolin Ritz (pers. com. 1987).

11. *Santa Catarina Palopó*. Santa Catarina and its neighbors San Antonio and Panajachel were originally Tzutujil but were taken over first by the Quiché, then by the Cakchiquel. Government interventions had a sorry impact on the Santa Catarina economy. For a time the government banned the cutting of the *tule* — once a source of income — because it threatened the environment of a rare duck called the Atitlán poc, which nested in the reeds. The government also introduced black bass into the lake, and these ate all the smaller fish preferred by the locals. The bass proved impervious to the old fishing methods. Consequently the people of Santa Catarina have had to resort to other means for making money: the men have to depend on seasonal work on the coast, and the women must sustain themselves with weaving.

12. *Panajachel*. As tourism developed in Guatemala in the 1970s, the lake became a favored locale, and many new hotels were built to accommodate the visitors. Many Panajachel locals were pressed into jobs as hotel workers and many have become Ladinoized in the process. Re professional weavers who supply the decorative center panel of Panajachel huipils see Tax 1953 (p. 152).

13. *Santa Cruz, San Marcos, and San Juan la Laguna*. The people of Santa Cruz and San Marcos la Laguna spoke Tzutujil in the Prehispanic period. As late as 1630, they were both subject to Santiago Atitlán, but by the late 17th century Santa Cruz was recorded as being a part of Sololá, a Cakchiquel stronghold. Cakchiquel is the language of both villages today.

San Juan can be reached by boat from Panajachel, or by a narrow dirt road, dusty in the dry season, and muddy when it rains. Today, they must rent back land that formerly belonged to them from their more prosperous neighbors in San Pedro la Laguna, who own half of San Juan's property, having bought it up in a period of crop failure and hard times. San Juan la Laguna and San Pedro la Laguna, although only two kilometers apart, are completely different in their outlook and practices, though both share the same Tzutujil tongue. Characterization of the way of life in San Juan is based on information from UCLA anthropologist David Morrill (pers. com.).

Santa Cruz costume of the 1930s is depicted in O'Neale 1945, pp. 82,122, fig.27g. All three villages have been described as poor even by Guatemalan standards. Braudel 1981, vol. 1 (p. 313) postulates that poverty is the prime reason for costume continuity.

14. *Quezaltenango - Totonicapán Basin*. Smallpox and a pulmonary plague epidemic were recorded in the *Annals of the Cakchiquels* (Brinton 1895). Other maladies unknown previously to local populations such as mumps, measles and typhus took a high toll. On the decimation of the Maya community in the 16th century, see MacLeod 1983; also Veblen cited in Lovell 1985 (pp. 143,148). Veblen's population survey was based on native and Spanish colonial documents recording

the numbers of Maya who fought in battles against the Spaniards. Alvarado, too, described Guatemala which he entered through this region as being well populated with many strong towns.

After the foot loom had been assimilated, it was only a few more steps to the technology of the draw loom that could create fine, elaborate textile patterns. Men's muslin shirts and *pantalones*, the kind that tie at the neckline and waist and calf, were still being marketed in the early 1960s under the name of the Cantel Mill, but are no longer available today.

15. *Olintepeque, Momostenango, and Santa María Chiquimula*. These villages lie on an old volcanic range. Severe erosion has left landmarks of rilled clay and pinnacles of volcanic ash *(riscos)* in the Momostenango area which are still the site of rituals called Eighth Monkey, performed by priests referred to as Chuch Kahua, who seek areas protected by vegetation in which to build their shrines. Allen Christiansen, an anthropologist and linguist who has lived in the area, sees Olintepeque as an isolated group that doesn't relate even to those close to them such as Zunil and Almolonga (pers. com. 1987). The first two are located near the area where the Quiché began their drive through Mam territory. This strategic movement effectively cut the Mam territory in two, separating the Quezaltenango region from the Mam center at Zaculeu, near present-day Huehuetenango. The *Popul Vuh* and the *Título Coyoi* mention large Prehispanic settlements here, and there are indications that cultural and political ties existed between the two groups prior to the take-over. Native chronicles also indicate that high ranking members of major Quiché lineage groups were put in control of large urbanized colonies here at a later date. Although no exact records exist to prove it, Olintepeque may be the site of the decisive battle between Tecum Uman, the Quiché prince in command of the Totonicapán area and his 8,400 warriors and Alvarado with his 135 Spanish cavalrymen, 120 infantry, and 400 Mexican allies from Tlaxcala and Cholula (Carmack 1981, p. 144). It was the first time the natives had seen either guns or men on horseback, and the results were disastrous for the native defenders. The reports say that the river ran red with blood. The river running through Olintepeque is called Xequijel which means "under blood." The huipil of Chiquimula in the 1930s was backstrap woven according to Wood & Osborne 1966 (pp. 136-37), but in the late 1960s and today it is foot loom woven. Because of the two-panel construction and shorter length of its huipils, and because of the differences in its skirt, Gwendolin Ritz (pers. com.) sees Santa María Chiquimula standing by itself.

16. *San Cristóbal Totonicapán, San Francisco el Alto, and San Andrés Xecul*. Re the possibility that these villages were given to Alvarado's Mexican allies, see Osborne 1965 (p. 20). According to Robinson 1987, the round hoop for embroidery was a Western import of the 18th century. Embroidery itself is considered by Robinson to be a Chinese invention (p. 68). Now embroidery machines are used by professionals and the machine embroidered huipils are a very popular item in the local markets and are bought and worn by women in other towns as well. The fact that they are cheaper certainly contributes to their popularity, but there is also a fascination with a machine-made product. In the 1960s many women in this area added decorative bands of braid or a saw-toothed appliqué of contrasting commercial fabric — usually taffeta or velvet — on or near the skirt bottom. Skirt lengths produced in this area are wider and of a lighter weight than the *morga* skirts of the Chimaltenango and Sacatepéquez regions.

17. *San Pedro Sacatepéquez, Totonicapán, and Santa Lucía Utatlán*. This Totonicapán is also referred to as San Miguel Totonicapán (in contrast to San Cristóbal Totonicapán, discussed above), and the name of the department is Totonicapán, as well. See McBryde 1947 on trade routes. In addition to textiles, Totonicapeños make chests, tables, chairs, and coffins, as well as ceremonial masks and dance costumes which are used all over the highlands and even as far as Mexico. Other industries are ceramics production, flour mills, and liquor distilleries. According to Osborne 1965 Totonicapán is a good place to study costume because there are still three distinct Quiché classes who have not mingled with the descendants of other tribes who settled here (pp. 148,149).

The people of Santa Lucía speak the same Quiché dialect as Nahualá and Santa Clara la Laguna according to Kaufman 1976. A cultural similarity with San Cristóbal in daily dress has been pointed out by McBryde 1947 (p. 53). Curiously, Gall

(op. cit., chap. 5, note 1) identifies the inhabitants as Cakchiquel. Its beginnings are unrecorded.

It is the rich who copy the costumes of the conquering group according to Braudel 1981, vol. 1 (p. 312). He cites the Indian Hindus copying the Moguls and the Turks copying the Asmanli sultans. This seems to be the case in Guatemala, too, for these festive huipils are worn only by rich Maya. The women of San Pedro keep alive an ancient ritual in honor of the corn goddess, carrying a dressed-up ear of corn in a procession through the village every year. Poetic rhythms dating back to the *Popul Vuh* are still in effect in Totonicapán (Allen Christenson, pers. com. 1987). Of the two Totonicapán festive huipils in the Taylor Museum, one is similar to ours; another is even more Spanish in style, with very elaborate lace forming a ruffled collar and cuffs embellished with floral embroidery and described as "distinctly Spanish in origin" (Conte 1984, pp. 88-90).

18. *Sacapulas and Aguacatán*. These two towns fit the pattern described by Fox 1978 of what he calls "environmental circumscription," whereby groups bounded by topographic barriers, separate but sharing a generally homogenous habitat and a common river system, become interacting populations. See Fox 1978 on Aguacatán's garden cultivation (p. 101), on the preservation of *parcialidades* (ancient units based on clan or kin groups associated with a particular area of land), and on Prehispanic sites suggesting that the original people of Sacapulas may have been related to the Ixil (p. 111). According to Delgado 1963 (p. 296) the kind of huipil seen in Plate 24 is from the Chalchitán canton.

See Kaufman 1975 on the Sacapultec dialect (p. 60). The only backstrap-woven Aguacatán huipil on record is owned by the Ixchel Museum and was pictured in a Japanese publication (*Textile Arts*, Spring 1984, p. 72). For a description of an early Aguacatán huipil see O'Neale 1945 (p. 250). An earlier skirt style from Sacapulas is illustrated in Wood & Osborne 1966 (p. 93).

19. *Santa Cruz del Quiché*. See Carmack 1981 (pp. 305-26) on the nexus of trade routes at Santa Cruz.

20. *San Mateo Ixtatán*. San Mateo Ixtatán's area is one of the most extensive land areas in the department of Huehuetenango and encompasses a wide range of impressive land forms — rolling hills as well as broken and stony terrain, cultivated plains and forests, rivers and swamps. Climate varies with elevation, cold in the mountains, and warm in the lower regions. The Chuj and the other linguistic groups surrounding them (the Jacalteca, Kanjobal, and Chol) are very small in number compared to the Quiché, Mam, and Cakchiquel of the west and central highlands. In Prehispanic times, a variety of plants yielded medicines and dyes to suit Maya needs as well as feathers from the exotic Quetzal bird, much esteemed by Mayan and Aztec royalty for their extravagant headdresses. Products now traded locally include cereals, potatoes, sugar cane, coffee, tobacco, and cocoa as well as rush mats (petates) and hats made from palm fiber. Limestone, lead and copper are mined in the mountains. On the earliest known style of huipil, see Conte 1984 (p. 58). On the styles of the 1930s, see Rowe 1981 (p. 145). Some of the huipils photographed by Masuoka and others in the '70s have a ruffled collar of imported fabric decorated with braid that seem to relate to the huipils of Soloma, Santa Eulalia, and San Juan Ixcoy.

21. *San Pedro la Laguna*. Paul 1974 presents a woman's point of view on the weavers of San Pedro la Laguna (see pp. 282,288).

22. *Santo Domingo Xenacoj and Sumpango*. The dialect spoken in these two villages is one shared with San Pedro Sacatepéquez to the east and Santiago Sacatepéquez to the southeast. Our last visit to Santo Domingo was in the early '80s, when we went with Susan Masuoka to celebrate a baptism in a home in the village. Although all three Maya women present were excellent weavers in the traditional Santo Domingo style, only one, the great grandmother of the baby wore a Santo Domingo huipil such as the one shown. The mother of the child wore a backstrap woven Patzún huipil with embroidered flowers around the neck which she said had been given to her by a friend. She said she liked its bright colors and liked wearing something different. The grandmother wore a trade huipil from Totonicapán, and she said she preferred it because it was lighter weight and more comfortable in the hot weather.

249. *Market women in San Juan Sacatepéquez.*

Costume and Society

The clothing one wears is always a statement of identity. In Guatemala in the 1960s, the daily costume clearly announced the wearer's village. To discerning eyes it could also reveal whether the wearer was old or young, widowed, married or single, rich or poor, tradition-oriented or favorable to change. And if the wearer was dressed for fiesta, or *cofradía* service, her costume clearly said so.

In every highland village, the most notable costumes are those worn for special occasions. The costumes worn for *cofradía* ceremonies are especially impressive, but many other occasions, religious and secular, call for special clothing. In addition to the usual rites of passage, such as weddings, baptisms, funerals, there are numerous religious festivals dotting the church calendar, such as Todos Santos (All Saints), Semana Santa (Holy Week), Corpus Cristi, and most importantly, the *fiesta titular,* in honor of the patron saint after whom one's village is named. Lesser church occasions, like novenas, and certain secular occasions, for example the annual installation of new public officials, also call for special attire.

The more affluent the community, the greater the range of huipil styles. Even where money is scarce, ceremonial costumes and particularly *cofradía* garments have a distinctive look. They may be styled so as to differ from daily dress, or they may have ordinary shape and style, but be fashioned of richer materials or embellished with unusual patterns. They may even be composed of daily garments which are worn in a special manner and thereby subtly transformed for ceremonial purposes. Some cofradía huipils are actually less decorated than the current daily styles and their simplicity reflects the costume traditions of an earlier time.[1]

Santo Tomás Chichicastenango *(Figure 251)*

The people of Chichicastenango are descended from the Quiché who ruled Utatlán, the great Prehispanic ceremonial and administrative center of the highlands. After it was captured and destroyed by Alvarado, its survivors were resettled in Chichicastenango, a nearby area that had been abandoned by the Cakchiquel. It was here, in the archives of the colonial church of Santo Tomás, that a priest discovered the *Popul Vuh*, considered the most important source of study for Quiché myth and ritual.

Chichicastenango's prestige is reflected in extraordinary concern for proper dress. Opulent to the eye and complex in patterns and techniques, its costumes evidence a proud heritage. The men's garments are like no other in Guatemala. Both the short, split-leg pants and the jacket *(saco)* are made of wool, their tailoring and embroidered decoration done by men. In the 1960s, women took great pride in their ability to dress themselves and the female members of their family with the products of their backstrap looms. Men also made important contributions to women's dress. They embroidered *fajas*, sewed *randas,* and produced the intricate appliqué and embroidery around the neckline of every huipil. Women wove the men's accessories *(tzutes* and *fajas)* and their own huipils and *tzutes* and in time took over some of the embroidery work from the men.

While the Maxeños (as Chichicastenango residents are called) are highly traditional, their costumes have nonetheless evolved over the course of fifty years. A photograph from the 1950s (fig. 250) shows us the huipil characteristic of that era: its background color was white, with supplementary decoration in red. Large double eagles filled the center panel (back and front), and smaller double eagles covered the shoulders on the side panels. Spread open flat, the design area formed a cross. An appliquéd black taffeta sunburst, outlined with chainstitch embroidery, encircled the neckline

250. People of Santo Tomás Chichicastenango.

251. Costumes of Santo Tomás Chichicastenango.

252 (below). Detail of the huipil seen in figure 251, center.

253. Detail of huipil shown in figure 251, right.

and four rosettes occupied opposing positions on the front, back, and shoulders.

Photographs from the Whitman Archive give us an idea of various changes taking place in the huipil during the 1960s. Out of 56 town, market, and church scenes photographed by Whitman in Chichicastenango, 44 women's huipils are clear enough to observe and classify. They seem to fall into three major groups, as well as a couple of minor ones. The oldest or most "traditional" style (Group A) is worn by old women. The prevailing style (Group B), accounting for over half the sample, is seen on women in their middle years. The newest style (Group C), like the oldest, appears on only a few — usually the young women of the village. The three costumes shown here, each worn in the 1960s, exemplify the three main huipils styles seen in the Whitman photographs. They also illustrate the affluence and variety available in the woman's daily dress during that period.[2]

Somber colors predominate in the costume seen on the mannequin at center. This huipil represents the earliest of the three styles (Group A) seen in the Whitman pictures. It resembles the 1950s huipil except that the colors are different and the weaver has chosen to substitute two of the usual four appliqued rosettes with a brocaded diamond form (fig. 252) — an interesting variant. Although weft decoration is cotton rather than the more prestigious silk, the quality of the weaving and the use of the rare brown *cuyuscate* in the ground fabric communicates status. Cotton threads are used for the intricate floral embroidery on the belt and for the *randa* of the skirt. The *tzute* is in the simple style of the 1960s with a red ground and black-and-white pinstripes; its two webs are joined with a cotton *randa*. The skirt is exceptionally fine, with precise ikat stripes, and a cotton and silk *randa*. All skirts are produced locally on foot looms.

The costume design seen to the left, matching Group B in the Whitman Archive, is the most popular style of the 1960s, and might be considered transitional. The double eagle is still visible on front and back, but small diamonds have begun to take shape within the basic design (fig. 253). Rows of zigzags, both small and large, frame the center panel at sides and bottom, and form a definite motif on the central sleeve. Although the cotton is dyed brown (not natural *cuyuscate*), this huipil reflects the highest economic and social status because of its lavish use of silk for all the supple-

254. *Costumes of San Juan Sacatepéquez.*

mentary weft brocading. Silk is also used to embroider the *faja* and the skirt *randa*.

The costume at right, corresponding to Group C of the Whitman sample, points towards future trends. Diamonds, zigzags, and stars have become larger in scale and more dominant in placement and coloring. The ground is once again brown, but wool has been used for brocading. Note the use of brighter, more contrasting colors and bolder designs. The center diamonds are an inch and a half long as compared with the three-eighths of an inch on Group B, and the zigzag block on the sleeve is considerably larger, measuring five by eight inches. The wool embroidered *faja* has geometric forms instead of the floral designs of the other two. The skirt does not employ ikat, but is a simple arrangement of pinstripes, embellished with a *randa*. The *tzute* in the basket has random designs in wool brocade, and a wool *randa*. Wool, while not as costly as silk, was more expensive than cotton and often preferred.

San Juan Sacatepéquez *(Figure 254)*

San Juan Sacatepéquez is the largest Maya township in the department of Guatemala. It is a flourishing floricultural center whose terraced slopes are planted in flowers that are sold all over Guatemala and to other countries as well. Energetic commerce takes place in a thriving Sunday market (fig. 249). The town's well-being is reflected in a wide variety of garments worn on special occasions, and in the exuberantly sophisticated coloring of the everyday huipil. This particular color combination, seen in only one other village, distinguishes the huipil of San Juan Sacatepéquez: it is the gold, red, mauve, and *cuyuscate* stripe. The flamboyant use of opposing colors, and the overlay of bold design on stripe creates an unusual and appealing dramatic tension. Most of the daily huipils from here are warp-striped, and the variety in striping seems infinite.

The three-webbed white ground *cofradía* huipil of San Juan Sacatepéquez, which always hangs outside the skirt, is seen on the kneeling mannequin. The brocaded rows on the central panel come almost to the bottom in back and are dense with birds and animals as well as double eagles and a feathered serpent. The side webs

255. *Woman in San Juan Sacatepéquez costume, photographed in Guatemala City.*

have rows of brocading across the shoulders only. Blue cotton fabric binds the neckline and forms the large centrally placed rosette, front and rear. The *cofradía* hairwrap in Totonicapán style, seen here being tied on the head, is traditionally given to a San Juan Sacatapéquez girl by her intended husband and comes to a twisted peak above the forehead.

The daily two-web huipil is so heavily brocaded that it covers up most of the warp-striped ground, though we can discern the purple/mauve stripes at center front. Buttonhole embroidery stitches frame the round neckline and a slit at center front, and the same blue thread forms ties. Across the chest is a motif in gold and blue which the women of this village identify as a plant form, although we believe it to be related to the ancient Maya feathered serpent motif. The wide sash is back-strap woven in the traditional gold, mauve, and red stripes.

The indigo skirt is of medium-weight with warp and weft stripes forming a small rectangular plaid; the mauve *randa* is worn horizontally at the hip-line and vertically in either the side or back. For some occasions the hair braid is interwoven at the nape of the neck with thick black or purple wool strands. Folded on the wooden storage box *(cofre)* is a two-paneled *tzute* with San Juan's traditional mauve and gold coloring. The brocaded rectangular panel in the center is characteristic of a ceremonial *tzute*. It is of the same weave and weight and almost the same size as a huipil.

The wedding huipil of San Juan Sacatepéquez, (seen at center, partially covered by the *cofre* lid) is also worn at baptisms. We see a simplified color palette and design common to a number of ceremonial garments, representing a carry-over of a style from a earlier period. Brocading is restricted to red and mauve, on a background of white with widely spaced mauve stripes, and a weft ribbed weave runs horizontally across the panels. A wide band of brocade is across the shoulders. It is also made of three webs with the *randa* in tiny blocks of red and mauve as is the *cofradía* huipil, and is bound at the neckline with blue. This garment has evidently been worn to a number of baptisms as the original blue neck binding has been replaced, although the original faded blue rosettes remain. In San Juan Sacatepéquez, ceremonial huipils are sewn together at the sides, unlike everyday huipils, which are not sewn but overlapped at the sides so as to cover the body underneath. The ceremonial huipil is worn over the everyday huipil.[3]

San Martín Jilotepeque *(Figure 256)*

The weaving of huipils is today an important source of income for the women of San Martín Jilotepeque. These three huipils, all from the 1960s, range from the simplest (on the mannequin's head) to the most complex (in her hands); yet they share a remarkable stylistic similarity. A much wider selection of styles and colors could be found there today.

An all-cotton white, purple, and indigo huipil is seen here folded on the mannequin's head, taking the place of a *tzute* (as is customary) in this village; but the same garment could also be worn as an everyday huipil or, because of its simplicity and retiring color, as a mourning huipil. The quality of weaving is tight and even, but with only two colors in the supplementary weft the work can proceed quickly and the cost for such a garment is modest both in time and material.

On the mannequin, a huipil with a ground of simple indigo cotton sets off an embellishment of considerable sophistication: some of the decorative threads are either rayon or silk, and eight different colors are incorporated into the weft brocade. The introduction of different fibers and colors complicates both the weaving and the process of design and adds to its cost.

The huipil held out for inspection demonstrates a skillful and highly artistic amplification of the basic brocade design, especially in the elaborate chest band. It is a special garment to be worn for an important ceremonial occasion, either *cofradía* or wedding. Still more colors of thread are used and the cost of these threads, both silk and lustrina (the best imported cotton) adds considerably to the cost of the garment. In addition, instead of having the simple unembellished split neck opening of the first two, it is bound in velvet ribbon at both the neck and arm holes and trimmed with velvet rosettes front and back. A fine multicolored *randa* adds further enhancement. An accomplished weaver might well own all three of these huipils like the ones shown here, and she would then use them as the social occasion indicated.[4]

The all-purpose indigo skirt is of medium weight, and it is held in place by a trade belt from Totonicapán. Given its well matched coloring, the belt might have been made especially for this village; however this may be only coincidence.

256. Costume of San Martín Jilotepeque.

257. *Costumes of Santa María de Jesús.*

Santa María de Jesús *(Figure 257)*

The costumes from Santa María de Jesús, a Cakchiquel-speaking village on the steep slopes of Volcano Agua near Antigua, are displayed here so as to illustrate the stylistic relationship of costumes within a family group. The grandmother figure (left) carries an indigo *tzute* brocaded in typical mourning colors, appropriate to a widow. The boy's backstrap-woven shirt is made from a textile that matches the red ground *tzute* carried by the mother. His shirt and pants mirror those that the father would wear for a festive occasion.

The foot-loom-woven skirts shown here conform to what was being worn in the 1960s. The skirt on the right is in typical Santa María de Jesús style, and since the 1970s this kind has been made by local weavers. Prior to that time, Santa María women bought their skirts from weavers in El Tejar, near Chimaltenango, who brought them to Santa María to sell; sometimes they brought the Chimaltenango style, shown on the grandmother, left. Unlike the other two, this skirt has no *randa* but is sewn together with flat-felled seams. Occasionally skirts of the Sololá style were also sold and worn here, as seen on the girl (center).

It is the huipils, however, that tell the most interesting story. Of special interest is the huipil on the grandmother mannequin, a style used for weddings, now lavishly embroidered with quetzals and other birds, rabbits, and flowers in multicolors on a dark ground. The embroidery was done by Santa María de Jesús men using age-old designs. Yet in markets in the Quezaltenango-Totonicapán area, far from the markets with which Santa María trades, this same huipil style is available. Certain local folktales hold that the village was founded "long ago" by a few married couples from the Quezaltenango area. Perhaps this explains the source of this unusual decorative treatment.

The huipils shown on the mother figure (right) and girl are also atypical when compared with other Cakchiquel styles. They are both brocaded all over in diamond forms. The Santa María style seems reminiscent of some early huipils from the Mam village of San Martín Sacatepéquez, especially in the motifs on the shoulder band (fig. 258).[5]

258. *Detail of the huipil seen in figure 257, right.*

259. Costume of Patzún.

260. Market in Patzún.

Patzún *(Figure 259)*

In Guatemalan villages, as all around the world, a wedding is an important event. Not all weddings are graced by lavish garments but for many who have a church ceremony the wedding huipil represents the highest expression of a weaver's skill. Sometimes, as in the case of the Cakchiquel village of Patzún, the wedding huipil also serves as a *cofradía* garment. For both occasions, it is worn outside the skirt, in the Prehispanic manner.

Patzún garments in the Museum's collection include not only several huipils from the 1960s but also three that antedate them, one of which is shown here. This one was made for ceremonial purposes, as evidenced by the extravagant use of silk around the neckline and the embroidery style, representing feathers. Older huipils like this are of a much heavier weave than later ones, and, being durable, might well have been worn into the 1960s. The same design was being produced during the 1960s, but the floss was of a brighter coloring.

The skirt shown here, made of heavy *morga*, is in the bold plaid style typical of the early 1960s and before. Ikat skirts of indigo and white dominated everyday wear, but ceremonial occasions call for the older style because of its more traditional aspect. Like most skirts this one is folded under at the top, pulled taut around the waist, and folded vertically at the hip. A sash of black-and-white wool, made in Chichicastenango, holds it at the top, and sometimes this is covered by a brocaded backstrap sash of the same width which is made in Patzún. The silk embroidered ceremonial headdress, called *paya*, is unique to Patzún. Designs characteristically combine Christian motifs with animal motifs that are probably pre-Christian, such as the double-headed bird or the jaguar. Tinsel-like braid borders the fabric rectangle, and silk tassels fall in front as shown. It is worn alone on the head for *cofradía* functions. For weddings, it is combined with a veil as seen here. This veil, in the form of a huipil without the neckhole, is made in Cobán.[6]

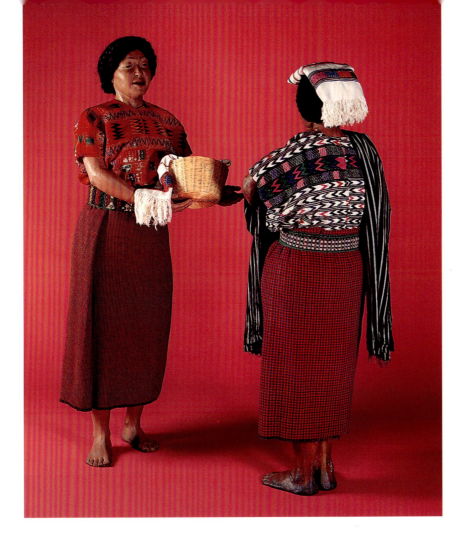

San Andrés Semetabaj *(Figure 261)*

While special widows' garments are not seen as often as wedding costumes, in the 1960s they were still worn in many places. Our example is from San Andrés Semetabaj, a small Cakchiquel village that lies on a shelf of land high above Lake Atitlán, where a fortuitous climate allows two commercial wheat crops a year along with the subsistence crops of corn, squash and beans. Headquarters for a regional government agricultural cooperative, San Andrés Semetabaj is highly Ladinoized. In spite of this, Maya traditions are still strong and huipils are still produced on backstrap looms.

The contrast between the regular huipil with its matching *servietta*, in bright colorings of red, green, and blue, and the huipil of mourning *(luto)*, or widow's huipil, which is distinguished by its softer, more muted tones, is evident here. The widow's headcloth is brocaded in the same mourning colors of blue, rose, and white. Her light-weight skirt of red-and-blue plaid is in an old style, as is her indigo-and-white warp-striped shawl.

Blue, lavender, and rose were favorite mourning colors during the 1960s, but now that weavers experiment so freely with non-traditional colorings, it is more difficult to identify widows.[7]

261 (above). Costumes of San Andrés Semetabaj.
262 (right). Faja seen in figure 261, right.

263 (right). Costume of San Antonio Aguas Calientes.

264 (below). Detail of the tzute in the basket shown in figure 263.

265. Weaver in San Antonio Aguas Calientes.

San Antonio Aguas Calientes *(Figure 263)*

The Cakchiquel women of San Antonio Aguas Calientes are often extolled as the best weavers in Guatemala. O'Neale described their huipil as the most elaborate and intricately woven in the highlands. They employ a number of difficult weaving techniques, including indigenous (single-faced) and imported (double-faced) ones, and find a steady market for their weaving in nearby Antigua, with its large foreign community and tourist trade. Weavers range from very conservative to highly innovative, and pay meticulous attention to details; good weavers attain high status in the community. Since the 1960s and possibly earlier there have also been local male foot loom weavers producing Totonicapán-type *cortes* and sashes for the local trade.

The huipil worn by the mannequin seen here is typical of the coloring most favored in the 1960s — tones of mauve and purple with accents in orange and red. The red ground cloth is completely covered with brocade above the waist. Row upon row are single-faced indigenous motifs, with emphasis on the shoulder and chest bands.

The huipil in the mannequin's hand has its own aesthetic story to tell. Mending patches of commercial material have been carefully selected to blend and enhance the color scheme of the original tattered huipil, evidencing the aesthetic sense of its repairer. The especially fine *tzute* draped in the basket (fig. 264) was woven in the 1930s. The skirt, woven locally, is cotton with a woolen weft; it was the most popular style and color of the middle to late 1960s. At that time the backstrap-woven sash was worn by both men and women, but the narrower belt woven in Totonicapán style was also an option for women then and is now preferred.[8]

Patzicía and Cerro de Oro *(Figure 266)*

In this plate we show costumes from two seemingly unrelated villages: one from Patzicía, a Cakchiquel-speaking village in the department of Chimaltenango, and the other from Cerro de Oro, a Tzutujil *aldea* in the department of Sololá. An examination of their costumes, however, indicated a relationship; and following this clue, we discovered an interesting historical connection. In 1880, after a crop failure and

*266. Costumes of Patzicía (left)
and Cerro de Oro (right).*

famine, a group from Patzicía migrated to Cerro de Oro, under the jurisdiction of Santiago Atitlán. The traditional civil religious hierarchy of Santiago Atitlán influenced some of the group to adopt the Tzutujil language and the dress of Santiago Atitlán (as in figure 179). Others, however, wanting to maintain their Cakchiquel ties, continued to speak Cakchiquel and wore the Patzicía costume in a modified version.

The traditional ceremonial huipil of Patzicía is worn outside the skirt in the manner of the overhuipils of the Chimaltenango area. The skirt is of *morga* in the bold plaid design of the 1960s and earlier. On the right is the modified huipil worn by the Cerro de Oro women. Both are backstrap woven, with a red ground and grouped warp pin stripes in various colors, but the brocaded pattern on the Cerro de Oro huipil is totally different and reflects their new location with soumak stylized water insects seen on other Lake village textiles (such as those of San Lucas Tolimán, Santa Catarina Palopó). The skirt, too, is *morga*, but in small discrete checks. As in Santiago Atitlán, the women do not wear sashes; the skirt is wrapped and an end corner is tucked in at the top.[9]

Santa María Cauqué and Santiago Sacatepéquez *(Figure 267)*

Usually there is little distinction between the clothing of a hamlet (*aldea*) and that of the town to which it belongs. Not so here. According to Gall, Santa María Cauqué once had *municipio* status. However in 1935 governmental decrees annexed it to Santiago Sacatepéquez as an *aldea*. In maintaining their own costume, the women of Santa María Cauqué reflect their individuality and loyalty to their own pre-1935 village.

The population of Santa María Cauqué is predominantly Catholic; Santiago Sacatepéquez is predominantly evangelical. Though converts to evangelism tend to give up their traditional *traje*, the women of Santiago Sacatepéquez have continued to wear theirs, providing the one splash of color in the evangelical parade that takes place annually in the capital. A small and very modest museum has also been established in the village showing the change of styles in the local huipil, indicating that

*267. Costumes of Santa María Cauqué (left)
and Santiago Sacatepéquez (right).*

they still think of themselves as Maya and place great value on their traditional costume.

The huipil of Santa María Cauqué is of a heavy-ribbed weave similar to the one from Santo Domingo Xenacoj. Narrowly spaced white pin stripes streak the red background, and the supplementary weft brocade repeats the same rectangular geometric motif in rows to the waist. The sash, backstrap woven like the huipil, has the same brocaded motifs. The skirt is of *morga* with regularly spaced pin stripes interrupted by groups of stripes in both the warp and the weft, and a narrow multicolored *randa*. On her head she carries a foot-loom-woven *tzute* popular in several Sacatepéquez villages, and in her hands is a backstrap-woven utility cloth particular to her village.

The Santiago Sacatapéquez huipil is also of a heavy weave and the brocade is of the Picked-pile technique, which indicates it may have been woven by a professional weaver in Santo Domingo Xenacoj as a special occasion huipil for a Santiago Sacatepéquez woman. The style of the sash is unique to this village and has multicolored woolen circles (like *Lifesaver* candies) hanging on braided wool threads from a narrow black and white striped belt. At least two different types of skirts are worn in this village — the striated *morga* like the one from Santo Domingo Xenacoj but without the *randa*, and a lighter weight all indigo skirt, also without a *randa*, as seen here. The large *tzute* (tied around a bundle) was prevalent in the village in the early 1960s. The most common everyday huipil style of the 1960s had row upon row of motifs, described locally as "eye of God" and "stairway to Heaven." The background fabric is always red and white with stripes, sometimes close together, other times wide apart.

Sololá, Nebaj, and Santa María de Jesús *(Figure 268)*

The three *cofradía* huipils shown here would never be seen in the same place in real life, since Sololá and Santa María de Jesús are widely separated Cakchiquel towns, while Nebaj is Ixil. Nor would a woman from one town dress a *santo* with strangers present. In spite of geographic separation and ethnic diversity, the costumes have been brought together in this photograph for the sake of comparison. The main feature they have in common outside their basic function is the grandeur,

268. Costumes of Sololá (left), Nebaj (center), and Santa María de Jesús (right).

if this word may be used, of each of them. It takes no great perception to see that these are not daily or ordinary garments, and it is not fanciful to say that each woman who wore such a huipil was conscious of her high duty in preserving the *costumbre* of her town.

The *cofradía* garment is usually thought of as the most elaborate of all Indian garments, but the degree is relative. *Cofradía* officers are responsible for providing their own official garments as well as paying for other fiesta expenses and some have fewer resources than others. Thus the *cofradía* costume itself may be relatively modest, like the fireworks, church decorations, and *aguardiente* provided for the occasion. Such is the case with the Sololá *cofradía* huipil on the left. The weave is relatively light, the thread less fine than sedalina, and the embroidery unassuming. Nevertheless in its basic design and decoration it has all the attributes of a typical *cofradía* huipil. It has three webs, is embellished around the neck, and most importantly, falls over the skirt in the Prehispanic style. A detail of a more lavish *cofradía* huipil from Sololá is seen on page 93 (fig. 134).

Less modest is the Nebaj *cofradía* huipil dating from the late 1950s or early 1960s whose central web combines silk with cotton in a fine weft-faced weave. The *cofradía* huipil from Santa María de Jesús is the most elaborate of the three. It is ample in width and length and silk has been lavishly used in the brocading, not only on the huipil but on its accompanying ceremonial *tzute*.

The Sololá figure to the left is shown dressing a saint figure in a small *camisa*. Sometimes such garments are commissioned by the *cofradía,* and made by the sacristans. Often they are made in fulfillment of a vow made to the saint. These small textiles are stored in the *cofradía* house and cared for by the women who wash and change them. The parading of the saints' figures is an occasion for ceremonial costume. For such processions the saints are often dressed in miniature garments exactly like those worn by the people of the town. A male saint may wear a *camisa*, as in figure 269. A female saint may wear a ceremonial huipil, perhaps a skirt and, on her head a proper headdress of ribbons or a *tzute*.[10]

The skirts seen here are of indigo and white *morga* plaid, heavier and bolder than the daily skirts, and typically used with ceremonial huipils. *Tzutes* are made specifically for ceremonial use. They are worn folded or draped on the head and, in the case of the Nebaj *tzute*, over a white veil.

269. Festival in Sololá.

270. Costumes of Chuarrancho (left) and San Pedro Sacatepéquez (G) (right).

San Pedro Sacatepéquez (G) and Chuarrancho *(Figure 270)*

The *cofradía* costumes seen above are notable examples of the distinct and cohesive style worn in villages of the Sacatepéquez, a Cakchiquel subgroup living in the departments of Sacatepéquez and Guatemala. San Pedro Sacatepéquez is acknowledged as an important weaving center and has probably influenced the weaving style of several other towns including Chuarrancho, which was at one time a dependency of San Pedro.[11]

Densely brocaded patterns in purple and red are characteristic of the ceremonial costumes of this area, and may be a survival from an earlier era. In both San Pedro and Chuarrancho, the ceremonial huipils are open down the sides, in contrast to daily huipils, which are closed. They are worn outside the skirt and covered with supplemental weft life forms. The ceiba tree is a common motif in San Pedro; the portal motif seems to be used only in Chuarrancho and both only on *cofradía* huipils. Osborne suggests that the bold patterns and thick appearance are a style once woven by noble Cakchiquel women which has persisted in ceremonial garb. Heavy buttonhole embroidery plus finer embroidered necklace-like star forms are typical neckline treatment on San Pedro huipils. Wedding huipils have a wider color range than those for *cofradía* wear and pinks, turquoise, mauve, and other pastels are set on a white ground. The *mano* band across the shoulders is usually purple, however.

The ceremonial huipil of San Pedro Sacatepéquez is all the more interesting for the unusual ways in which it is worn. During procession at the patron saint's feast day it is draped over the head and shoulders like a *tzute*. At weddings the *cofradía* huipil is hung on the back of a married woman, over her festive huipil. At processions, the marriage huipil is worn inside out.

Notes

1. *Costume and Society*. Any given festive occasion is certain to involve one or more of the following: marimba concerts, chirimia and drum music, dances with elaborate rented costumes and masks, mock bullfights, rockets and firecrackers, incense, flowers, pine boughs, the recitation of Latin prayers, and the consumption of *aguardiente*, a local liquor.

2. *Santo Tomás Chichicastenango*. See Carmack 1981 on the early history of the Quiché. The Nahua-speaking forebears of the Quiché entered Guatemala from Mexico in small bands bent on conquest, bringing with them cultural patterns of the northern peoples: military conquest, commoner-aristocratic social ranking, human sacrifice, lineage organization, ritual calendrics, and dualism and cardinal point orientation in religious symbolism (Carmack 1981, p. 6). It is believed that most of them married local women. The Quiché language evolved out of the marriage of the conquerors' Nahua dialect and the local Maya dialect. During the mid-1960s and before, the market at Chichicastenango was geared to local Maya trade; ceramic dishes, candles, incense, flower petals and *aguardiente* did a more thriving business than textiles. There were skirts, foot-loom-woven by Ladinos in the village, black and white wool *fajas* to be embroidered later by men, and *tzutes*. A shop on the plaza sold thread to Chichicastenango weavers and embroiderers and handled a few examples of their work. By the mid-1970s, market products were increasingly geared toward the tourist trade. Merchants from Totonicapán dominated with their foot-loom-woven goods, not worn by locals. The weavers shop now began to sell backstrap woven textiles from Chiquimula, San Juan Cotzal, Sololá, and other distant and different places. By the 1980s, the decline in tourist trade as a result of guerrilla and army fighting in the Quiché area was pitifully evident. On men's contributions to women's dress, see Bunzel 1952 (p. 60). The style of the huipil in the Blank photo is the same one described by O'Neale from her 1930's research, pictured by Rowe 1981 (p. 88). They were still worn by a few old women in the 1960s. Certainly very little change took place between the turn of the century and the 1950s. The Museum's collection is particularly fine in costumes and ancillary textiles from Chichicastenango, so we can examine in greater detail the colorings and patterns from our own examples.

3. *San Juan Sacatepéquez*. According to Fox 1978 (p. 203), the people of San Juan are descended from the Akahal, a separate tribal group taken over by the Cakchiquel shortly before the Spanish Conquest. Rowe 1981, Osborne 1935, Wood and Osborne 1966, and Delgado 1963 have all noted the range of everyday huipil styles. San Raimundo is the only other village using the distinctive color combination of gold, red, mauve and *cuyuscate*. The only difference between the two is in the particular way a pine tree is depicted in the brocading according to Cherri Pancake (pers. com. 1976), or in a subtle stripe configuration with more white showing (Susan Turner, pers. com. 1988). Linguistically San Juan Sacatepéquez is related to San Raimundo, San Martín Jilotepeque, Chuarrancho, and Ayampuc (Kaufman 1975, p. 63). Gwendolin Ritz provided information about local nomenclature for the design form we refer to as 'feathered serpent.'

4. *San Martín Jilotepeque*. The San Martín huipil relates stylistically to that of San Antonio Aguas Calientes (see Chapter 4, p. 126).

5. *Santa María de Jesús*. Thanks to linguist Don Cheney and his wife Gretchen, a weaver, who have lived and done research in the village, for the information on embroidery traditions. Linguistics as well as folklore offers clues as to the origins of Santa María de Jesús. Stephen Stewart, a linguist in Guatemala City, found the Santa María dialect to be unlike any other Cakchiquel dialects. Lovell 1985 (p. 80) is the source of the citation re Maya awareness of differences in social affiliation.

It is interesting to note that a town and a volcano, both named Santa María de Jesús, exist in the Quezaltenango area, not far from San Martín Sacatepéquez. I suspect a historic connection between these areas, and that early settlers of Santa María de Jesús came from one of the Mam enclaves that were dispossessed to make room for Alvarado's cohorts. I do not mean to suggest that styles have remained constant for 400 years, but rather that Mam symbolic motifs, represented here by the multiple diamonds, may have persisted. An important aspect of tradition is the enduring reverence for one's ancestors. Referring to the Mam people, Lovell says "the Indians were always acutely aware of the differences both between and within their traditional social affiliations. Some communities congregated elsewhere continued to exist and are still in existence today." This suggests a broader kinship, the patrilineal clan of an earlier time. Fox's theory of "regionalism" describes the tendencies of highland populations to maintain ethnic continuity even after inclusion within other Conquest systems (1978, pp. 275-6).

6. *Patzún*. Copies of the *paya* shown here and others became extremely popular with the tourist trade of the 1970s and were produced for sale in all size, colors, and fibers. I am indebted to Gwendolin Ritz for the distinction between *cofradía* and wedding uses of the headdress.

7. *San Andrés Semetabaj*. Warren 1978 (p. 24) discusses the strength of Maya traditions in San Andrés Semetabaj. San Andrés still maintains cultural affinities with Cakchiquel villages in the Chimaltenango area, especially Tecpán and Santa Apolonia. Re mourning colors, owing to the political massacres of the early 1980s, there are many widows, young and old, who cannot afford the luxury of a special huipil for themselves. Foot loom weavers in the Totonicapán-Quezaltenango area continue to produce huipils in widow's colorings, however.

8. *San Antonio Aguas Calientes*. Several villages in the region share the same Cakchiquel dialect that is spoken in San Antonio Aguas Calientes (Kaufman 1975, p. 61). They are San Andrés Itzapa, Parramos, Alotenango, Duenas, and Santa Catarina Barahona. The huipils of San Andrés and Duenas bear a close resemblance to those of San Antonio. In Antigua, San Antonio Aguas Calientes weavers now ply their trade in hotels and pensions, in church courtyards, the main plaza, and on the streets as well as in the marketplace. The road to their village is dotted with weaving shops. Women weavers have even been sent to exhibit their talents at trade fairs in the United States and Europe. It is hardly surprising that in this village a few young men have taken up the backstrap loom. So intense is the competition that family disputes can arise over weaving sales. Now, the weaving of textiles, some in the styles of other villages, seems to provide a more lucrative economic base than weaving rush mats and cultivating fruit and vegetables. Costume colors have changed in San Antonio since the 1960s. At a later period, the color orange predominated with turquoise and blue accents and the banding was more apt to have grape or flower designs in the mano and chest positions. This comprehensive collection has given us an opportunity to study in depth the change from indigenous to Europeanized motifs introduced into San Antonio in the late 19th century probably by nuns. The variety of artifacts (sleighs, bicycles, etc.) and flora and fauna introduced into Guatemala weaving by means of brocading pattern books makes a story all its own.

9. *Patzicía and Cerro de Oro*. On the migration from Patzicía to Cerro de Oro, see McBryde 1947 (p. 90).

10. *Sololá, Nebaj, and Santa María de Jesús*. On the names of decorative motifs in Sololá, see Mayén de Castellanos 1986 (p. 61). While the typical *cofradía* huipil from Sololá is three-webbed, we have seen one constructed of two webs.

The place and type of care given to the textiles used for *santos* probably varies from town to town and even, according to Asturias de Barrios 1985 (p. 54), from *cofradía* to *cofradía*. In San Pedro Sacatepéquez the women care for and clean the garments, but the men actually change them on the figures since the saints are too high for the women to reach and too heavy to lift down. Not all saint figures are dressed in handwoven Maya costume; some wear silks and satins of commercial manufacture, or have European-style clothing carved along with their bodies.

11. *San Pedro Sacatepéquez and Chuarrancho*. On the persistence of the style once woven by noble Cakchiquel women, see Osborne 1975 (p. 76).

Appendices

APPENDIX 1A: COTÓN

TOWN	LANGUAGE	USE AND NAME	DESCRIPTION	SOURCE
Acatenango	Cakchiquel	*gabán*	black wool, waist length unsewn sleeves	Delgado 1963:281
Cajolá	Southern Mam	*cotón*	grey and white striped wool treadle woven, to thigh	Delgado 1963:320
Chichicastenango	Quiché	*kotonn, chaket* for municipal officials daily – joined at bottom	1) bl. wool, fringed, heavily embroidered 2) same, but front with 2 pieces joined at bottom (more common)	Rodas et al 1940: figs. 17, 18, 27 Rowe 1981:91, fig. 75
Colotenango	Mam	worn by mature man *jerga, capixaj*	22" tan and white vertical stripes	Mejía de Rodas 1987:62 Valladares 1957:84 Delgado 1963:304
Nahualá	Quiché	ceremonial; daily for warmth	like a short *capixay* with sleeves not used black wool	Susan Masuoka Rowe 1981:79, 82, fig. 63
Parramos	Cakchiquel	daily	white cotton sleeveless, fringed and long in back, worn belted	Wood and Osborne 1966:10, pl. 41
San Andrés Sajcabajá	Quiché	?	red cotton, colored pinstripes, fringe	Delgado 1963:336
San Martín Jilotepeque	Cakchiquel	*cotón cerrado*	hip length wool, open sleeves	Delgado 1963:283
Santiago Atitlán	Tzutujil	ceremonial	Sololá-type, checked wool worn until 1910	Rowe 1981:70, fig. 31 O'Neale 1945: 211
Santiago Chimaltenango	Mam	daily	black and white wool, woven by women, to hips	Wagley 1949:pl. 2a, 3a
Sololá	Cakchiquel	ceremonial, *sacro, cerrado, koton*	closed jacket of blue/wh striped or checked wool, usually with appliqué or embroidery	O'Neale 1945: 299 Mayén de Castellanos 1986: foto 26, 34, dibujo 14
Todos Santos	Mam	*capixay*	waist length, sleeves not sewn, dark twill weave	Osborne 1975:161 O'Neale 1945:303 La Farge 1931:16

APPENDIX 1B: CAPIXAY

TOWN	LANGUAGE	USE	NAME AND DESCRIPTION	SOURCE
Cobán	Kekchi	?	? dark wool "ample cloaks"	Morelet cited in Delgado 1963:268
Comalapa	Cakchiquel	ceremonial shoulder-covering cape	? bl. wool, cape, ankle length, **has (prob. a large collar called vallon [wallon])	Delgado 1963:282 (from old photo)
Jacaltenango	Jacalteca	? sleeves	? bl. wool, rectangular tunic, short open	La Farge, O. and Byers 1931:26, 36
Jocotenango	Cakchiquel	ceremony?	? perfect *capixay* in all details	Maudslay & Maudslay 1899:p.37 ill.
Joyabaj	Quiché	worn by older men, esp. officials	? rectangular, long, fringed at back	O'Neale 1945:268
Nebaj	Ixil	ceremony?	? all details present 9/22/88	Fisher, A.S. 1983:fig. and letter

Panajachel	Cakchiquel	warmth	COTON. natural dk. br. or bl. wool, long, front shorter, fringed, open	O'Neale 1945:287
Parramos	Cakchiquel	?	no description, merely mentioned as being worn	Osborne 1975:154
Patzún	Cakchiquel	?	? bl. natural wool, sleeveless, open at sides, longer in back than front, fringe	Maudslay & Maudslay 1899:42 and ill. same page
Salamá	No Mayan language any more- Spanish	?	? wool, recessed sleeves, fringe, 34" l.	O'Neale 1945:296
San Antonio Aguas Calientes	Cakchiquel	?	CODIARTE. bl. wool, rectangular, seams open, sleeves recessed under shoulder, 39" l. x 46" in back, fringed	Osborne 1975:154, 161 O'Neale 1945:252 FMCH has an example
San Antonio Palopó	Cakchiquel	?	? bl/brown twill weave wool, rectangle, 31" l., 36" l. back, fringed, sleeves open	O'Neale 1945:286 Maudslay 1899:55, pl.11
San Juan Atitán	Mam	warmth	CAPIXAJ. dark wool, open seams, 44" l., longer in back, fringe	Delgado 1963:301 MCH has two examples
San Juan Ixcoy	Kanjobal (N. Mam)	?	HOPIL. treadle-woven, dark wool, to knee	Delgado 1963:305
San Juan la Laguna	Tzutujil	ceremony?	? all details present except front 2" longer than back	Fisher, A.S. 1983:fig. and letter 9/22/88
San Marcos la Laguna	Tzutujil	?	? dk wool, no seam sewed, must be about 45" l. because similar to Santiago Atitlan – need 3 or 4 varas to make	Tax 1937:434 O'Neale 1945:273
San Martín Sacatepéquez	Mam	warmth	? dk. wool, rectangular, all seams open, 60" l. in front, back longer, fringed	Delgado 1963:330 O'Neale 1945:276 FMCH has an example
San Mateo Ixtatán	Chuj	?	? "black wool tunic"	La Farge, O. and Byers 1931:215
San Miguel Acatén	Kanjobal	?	? to the knee, fringed	Osborne 1975:161
San Pablo la Laguna	Tzutujil	?	? dk. wool, rectangular, all seams open, length to knees in front, longer in back	O'Neale 1945:284
San Pedro Soloma	Kanjobal	warmth	? dk. wool, rectangular, no mention of open sides, 34" l. x 37" l. in back	O'Neale 1945:300
Santa Catarina Palopó	Cakchiquel	?	? similar to San Antonio Palopó	O'Neale 1945:286
Santa Cruz la Laguna	Cakchiquel	?	? rectangular tunic, shorter in front, totally useless sleeves only — cm. wide	Fisher, A.S. 1983: fig. 10
Santa Eulalia	Kanjobal	?	? bl. wool, rectangular, sleeves and sides unsewed, long and longer in back	La Farge, O. and Byers 1931: fig. 64 ill. and p.228 O'Neale 1945:213
Santa María Chiquimula	Quiché	?	CHAMARRA. bl/wh. wool, no size given	Delgado 1963:369
Santiago Atitlán	Tzutujil	said to be ceremonial but used daily	? dark wool, rectangular, no mention of open seams, 46" l. x 50" l. in back – similar to San Marcos	Tax 1937:434 O'Neale 1945:211, 297
Sololá	Cakchiquel	ceremonial - worn only by *cofrades*	KAWANO. dk wool, rectangular, sleeves partly open (and arms not in sleeves), 38" l. x 44" l. in back,* fringed†	Mayén de Castellanos 1986:73, foto 24 O'Neale 1945:299
Tecpán (in 1840)	Cakchiquel	?	? blue (not black) "cloak" with hood like Arab burnouse	Stephens, J.L. 1842, II: 147
Zacualpa	Quiché	?	? twilled bl. wool, open, shoulders recessed, 50" l. fringed	O'Neale 1945:305, fig. 54p

*In 1936 — in 1986 front very short and back long. †Not fringed in the 1980's. **May not be a capixay.

APPENDIX 2: RODILLERA OR PONCHITO

TOWN	LANGUAGE	USE AND NAME	DESCRIPTION	SOURCE
Chivinal	Mam	?	KILT white wool, bl. pinstripes – worn above knee	Osborne 1975:159
Comalapa	Cakchiquel	*xérka*	APRON bl/wh wool – small 56" x 25", secured by sash similar to woman's faja	Asturias 1985:51, photo 13
Comitancillo	Mam	?	KILT white wool, bl. pinstripes – worn above knee	Osborne 1975:159
Concepción Tutuapa	Mam	?	KILT white wool, bl. pinstripes – worn above knee	Osborne 1975:159
Huehuetenango	Mam	?	KILT wool, checked	O'Neale 1945:266
Ichiguán	Mam	?	KILT white wool, bl. pinstripes – worn aboveknee	Osborne 1975:159
Joyabaj	Quiché	?	KILT blue/white wool checks	O'Neale 1945:268 Wood/Osborne 1966: pl. 26
Nahualá	Quiché	daily wear	KILT bl/wh wool, short fringe – secured by belt, one or both back ends turned back 6"; ends thus meet	Osborne 1975:159 Rowe 1981:ill. fig. 51, 58, 59
Panajachel	Cakchiquel	?	KILT bl/wh wool, fringed, small 52" x 27"	O'Neale 1945:287 Tax, pc 4/6/84
Patzicía	Cakchiquel	?	KILT	Osborne 1975:150 ill.
Patzún	Cakchiquel	?	APRON checked	Whitman Archive (see fig. 45)
Sacapulas	Quiché	?	black & white wool woven by men	O'Neale 1945:15
San Andrés Semetabaj	Cakchiquel	?	APRON checked	Warren 1978:photo 4, 9, 10, 13
San Antonio Palopó	Cakchiquel	?	KILT open front left, fringed wool bl/wh covers pants	O'Neale 1945:286 Tax, pc 4/6/84
San Martín Jilotepeque	Cakchiquel	?	KILT wool, held by red sash, blue/white checks	Delgado 1963:284 Osborne 1975:154
San Miguel Ixtahuacán	Mam	?	KILT white wool, bl. pinstripes – worn above knee	Osborne 1975:159
San Pedro Jocopilas	Quiché	?	KILT bl/wh wool	O'Neale 1945:268, 15
San Sebastián Huehuetenango	Mam	*lanter* (from *delanter* = apron)	KILT woven on backstrap loom by women, bl. with white warp pins	Sperlich & Sperlich 1980:119, pl. 13
Santa Apolonia	Cakchiquel	?	APRON	Osborne 1975:245 ill.
Santa Catarina Ixtahuacán	Quiché	?	KILT bl/white checked wool cover short trousers	von Tempsky 1858:363 Osborne 1975:153
Santa Catarina Palopó	Cakchiquel	?	KILT bl/wh wool, secured by banda	O'Neale 1945:286 Osborne 1975:192 ill.
Santa Cruz la Laguna	Cakchiquel	?	KILT bl. wool with wh. stripes in both directions – secured by belt & banda; worn long, below knees	O'Neale 1945:264 Tax, pc 4/6/84
Santiago Atitlán	Tzutujil	?	KILT bl/wh wool	Osborne 1975:241 ill.
Santiago Chimaltenango	Mam	?	short "apron" bl. & white wool & woven by women	Wagley 1949:123
Sololá	Cakchiquel	?	KILT bl/wh wool, short fringe - so long belt doesn't catch all (falls in loop)	O'Neale 1945:298

Tacaná	Mam	?	KILT white wool, bl. pins – worn above knee	Osborne 1975:159
Tecpán	Cakchiquel	?	KILT wool, med. & light blue checks, with or without fringe	O'Neale 1945:209, 302
Zacualpa	Quiché	?	black wool cross-barred with inconspicuous white – thoroughly felted	O'Neale 1945:305

APPENDIX 3: SPLIT OVERPANTS

TOWN	LANGUAGE	USE AND NAME	DESCRIPTION	SOURCE
Cajolá	Southern Mam	?	bl. wool overpants like Olintepeque over white cotton drawers	Delgado 1963:320
Cantel	Quiché	ceremonial	cut like Todos Santos	Wood/Osborne 1966: pl. 49.
Comalapa	Cakchiquel	ceremonial *(cofradía* only*)*	black wool to below the knees, over white calzoncillos	Asturias 1985:53, 85 ill. Delgado 1963:282
Concepción Chiquirichapa	Southern Mam	?	like Olintepeque	Delgado 1963:323
Concepción Tutuapa	Southern Mam	mantilla – diaper, old men, especially officials	woven like a loincloth	Osborne 1975:159
Olintepeque	Quiché	ceremonial only	commercial bl. wool, ankle length over white cotton drawers and lace, button like Todos Santos, embroidered	Delgado 1963:326 Wood and Osborne 1966, pl. 46
Patzún	Cakchiquel	daily 1893	black wool, knee length loose trousers over embroidered white underdrawers, side slit	Whitman Archive, fig. 49 Maudslay & Maudslay 1899:42 O'Neale 1945:191
Quezaltenango	Quiché	marriage	worn over white banded calzoncillos — cut like Todos Santos, embroidered pocket?	Osborne 1975:215 ill.
San Juan Ostuncalco	Southern Mam	?	similar in cut to Olintepeque but no embroidery on plain drawers	Delgado 1963:327
San Juan Sacatepéquez	Cakchiquel	ceremonial *(cofradía)*	short, dark wool, split on side	Rowe 1981:54, p.60, 61 ill. O'Neale 1945:192, 269
San Martín Jilotepeque	Cakchiquel	ceremonial *(cofradía)*	split front, buttoned like Todos Santos and 1 button low on thigh	Osborne 1975:214 ill.
San Miguel Totonicapán	Quiché	ceremonial	cut like Todos Santos	Osborne 1975:214 ill.
San Pedro Soloma	Kanjobal	?	mentioned, not described	O'Neale 1945:190
Sololá	Cakchiquel	ceremonial *(cofrades, alguaciles, regidores)*	wool over daily pants – side split, full length	Maudslay & Maudslay 1899:28 ill. O'Neale 1945:191, 298 Mayén de Castellanos 1986:71 ill., fotos 23,24
Sumpango	?		overpants are described and illustrated as not being slit, but are worn over white underpants which show only because they are longer than the overpants	Wood/Osborne 1966:pl. 11
Tecpán	Cakchiquel	ceremonial *(cofradía)*	bl. wool over lace embroidered whitepants, blue trousers open at knee, strange cut	Osborne 1975:219 Stephens 1842:II, 147
Todos Santos	Mam	daily	wool, split up front, of intricate cut, 4 buttons each side	O'Neale 1945:191 Rowe 1981: fig.121
Totonicapán	Quiché	ceremonial	long black, very elaborately decorated and embroidery	Osborne 1975:214 ill.

APPENDIX 4A: MAYA NAMES FOR MEN'S COSTUME PARTS

ENGLISH	SPANISH	NATIVE NAME	MAYA LANGUAGE	TOWN	SOURCE
*capixay**	*capisayo* *capusay* (Basque)	*kapixhaay* *xyal*	Northern Mam Quiché	San Ildefonso Ixtahuacán Nahualá	Proyecto Linguistico 1979, pc Masuoka 1988, pc
drawers	*calzón, calzones*	*kurson* *carsoon*	Cakchiquel Ixil	Sololá Chajul	Mayén de Castellanos 1986:132 Masuoka 1988, pc
*gabán**	*gabán*	*kawáno*	Quiché	Sololá	Mayén de Castellanos 1986:73
hip cloth	*rodillera, ponchito*	*xérka* (from Spanish *xerga* = coarse wool) *xérka*	Cakchiquel Cakchiquel	Comalapa Sololá	Asturias 1985:115 Mayén de Castellanos 1986:134
closed jacket, round jacket	*cotón*	*koton* *po7t koton* *jeerga* (from Spanish *xerga* = coarse wool)	Cakchiquel Cakchiquel Northern Mam	Sololá Comalapa Colotenango	Mayén de Casatellanos 1986:132 Asturias 1985:113 Mejía de Rodas 1987:127
open jacket	*chaqueta*	*chaqueta*	Cakchiquel	Sololá	Mayén de Castellanos 1986:131
overpants	*sobrepantalón* *sobrepantalones*	*estameya* (from serge = *estameña* in spanish)	Cakchiquel	Sololá	Mayén de Castellanos 1986:131
sash	*banda, cincho*	*siinch*	Northern Mam	San Ildefonso Ixtahuacán	Proyecto Linguistico 1979, pc
shirt	*camisa*	*camish,* *kamxa7*** *cam'ix* *kamixhj* *camis*	Cakchiquel Cakchiquel Quiché Northern Mam Ixil	San Juan Sacatepéquez Comalapa Nahualá San Ildefonso Ixtahuacán Chajul	Pang 1963:292 Asturias 1985:111 Masuoka 1988, pc Proyecto Linguistico 1979, pc Masuoka 1988, pc
trousers	*calzoncillos*	*kasion*	Cakchiquel	Comalapa	Asturias 1985:111

*There is no English term for this garment. **Both the Proyecto Linguistico and the Ixchel Museum use the "7" in place of the apostrophe.*

APPENDIX 4B: MAYA NAMES FOR WOMEN'S COSTUME PARTS

ENGLISH	SPANISH	NATIVE NAME	MAYA LANGUAGE	TOWN	SOURCE
hair ribbon	*cinta*	*xak'ap* *xo'op*	Quiché Cakchiquel	Nahualá Panajachel	Masuoka 1988, pc Kieffer 1975, pc
huipil*	*	*po7t* *po7t*	Cakchiquel Cakchiquel	Comalapa Sololá	Asturias 1985:112 Mayén de Castellanos 1986:133
		po't *po't* *po'ot* *klo7j*	Quiché Cakchiquel Kekchi Northern Mam	Nahualá Panajachel Cobán San Ildefonso Ixtahuacán	Masuoka 1988, pc Kieffer 1975, pc Dieseldorff 1984:37 Proyecto Linguistico 1979, pc
sash or belt	*faja*	*b'ano ky'itzb'aj*	Northern Mam	San Ildefonso Ixtahuacán	Proyecto Linguistico 1979
shawl	*panuelo, rebozo*	*q'ub'el* *su't, perraj* *xhi7wil*	Cakchiquel Quiché Northern Mam	Comalapa Nahualá San Ildefonso Ixctahuacán	Asturias 1985:113 Masuoka 1988, pc Proyecto Linguistico 1979
skirt	*refajo, corte*	*uk* *uk* *uk* *uq* *uc'* *aamj*	Cakchiquel Cakchiquel Quiché Cakchiquel Kekchi Northern Mam	San Juan Sacatepéquez Panajachel Nahualá Comalapa Cobán San Ildefonso Ixtahuacán	Pang 1963:292 Kieffer 1975, pc Masuoka, pc Asturias 1985:115 Dieseldorff 1984:37 Proyecto Linguistico 1979, pc
utility cloth	*tzute***	*su7t* *su't* *(t)su't*	Cakchiquel Quiché Cakchiquel	Sololá Nahualá Panajachel	Mayén de Castellanos 1986:132, 133 Masuoka 1988, pc Kieffer 1975, pc

*There is no English nor Spanish term for this garment. **Hispanization of su't.*

References Cited

Alfonso X El Sabio
1979   *Cantigas de Santa María.* (Codice T.I.1) facsimile edition. Madrid: Biblioteca San Lorenzo el Real de El Escorial. Orig. pub. 13th c.

Allen, Max
1981   *The Birth Symbol in Traditional Women's Art from Eurasia and the Western Pacific.* Toronto: Museum for Textiles. Catalog from Toronto Museum.

Anawalt, Patricia R.
1979   "The Ramifications of Treadle Loom Introduction in 16th-Century Mexico." In *Looms and their Products: Irene Emery Roundtable on Museum Textiles 1977 Proceedings*, edited by Irene Emery and Patricia Fiske. Washington, D.C.: The Textile Museum.
1981   *Indian Clothing before Cortes.* Norman, Ok: University of Oklahoma Press.

Anderson, Marilyn
1978   *Guatemalan Textiles Today.* New York: Watson-Guptill Publications.

Anderson, Marilyn, and Johnathan Garlock
1988   *Granddaughters of Corn: Portraits of Guatemalan Women.* Willimantic: Curbstone Press.

Anderson, Ruth Matilda
1979   *Hispanic Costume 1480-1530.* Hispanic notes and monographs. Peninsular series. New York: The Hispanic Society of America.

Annis, Sheldon
1987   *God and Production in a Guatemala Town.* Austin: University of Texas Press.

Arco, Ricardo del
1924   *El traje popular altoaragones; aportación el estudio del traje regional español.* Huesca, Spain.

Arriaga Ochoa, Antonio
1938   *Organización social de los Tarascos.* Morelia, Mexico: Departamento de Extension Universitaria.

Ashelford, Jane
1983   *The Sixteenth Century*, vol. 1 of *A Visual History of Costume.* London: Batsford, and New York: Drama Book Publishers.

Asturias de Barrios, Linda
1985   *Comalapa: Native Dress and its Significance.* Guatemala City: Ixchel Museum. Also published in Spanish.

Beals, Ralph L.
1967   "Acculturation." In *Handbook of Middle American Indians*, vol. 6, edited by Robert Wauchope. Austin: University of Texas Press.

Benítez, José R.
1946   *El traje y el adorno en México.* Guadalajara, Mexico: Imprenta Universitaria.

Bernis, Carmen
1962   *Indumentaria española en tiempos de Carlos V.* Madrid: Instituto Diego Velazquez, del Consejo Superior de Investigaciónes Scientificas.

Bernis Madrazo, Carmen
1956   *Indumentaria medieval española.* Madrid: Instituto Diego Velazquez, del Consejo Superior de Investigaciónes Scientificas.

Bjerregaard, Lena
1977   *Techniques of Guatemalan Weaving.* New York: Van Nostrand Reinhold.

Boyd-Bowman, Peter
1964-8   *Indice geobiográfico de cuarenta mil pobladores españoles de America en el siglo XVI.* Bogotá: Instituto Caro y Cuervo.
1973a   *Patterns of Spanish Emigration to the New World (1493-1580).* Special Studies, SUNY at Buffalo Council on International Studies, no. 34. Buffalo.
1973b   "Spanish and European Textiles in Sixteenth Century Mexico." *The Americas*, 29 (3). Washington, D.C.: Academy of American Franciscan History.
1987   *Léxico Hispanoamericano del siglo XVI.* Spanish series, no. 42. Madison: Hispanic Seminary of Medieval Studies, Ltd.

Braun, Joseph
1907   *Die Liturgische Gewandung in Occident und Orient.* Freiburg: Herder im Breisgan.

Braudel, Fernand
1972-3   *The Mediterranean and the Mediterranean World in the Age of Philip II.* 2 vols., translated from French by Siân Reynolds. New York: Harper and Rowe.
1981   *The Structures of Everyday Life*, vol. 1 of *Civilization and Capitalism*, translated from French by Siân Reynolds. London: Collins.
1982   *The Wheels of Commerce*, vol. 2 of *Civilization and Capitalism*, translated from French by Siân Reynolds. New York: Harper and Rowe.

Brinton, Daniel G., editor
1895   *Annals of the Cakchiquels.* Library of Aboriginal Literature, No. 6. Philadelphia.

Bruhns, Karen Olsen
1988   "Yesterday the queen wore...an analysis of women and costume in the public art of the late Classic Maya." In *The Role of Gender in Precolumbian Art and Architecture*, edited by Virginia E. Miller. Lanham, Md: University Press America.

Bunzel, Ruth
1967   *Chichicastenango, a Guatemalan Village.* Publications of the American Ethnological Society, No. 22. New York. Orig. pub. 1952.

Butler, Mary
1935   "A Study of Maya Moldmade Figurines." *American Anthropologist*, 37 (4).

Carmack, Robert M.
1981   *The Quiche Mayas of Utatlán.* Civilization of the American Indian Series. Norman, Oklahoma: University of Oklahoma Press.
1986   "Ethnohistory of the Guatemalan Colonial Indian." In *Ethnohistory*, Supplement 4 to *Handbook of Middle American Indians*, edited by Victoria Bricker and Ronald Spores. Austin: University of Texas Press.

Chavero, Alfredo
1979   *El lienzo de Tlaxcala.* Mexico: Editorial Cosmos. Orig. pub. 1892.

Childs, Carla P., and Patricia Greenfield
1980   "Informal Modes of Learning and Teaching: the Case of Zinacanteco Weaving." In *Studies in Cross-Cultural Psychology*, edited by Neil Warren, vol. 2. London: Academic Press.

Christian, William A., Jr.
1981   *Local Religion in Sixteenth Century Spain.* Princeton University Press.

Cline, Howard F.
1972   "Ethnohistorical Regions of Middle America." In *Handbook of Middle American Indians,* vol. 12, edited by R. Wauchope. Austin: University of Texas Press.

Coggins, Clemency
1985   "Maya Iconography." In *Maya Treasures of an Ancient Civilization,* edited by Flora S. Clancy et al. New York: Harry S. Abrams, in association with the Albuquerque Museum.

Coggins, Clemency, and O.C. Shane, 3rd, editors
1984   *Cenote of Sacrifice.* Austin: University of Texas Press.

Conte, Christine
1984   *Maya Culture and Costume.* The Taylor Museum of the Colorado Springs Fine Arts Center.

Cordóva, Fray Matías de
1932   "Utilidades de que todos los Indios y Ladinos se vistan y calcen a la Española, y medios de conseguirlo sin violencia, coacción ni mandato." In *Un fraile procer y una fabula poema,* by Flavio Guillen. Guatemala City: Tipografia Nacional. Orig. pub. 1798.

Cordry, Donald, and Dorothy Cordry
1968   *Mexican Indian Costumes.* The Texas Pan American Series. Austin: University of Texas Press.

Cruz Cano y Olmedillo, Juan de la
1823   *Delineations of the Most Remarkable Costumes of the Different Provinces of Spain.* London: H. Stokes.

Delgado, Hilda [see also Pang]
1963   *Aboriginal Guatemalan Handweaving and Costume.* Ph.D. dissertation, Indiana University. University Microfilms Inc., Ann Arbor, Michigan.

Deuss, Krystyna
1981   *Indian Costumes from Guatemala.* No place given. K. Deuss.

De Vries, Ad
1984   *A Dictionary of Symbols and Imagery.* New York: Elsevier Science Publishing, Inc.

Diaz del Castillo, Bernal
1927   *The True History of the Conquest of Mexico.* Translated by Maurice Keatinge, Esq. New York. (Also 1957, translated and edited by Albert Idell, New York: Doubleday.) Orig. pub. 1568.

Dieseldorff, Dr. Herbert Quirín
1984   *X Balam Q'ué, El Pájaro Sol: El traje regional de Cobán.* Guatemala: Museo Ixchel.

Early, John D.
1983   "A Demographic Survey of Contemporary Guatemalan Maya." In *Heritage of Conquest; Thirty Years Later,* edited by Carl Kendall, John Hawkins, Laurel Bossen. Albuquerque: University of New Mexico Press.

Ekholm, Susanna M.
1979   "The Lagartero Figurines." In *Maya Archaeology and Ethnohistory: Cambridge Symposium on Recent Research in Mesoamerican Archaeology,* edited by Norman Hammond and Gordon R. Willey. Austin: University of Texas Press.

Eliade, Mircea
1959   *The Sacred and the Profane: The Nature of Religion.* Harvest Books. New York: Harcourt Brace and World, Inc.

Farriss, Nancy
1984   *Maya Society under Colonial Rule.* Princeton: Princeton University Press.

Fisher, Abby Sue
1983   *European Influences on Clothing Traditions in Highland Guatemala.* Unpublished MA Thesis, Cal. State Univ. Chico.

Foster, George F.
1953   "Cofradía and compadrazgo in Spain and Spanish America" *Southwestern Journal of Anthropology* 9 (1). New Mexico.
1960   *Culture and Conquest.* Viking Fund Publications in Anthropology, 27. New York: Wenner-Gren Foundation for Anthropological Research. Chicago: Quadrangle Books.

Fox, John W.
1978   *Quiché Conquest.* Albuquerque: University of New Mexico Press.

Fuente, Julio de la
1967   "Ethnic Relationships." In *Handbook of Middle American Indians,* vol. 6, edited by Manning Nash. Austin, Texas.

Fuentes y Guzmán, D. Francisco Antonio de
1932   "Recordación Florida." In *Biblioteca "Goathemala,"* vol. 6. Guatemala: Guatemala Sociedad de Geografía e Historia.

Gage, Thomas
1969   *Travels in the New World,* edited by J. Eric S. Thompson. University of Oklahoma, Norman. Orig. pub. 1648.

Gall, Francis
1976-83   *Diccionario Geográfico de Guatemala.* 4 vols. Guatemala, C.A.: Instituto Geográfico Nacional.

Gayton, A. H.
1967   "Textiles and Costumes." In *Handbook of Middle American Indians,* vol. 6, edited by Robert Wauchope. Austin: University of Texas Press.

Gibson, Charles
1964   *The Aztecs under Spanish Rule: A History of the Indians of the Valley of Mexico, 1519-1810.* Stanford: Stanford University Press.
1967   *Tlaxcalla in the Sixteenth Century.* Stanford: Stanford University Press. Orig. pub. 1952.

Gillin, John P.
1957   *The Culture of Security in San Carlos.* Middle American Research Institute Publication No. 16. New Orleans: Tulane University.

Glassman, Paul
1978   *Guatemala Guide.* Moscow, Vermont & Dallas: Passport Press.

Gómez de Cervantes, Gonzalo
1944   *La vida economica y social de Nueva España al finalizar del siglo XVI.* Mexico. Orig. pub. 1599.

Gómez-Tabanera, J.M.
1950   *Trajes populares y costumbres tradicionales.* Madrid: Editorial Tesoro.

Greenfield, Patricia, and Jean Lave
1982   "Cognitive Aspects of Informal Education. " In *Cultural Perspectives on Child Development,* edited by Daniel A. Wagner. San Francisco: W.H. Freeman.

Hagan, Alfred J.
1972   "An Analysis of the Hand Weaving Sector of the Guatemalan Economy." Ph.D. dissertation, University of Texas at Austin. University Microfilm 72-2342.

Holleran, Mary P.
1949   *Church and State in Guatemala.* Columbia University Studies in the Social Sciences, no. 549. New York: Columbia University Press.

Hoyos Sancho, Nieves de

1954   *El traje regional en España.* Temas españolas, 123. Madrid: Publicaciones Españolas.

Johnson, Irmgard

1959   "Hilado y Tejido." In *Esplendor de México Antiguo,* edited by Raúl Noriega et al. 2 vols. Mexico.

Kaufman, Terrence

1976   *Proyecto de alfabetos y ortografías para escribir las lenguas mayances.* Antigua: Editorial José de Piñeda Ibarra. Orig. pub. 1970.

King, Arden R.

1974   *Cobán and the Verapaz.* Middle American Research Series, No. 37. New Orleans: Tulane University.

La Farge, Oliver

1947   *Santa Eulalia.* Chicago: University of Chicago Press.

1962   "Maya Ethnology: the Sequence of Cultures." In *The Maya and Their Neighbors.* New York: D. Appleton-Century Co. Orig. pub. 1940.

La Farge, Oliver, and Douglas Byers

1931   *The Year Bearer's People.* Middle American Research Institute, no. 3. New Orleans: Tulane University.

Lincoln, Jackson S.

1945   *An Ethnological Study of the Ixil Indians.* University of Chicago Microfilm Collection of Mss. on Middle American Cultural Anthropology, no. 1. Chicago.

Lovell, W. George

1985   *Conquest and Survival in Colonial Guatemala: A Historical Geography of the Cuchumatán Highlands, 1500-1821.* Kingston: McGill, Queen's University Press.

Luján Muñoz, Luis

1978   "La indumentaria indigena de Guatemala segun las fuentes historicas del siglo XVII." In *Anales de la Sociedad de Geografía e Historia de Guatemala,* Tomo 51.

MacLeod, Murdo J.

1973   *Spanish Central America: a Socioeconomic History, 1520-1720.* California Library Reprint Series. Berkeley: University of California Press.

1983a   "Ethnic Relations and Indian Society in the Province of Guatemala, ca.1620-ca.1800." In *Spaniards and Indians in Southeastern Mesoamerica,* edited by Murdo J. MacLeod and Robert Wasserstrom. Latin American Studies Series. Lincoln: University of Nebraska Press.

1983b   "Papel Social y Económica de las Cofradías Indigenas de la Colonia en Chiapas." *Mesoamérica,* 5. Antigua.

Madsen, William

1967   "Religious Syncretism." In *Handbook of Middle American Indians,* vol. 6, edited by Robert Wauchope. Austin: University of Texas Press.

Maler, Teobert

1901   "Researches in the Central Portion of the Usumatsintla Valley." In *Memoirs of the Peabody Museum of American Archaeology and Ethnology,* vol. 2, no. 1.

Maudslay, Anne Cary and A.P. Maudslay

1899   *A Glimpse at Guatemala.* London: J. Murray.

Mayén de Castellanos, Guisela

1986   *Tzute y jerarquía en Sololá.* Guatemala: Museo Ixchel.

Maynard, Eileen Anne

1963   "The Women of Palín: a Comparative Study of Indian and Ladino women in a Guatemalan village." Ph.D. dissertation, Cornell University, New York. University Microfilms Inc. Ann Arbor, Michigan.

McBryde, Felix Webster

1934   *Sololá: a Guatemalan Town and Cakchiquel Market Center.* Middle American Research Institute, no. 5. New Orleans: Tulane University.

1947   "Cultural and Historical Geography of Southwest Guatemala." Smithsonian Institution Institute of Social Anthropology Publication no. 4. Washington, D.C.: Smithsonian Institution.

Mejía de Rodas, Idalma, Rosario M. de Polanco, and Linda Asturias de Barrios

1987   *Cambio en Colotenango.* Guatemala: Museo Ixchel.

Morris, Walter F., Jr.

1984   *A Millenium of Weaving in Chiapas: An Introduction to the Pellizzi Collection of Chiapas Textiles.* Privately published.

Ms.   "Fall Fashions: Lagartero Figurine Costume at the end of the Classic Period." Paper presented at 5th Palenque Round Table in 1982. Later published in Austin: University of Texas Press, 1985.

1987   *The Living Maya.* New York: Harry M. Abrams, Inc.

Nash, Manning

1958   *Machine Age Maya.* Memoirs of the American Anthropological Association, no. 87. Menasha, Wisconsin.

O'Neale, Lila M.

1945   *Textiles of Highland Guatemala.* Carnegie Institution of Washington, no. 567. Washington, D.C.

Orellana, Sandra

1984   *The Tzutujil Maya: Continuity and change, 1250-1630.* The Civilization of the American Indian Series, vol. 162. Norman: University of Oklahoma Press.

Osborne, Lilly de Jongh

1935   *Textiles of Guatemala..* Middle American Research Series, no. 6. New Orleans: Tulane University.

1975   *Indian Crafts of Guatemala and El Salvador.* Norman: University of Oklahoma Press. Orig. pub. 1965.

Pancake, Cherri

1976   *The Costumes of Rural Guatemala.* Museo Ixchel de Textiles, Guatemala.

1977   "Textile Traditions of the Highland Maya: Some Aspects of Development and Change." Paper delivered at International Symposium on Maya Art. Guatemala City, Guatemala.

Pang, Hilda Delgado (see also Delgado)

1969   "Figurines of Backstrap Loom Weavers from the Maya Area." In *Verhandlungen des XXXVIII Internationalen Amerikanistenkongresses* 1968, band 1.

1977   "Similarities Between Certain Early Spanish, Contemporary Spanish Folk, and Mesoamerican Indian Textile Design Motifs." In *Ethnographic Textiles of the Western Hemisphere: Irene Emery Roundtable on Museum Textiles 1976 Proceedings.* Washington, D.C.: The Textile Museum.

Paul, Lois

1974   "The Mastery of Work and the Mystery of Sex in a Guatemalan Village." In *Woman, Culture, and Society,* edited by M.Z. Rosaldo and Louise Lamphere. Stanford: Stanford University Press.

Prechtel, Martin, and Robert S. Carlsen

1988   "Weaving and the Cosmos Amongst the Tzutujil Maya of Guatemala." *Res,* 15, Spring 1988. Peabody Museum, Harvard.

Reina, Ruben E.

1966   *The Law of the Saints: A Pokomam Pueblo and Its Community Culture.* Indianapolis and New York: Bobbs-Merrill Co.

Remesal, Fray

1932   *Historia General, Chiapa y Guatemala,* vol. 2 of 5 vols. Guatemala.

Ribeiro, Aileen
1983 "The Eighteenth Century," vol. 3 of *A Visual History of Costume.* London: B.T. Batsford; New York: Drama Book Publishers.

Robinson, Natalie V.
1987 "Mantones de Manila — Their Role in China's Silk Trade." *Arts of Asia* (Jan-Feb).

Rodas N., Flavio, Ovidio Rodas Corzo, and F. Hawkins
1940 *Chichicastenango, the Kiché Indians.* Guatemala

Rowe, Ann Pollard
1981 *A Century of Change in Guatemalan Textiles.* New York: The Center for Inter-American Relations. Distributed by the University of Washington Press, Seattle.

Sahagún, Fray Bernardo de
1950-69 *The Florentine Codex: General History of the Things of New Spain,* translated by Arthur J.O. Anderson, and Charles Dibble. Monographs of the School of American Research. Santa Fe: School of American Research; Salt Lake City: University of Utah. 12 vols.

Schele, Linda, and Mary Ellen Miller
1986 *The Blood of Kings: Dynasty and Ritual in Maya Art.* Fort Worth, Texas: Kimbell Art Museum.

Siegel, Morris
1941 "Religion in Western Guatemala: A Product of Acculturation." In *American Anthropologist* NS, 43. Washington, D.C.: American Anthropological Association.

Simpson, Lesley Bird
1960 *The Laws of Burgos of 1512-1513.* San Francisco: J. Howell.

Snowden, James
1979 *The Folk Dress of Europe.* New York: Mayflower Books.

Sperlich, Norbert, and Elizabeth Katz Sperlich
1980 *Guatemalan Backstrap Weaving.* Norman: University of Oklahoma Press.

Start, Laura E.
1980 *The McDougall Collection of Indian Textiles from Guatemala and Mexico.* Pitt Rivers Museum. Oxford: Oxford University Press. Orig. pub. 1948.

Stephens, John L.
1842 *Incidents of Travel in Central America, Chiapas and Yucatán.* London.

Stoll, Dr. Otto
1886 *Guatemala, Reisen und Schilderungen aus den jahren 1878-1883,1886.* Leipzig: F. A. Brockhaus.
1889 *Die Ethnologie des Indiannstämme von Guatemala.* Leiden: P.W.M. Trap; New York: E. Stieger & Co.

Tax, Sol
1947 *Notes on Santo Tomás Chichicastenango.* Microfilm Collection of Mss. on Middle American Cultural Anthropology, no. 16. Chicago: University of Chicago Library.
1953 *Penny Capitalism: a Guatemalan Indian economy.* Institute of Social Anthropology Publication No. 16. Washington, D.C.: Smithsonian Institution.

Tax, Sol, and Robert Hinshaw
1969 "The Maya of the Midwestern Highlands." In *Handbook of Middle American Indians: Ethnology,* part 1, vol. 7, edited by Evon Z. Vogt. Austin: University of Texas Press.

Tedlock, Barbara
1985 *Time and the Highland Maya.* Albuquerque: University of New Mexico Press. Orig pub. 1982.

Tedlock, Barbara, and Dennis Tedlock
1985 "Text and Textile: Language and Technology in the Arts of the Quiche Maya," *Journal of Anthropological Research,* 41 (2).

Tempsky, Gustav von
1858 *Mitla: A Narrative of Incidents and Personal Adventures on a Journey to Mexico.* London.

Terga, Rev. Padre Ricardo, and Emilio Vásquez Robles
1977 "Tactic: El Corazón del Mundo." *Guatemala Indigena,* 12 (3-4).

Thompson, J. Eric S.
1966 *The Rise and Fall of Maya Civilization.* Norman: University of Oklahoma Press. Orig. pub. 1954.
1972 *Maya History and Religion.* Norman: University of Oklahoma. Orig. pub. 1970.

Torre Revello, José
1943 "Merchandise brought to America by the Spaniards (1534-1586)." *The Hispanic American Historical Review,* 23 (4). Durham, N.C.: Duke University Press.

Turok, Marta
1974 *Symbolic Analysis of Contemporay Mayan Textiles.* BA Thesis, Tufts University, Boston.

Valladares, León A.
1957 *El hombre y el maiz: etnografía y etnopsicología de Colotenango.* Mexico.

Veblen, T.T.
1977 "Native Population Decline in Totonicapán, Guatemala." In *Annals of the Association of American Geographers,* vol. 67, no. 4.

Violant y Simorra, Ramón
1949 *El Pirineo, Espanol: vida, usos, costumbres, creencias y tradiciones de une cultura milenaria que desaparece.* Madrid: Editorial Plus-Ultra.

Wagley, Charles
1941 *Economics of a Guatemalan village. Memoirs of the American Anthropological Association,* no. 58. Supplement to the American Anthropologist, vol. 43, Part 3. Menasha, Wisconsin: American Anthropological Association.
1949 *The Social and Religious Life of a Guatemalan Village. Memoirs of the American Anthropological Association,* no. 71. Menasha, Wisconsin: American Anthopological Association.

Warren, Kay B.
1978 *The Symbolism of Subordination: Indian Identity in a Guatemalan Town.* Texas Pan American Series. Austin: University of Texas Press.

Watanabe, John M.
1981 "Cambios económicos en Santiago Chimaltenango, Guatemala." *Mesoamérica,* 2 (June 1981). Antigua, Guatemala.

Wilhite, Rita M.
1977 *First Language Acquisition: Textile Design Terminology in Cakchiquel/Maya.* Ph.D. dissertation, Washington University, St. Louis, Mo. University Microfilm 77-21,043.

Wood, Josephine, and Lilly de Jongh Osborne
1966 *Indian Costumes of Guatemala.* Graz, Austria: Akademische Druck-u Verlagsanstalt.

Object Information and Illustration Sources

Page 1. Photograph, Whitman Archive, 1960s.
Pages 2-3. Photograph, Whitman Archive, 1960s.
Page 3. Huipil, Patzún, X75-780a. Gift of Caroline and Howard West.
1. Photograph, Susan Masuoka, 1978.
2. Photograph, Whitman Archive, 1960s.
3. Photograph, Laurie Levin, 1970s.
4. Instituto Nacional de Antropología e Historia, Mexico City.
5. Photograph, Copyright © Justin Kerr, 1985.
6. Drawing, Wes Christensen.
7. Photograph, Copyright © Justin Kerr, 1980.
8. Drawing, Wes Christensen.
9. Photograph, Copyright © Justin Kerr, 1976.
10. Colleción Museo Nacional de Arqueología y Etnología de Guatemala. Photograph, Sr. Rodolfo Rodriguez.
11. Photograph, Whitman Archive, 1960s.
12. Collection of Caroline & Howard West. Photograph, Richard Todd.
13. Collection of Caroline & Howard West. Photograph, Richard Todd.
14. Instituto Amatller de Arte Hispanico, Barcelona, Foto 18646. Courtesy of Richard Dunlap.
15. Drawing from Sahagún 1969, vol. 6, p. 201.
16. Photograph, Copyright © Rosalind Solomon, 1986.
17. Photgraph courtesy of National Museum of the American Indian. Smithsonian Institution, Neg. no. 38440.
18. Photograph, Whitman Archive, 1960s.
19. Photograph, Whitman Archive, 1960s.
20. Photograph, Laurie Levin, 1970s.
21. Drawing, Linda Schele.
22. Photograph, Laurie Levin, 1970s.
23. Photograph, Whitman Archive, 1960s.
24. Photograph, Whitman Archive, 1960s.
25. Photograph, Susan Turner, 1980.
26. Sandals, X80-969a/b. Anonymous Gift.
27. Photograph, Susan Turner, 1979.
28. From Gómez de Cervantes 1599, folio V. Photograph courtesy of the Trustees of the British Museum.
29. Drawing from Fuentes y Guzmán 1932, vol. 3, p. 393.
30. Photograph, Whitman Archive, 1960s.
31. Instituto Amatller de Arte Hispanico, Barcelona, Foto 19066. Courtesy of Richard Dunlap.
32. Costume incl bag, Chichicastenango X64-956a-f. Museum Purchase.
32. Jacket, Nebaj, X76-89. Museum Purchase.
32. Cotón, Soloma. X78-1677. Museum Purchase.
33. Saco, X79-198b. Gift of Michelle Jacobson-Ram.
34. Drawing, Shirley Hulsey.
35. Photograph. Laurie Levin, 1970s.
36. Drawing, Shirley Hulsey.
37. Bag, Nahualá, X76-1219. Gift of Caroline and Howard West. Photograph, Andrew West.
37. Bag, Sololá, X76-1217. Gift of Caroline and Howard West. Photograph, Andrew West.
38. Photograph, Laurie Levin, 1970s.
39. Drawing, Shirley Hulsey.
40. Drawing, Shirley Hulsey.
41. Photograph courtesy of the Trustees of the British Museum.
42. Photograph from Arco 1923, p. 52.
43. Photograph from Alfonso X el Sabio 1979 (facsimile edition).
44. Photograph from Alfonso X el Sabio 1979 (facsimile edition).
45. Photograph, Whitman Archive, 1960s.
46. Instituto Amatller de Arte Hispanico, Barcelona, Foto 19069. Courtesy of Richard Dunlap.
47. Photograph, Laurie Levin, 1970s.
48. Illustration from Cruz Cano y Olmedillo 1823.
49. Photograph, Whitman Archive, 1960s.
50. Drawing, Shirley Hulsey.
51. Huipil, San Lucas Tolimán, X76-1158. Photograph, Andrew West.
52. Pants, Santa Catarina Palopó, X80-944. Photograph, Andrew West.
53. Huipil, Palín, X78-780. Gift of Gordon L. Smith.
54. Photograph, Susan Turner, 1977.
55. Drawing, Shirley Hulsey.
56. Drawing, Shirley Hulsey.
57. Drawing, Shirley Hulsey.
58. Drawing, Shirley Hulsey.
59. Huipil, Jacaltenango, X86-1236. Gift of Caroline and Howard West.
60. Huipil, Soloma, X78-1674. Museum Purchase.
61. Huipil, Magdalena Milpas Altas, X75-785b. Gift of Caroline and Howard West.
62. Huipil, Joyabaj, X76-1196. Gift of Caroline and Howard West.
63. Huipil, Patzicía, X76-866. Gift of Caroline and Howard West.
64. Huipil, Tecpán, X77-1201. Gift of Caroline and Howard West.
65. Huipil, Olintepeque, X76-1232. Gift of Caroline and Howard West.
66. Huipil, San Pedro Sacatepéquez. 74-1468. Gift of Dr. & Mrs. Aaron Nisenson.
67. Huipil, San Miguel Chicaj. 80-942. Gift of Caroline and Howard West.
68. Huipil, Santa María de Jesús. 75-793. Gift of Caroline and Howard West.
69. Huipil, Totonicapán. 80-937. Gift of Caroline and Howard West.
70. Huipil, San Gaspar Ixchel. 80-987. Anonymous Gift.
71. Drawing from Codex Lienzo de Tlaxcala, 1892.
72. Drawing, Shirley Hulsey.
73. Drawing, Shirley Hulsey.
74. Drawing, Shirley Hulsey.
75. Drawing, Shirley Hulsey.
76. Drawing, Shirley Hulsey.
77. Corte, Patzicía, X80-924. Gift of Caroline and Howard West.
78. Corte, San Juan Sacatepéquez, X75-784b. Gift of Caroline and Howard West.
79. Corte, Soloma, X83-188. Gift of Caroline and Howard West.
80. Corte, San Pedro Sacatepéquez X76-1137. Gift of Caroline and Howard West.
81. Corte, San Rafael Petzal, X91-565. Gift of Caroline and Howard West.
82. Corte, San José Nacahuil, X80-955. Gift of Caroline and Howard West.
83. Corte, San Miguel Chicaj, X84-1135. Gift of Caroline and Howard West.
84. Corte, Zunil, X84-1133. Gift of Dorthy M. Cordry in memory of Donald B. Cordry.
85. Corte, San Andrés Xecul, X83-189. Gift of Caroline and Howard West.
86. Photograph, Susan Masuoka, 1978.
87. Corte, Sacapulas, X84-1129. Gift of Caroline and Howard West.
88. Corte, San Cristóbal Totonicapán, X83-55. Gift of Caroline and Howard West.
89. Photograph, Susan Masuoka, 1978.
90. Ikat cloth, Eastern Thailand or Laos. Lent by Caroline and Howard West.
91. Ikat cloth, Totonicapán, X84-1136. Gift of Caroline and Howard West.
92. Corte, Salcajá, X84-1142. Gift of Caroline and Howard West.
93. Tzute, Zunil, X76-1241. Gift of Caroline and Howard West.
94. Tzute, Panajachel, X75-39e. Museum Purchase.
95. Perraje, Alta Verapaz, X76-858. Museum Purchase.
96. Photograph, Whitman Archive, 1960s.
97. Perraje, Santiago Atitlán, X75-786d. Gift of Caroline and Howard West.
98. Perraje, Santiago Atitlán, X77-1150. Gift of Caroline and Howard West.
99a. Faja, San Antonio Aguas Calientes. 64-954d. Museum Purchase.
99b. Faja, Tecpán, X81-307. Gift of Caroline and Howard West.
99c. Faja, San Marcos la Laguna, X80-1094. Gift of Mary Price
99d. Faja, Chajul, 84-1152. Gift of Caroline and Howard West.
99e. Faja, Santa María de Jesús, X75-794. Gift of Caroline and Howard West.
99f. Faja, Sololá, X75-777d. Gift of Caroline and Howard West.
99g. Faja, Comalapa, X76-1178b. Gift of Caroline and Howard West.
99h. Faja, Palín, X76-1171. Gift of Caroline and Howard West.
100a. Faja, Chuarrancho, X76-1190. Gift of Caroline and Howard West.
100b. Faja, San Pedro Sacatepéquez, X76-1188. Gift of Caroline and Howard West.
100c. Faja, Chichicastenango, X76-1201b. Gift of Caroline and Howard West.
101. Faja, Santiago Sacatepéquez, X76-827. Museum Purchase.
102a. Faja, Todos Santos, X75-781c. Gift of Caroline and Howard West.
102b. Faja, Almolonga, X80-949. Gift of Caroline and Howard West.
102c. Faja, Aguacatán, X84-1177. Gift of Caroline and Howard West.
102d. Faja, San Juan Ostuncalco, X76-1235. Gift of Caroline and Howard West.
103a. Faja, Totonicapán, X84-1162. Gift of Caroline and Howard West.
103b. Faja, San Francisco el Alto, X77-1141. Gift of Caroline and Howard West.
103c. Faja, Santa Lucía Utatlán, X84-1158. Gift of Caroline and Howard West.
103d. Faja, Quezaltenango, X84-1177. Gift of Caroline and Howard West.
103e. Faja, Salcajá, X77-1212. Gift of Caroline and Howard West.
103f. Faja, San Antonio Aguas Calientes, X77-849. Gift of Mr. Leonard G. Field
104. Photograph, Susan Turner, 1976.
105a. Cinta, Chajul, X76-1204. Gift of Caroline and Howard West.
105b. Cinta, Aguacatán, X75-806. Gift of Caroline and Howard West.
105c. Cinta, Rabinal, X76-842. Museum Purchase.
105d. Cinta, San Juan Ostuncalco, X76-1234. Gift of Caroline and Howard West.
106. Cinta, Totonicapán, X66-3277. Gift of Vilma Matchette.
107. Tupui, Cobán, X64-955c. Gift of Don E. Willever.
108. Cinta, Santa María Chiquimula, X76-1191. Gift of Caroline and Howard West.
109a. Ribbon, China, X84-1155. Gift of Caroline and Howard West.
109b. Cinta, Jacaltenango, X84-1161. Gift of Caroline and Howard West.
109c. Cinta, San Martín Sacatepéquez, X84-1166. Gift of Caroline and Howard West.
110a. Textile, San Juan Sacatepéquez. Lent by Caroline and Howard West.
110b. Textile, San Juan Sacatepéquez. Lent by Caroline and Howard West.
110c. Textile, San Juan Sacatepéquez. Lent by Caroline and Howard West.
110d. Textile, San Juan Sacatepéquez. Lent by Caroline and Howard West.
110e. Textile, San Juan Sacatepéquez. Lent by Caroline and Howard West.
110f. Textile, San Juan Sacatepéquez. Lent by Caroline and Howard West.
111. Huipil, San Pedro Sacatepéquez, X91-561. Gift of Caroline and Howard West.
112. Huipil, Ixtahuacán, X77-1163. Gift of Caroline and Howard West.
113. Huipil, Sololá, X83-43. Gift of Caroline and Howard West. Photograph, Andrew West.
114. Huipil, Sololá, X77-1156. Gift of Caroline and Howard West. Photograph, Andrew West.
115. Huipil, Todos Santos, X83-416. Gift of Thomas K. Curtis; Todd P. Curtis; Caroline C. Bramhall; Sandra G. Lovell and S. Premena in memory of Caroline P. Greene. Photograph, Andrew West.
116. Huipil, Todos Santos, X91-568. Gift of Caroline and Howard West. Photograph, Andrew West.
117. Huipil, Santiago Atitlán, X76-92. Museum Purchase. Photograph, Andrew West.
118. Huipil, Santiago Atitlán, X75-786a. Gift of Caroline and Howard West. Photograph, Andrew West.

119. Huipil, Santiago Atitlán, X77-1148. Gift of Caroline and Howard West. Photograph, Andrew West.
120. Huipil, Todos Santos, X75-781a. Gift of Caroline and Howard West. Photograph, Andrew West.
121. Huipil, Mixco, X84-1124. Gift of Caroline and Howard West.
122. Huipil, Totonicapán, X76-1221. Gift of Caroline and Howard West.
123. Tzute, San Antonio Aguas Calientes, X83-421. Gift of Thomas K. Curtis; Todd P. Curtis; Caroline C. Bramhall; Sandra G. Lovell and S. Premena in memory of Caroline P. Greene.
124. Faja, Sololá, X75-777d. Gift of Caroline and Howard West.
125. Huipil, Santo Domingo Xenacoj. 76-826. Museum Purchase.
126. Huipil, Zacualpa, X75-813. Gift of Caroline and Howard West.
127. Pantalones, Santa Catarina Palopó, X75-1459. Gift of Caroline and Howard West.
128. Huipil, San Andrés Xecul, X76-870. Museum Purchase.
129. Huipil, Santa María Chiquimula, X80-950. Gift of Caroline and Howard West.
130. Huipil, Sumpango, X75-779a. Gift of Caroline and Howard West.
131. Huipil, Santa Barbara, X75-803. Gift of Caroline and Howard West.
132. Huipil, San Mateo Ixtatán, X75-801. Gift of Caroline and Howard West.
133. Huipil, Santiago Atitlán, X77-1148. Gift of Caroline and Howard West.
134. Huipil, Sololá. Lent by Caroline and Howard West.
135. Huipil, Nebaj. Lent by Caroline and Howard West.
136. Huipil, San Juan Cotzal. Lent by Caroline and Howard West.
137. Huipil, San Sebastian Huehuetenango, X80-977b. Anonymous Gift.
138. Corte, San Pedro Sacatepéquez, X83-36. Gift of Caroline and Howard West.
139. Huipil, San Francisco el Alto, X80-929. Gift of Caroline and Howard West.
140. Collar, Quezaltenango, X84-1169. Gift of Caroline and Howard West.
141. Huipil, San Martín Sacatepéquez, X76-1139. Gift of Caroline and Howard West.
142. Huipil, Santa Catarina Pasac, X76-534a. Museum Purchase.
143. Huipil, Santa María de Jesús, X75-792. Gift of Caroline and Howard West.
144. Fabric, Salcajá, X76-1222. Gift of Caroline and Howard West.
145. Huipil, San Andrés Semetabaj, X84-1127. Gift of Caroline and Howard West.
146. Morral, Colotenango, X80-1037. Anonymous Gift.
147. Drawing, Shirley Hulsey.
148. Trade huipil strip, Totonicapán. Lent by Caroline and Howard West.
149. Huipil, San Jose Nacahuil, X83-46. Gift of Caroline and Howard West.
150. Tzute, Chimaltenango, X83-61. Gift of Caroline and Howard West.
151. Pantalones, Chichicastenango, X64-956b. Museum Purchase.
152. Pantalones, Santiago Atitlán, X69-951. Gift of Mr. Richard Oaks.
153. Pantalones, Santiago Atitlán, X87-1149. Gift of Caroline and Howard West.
154. Huipil, Nebaj, X75-782. Gift of Caroline and Howard West.
155. Tzute, Santa María de Jesús, X75-792. Gift of Caroline and Howard West.
156. Paya, Patzún. Lent by Caroline and Howard West.
157. Tzute, Palín, X91-557. Gift of Caroline and Howard West.
158. Banda. Nahualá. Lent by Caroline and Howard West.
159. Textile, Quezaltenango, X78-497. Gift of Bette S. Chase.
160. Huipil, San Pedro Sacatepéquez, X76-1187. Gift of Caroline and Howard West.
161. Banda. San Juan Ostuncalco, X91-559. Gift of Caroline and Howard West.
162. Huipil, San Juan Cotzal, X76-1206. Gift of Caroline and Howard West.
163. Perraje. Chajul, X76-104. Museum Purchase.
163. Cinta, Chajul, X76-1204. Gift of Caroline and Howard West.
163. Huipil, Chajul, X76-91. Museum Purchase.
163. Faja, Chajul, X86-1228. Gift of Caroline and Howard West.
163. Corte, Chajul, X83-188. Gift of Caroline and Howard West.
163. Cinta, Nebaj, X86-1245. Gift of Caroline and Howard West.
163. Huipil, Nebaj, X75-782. Gift of Caroline and Howard West.
163. Faja, Nebaj, X76-1208. Gift of Caroline and Howard West.
163. Corte, Nebaj, X76-1207. Gift of Caroline and Howard West.
163. Perraje. Nebaj, X76-1211. Gift of Caroline and Howard West.
163. Huipil, San Juan Cotzal, X76-1206. Gift of Caroline and Howard West.
163. Faja, San Juan Cotzal, X76-838b. Museum Purchase.
163. Corte, San Juan Cotzal, X83-37. Gift of Caroline and Howard West.
163. Perraje, San Juan Cotzal, X76-1205. Gift of Caroline and Howard West.
164. Photograph, Susan Turner, 1975.
165. Huipil, Sacapulas, X81-308. Gift of Caroline and Howard West. Photograph, Andrew West.
166. Photograph, John Blanton, 1975.
167. Camisa, San Martín Sacatepéquez, X75-13a. Gift of Dr. and Mrs. Peter Furst.
167. Banda, San Martín Sacatepéquez, X86-1234. Gift of Caroline and Howard West.
167. Pantalones, San Martín Sacatepéquez, X75-13b. Gift of Dr. and Mrs. Peter Furst.
167. Camisa, San Martín Sacatepéquez, X83-222a. Gift of Frieda Whitman Ellsworth.
167. Banda, San Martín Sacatepéquez, X83-222c. Gift of Frieda Whitman Ellsworth.
167. Pantalones, San Martín Sacatepéquez, X83-222b. Gift of Frieda Whitman Ellsworth.
167. Cinta, San Martín Sacatepéquez, X84-1166. Gift of Caroline and Howard West.
167. Huipil, San Martín Sacatepéquez, X76-1139. Gift of Caroline and Howard West.
167. Faja, San Martín Sacatepéquez, X83-79. Gift of Caroline and Howard West.
167. Corte, San Martín Sacatepéquez, X83-25. Gift of Caroline and Howard West.
167. Cinta, Concepción Chiquirichapa, X84-1165. Gift of Caroline and Howard West.
167. Huipil, Concepción Chiquirichapa, X76-1238. Gift of Caroline and Howard West.
167. Corte, Concepción Chiquirichapa, X83-26. Gift of Caroline and Howard West.
167. Faja, Concepción Chiquirichapa, X83-80. Gift of Caroline and Howard West.
168. Perraje, San Martín Sacatepéquez. Lent by Caroline and Howard West.
169. Camisa, San Martin Sacatepéquez. Lent by Caroline and Howard West.
170. Huipil, Palín, X78-780. Gift of Gordon L. Smith.
170. Tzute, Palín, X76-1172. Gift of Caroline and Howard West.

170. Faja, Palín, X76-1171. Gift of Caroline and Howard West.
170. Corte, Palín, X80-925. Gift of Caroline and Howard West.
170. Tzute, Palín, X66-1136. Gift of Dr. & Mrs. Ralph Beals.
171. Photograph, Susan Turner, 1980.
172. Photograph, Dan Clement, 1970s.
173. Hair Wrap, Tamahú, X91-567. Gift of Caroline and Howard West.
173. Huipil, Tamahú, X74-1480. Gift of Dr. and Mrs. Aaron Nisenson.
173. Corte, Tamahú, X84-176. Anonymous Gift.
173. Huipil, Tactic, X76-1145. Gift of Caroline and Howard West.
173. Huipil, Tactic, X76-854. Museum Purchase.
173. Chachal, Tactic, X76-1164. Gift of Caroline and Howard West.
173. Corte, Tactic, X84-177. Anonymous Gift.
174. Huipil, Tactic, X76-1145. Gift of Caroline and Howard West.
175. Huipil, San Pedro Carchá, X76-1146. Gift of Caroline and Howard West.
175. Corte, San Pedro Carchá, X76-1470. Museum Purchase.
175. Huipil, San Pedro Carchá, X80-191. Gift of Gordon Frost.
175. Huipil, Cobán, X64-955a. Museum Purchase.
175. Corte, Cobán, X64-955b. Museum Purchase.
175. Tupui, Cobán, X64-955c. Museum Purchase.
176. Huipil, Cobán, X64-955a. Museum Purchase.
177. Photograph, Polly Blank, 1949.
178. Photograph, Whitman Archive, 1960s.
179. Cinta, Santiago Atitlán, X75-786e. Gift of Caroline and Howard West.
179. Huipil, Santiago Atitlán, X77-1148. Gift of Caroline and Howard West.
179. Corte, Santiago Atitlán, X75-786b. Gift of Caroline and Howard West.
179. Perraje, Santiago Atitlán, X75-786d. Gift of Caroline and Howard West.
179. Camisa, Santiago Atitlán, X76-248. Museum Purchase.
179. Banda, Santiago Atitlán, X77-1152. Gift of Caroline and Howard West.
179. Pantalones, Santiago Atitlán. 77-1149. Gift of Caroline and Howard West.
180. Photograph, Whitman Archive, 1960s.
181. Cinta, Santiago Atitlán, X75-786b. Gift of Caroline and Howard West.
182. Photograph, Caroline West, 1980s.
183. Cinta, Zunil, X76-97c. Museum Purchase.
183. Huipil, Zunil, X76-97a. Museum Purchase.
183. Faja, Zunil, X76-1239. Gift of Caroline and Howard West.
183. Corte, Zunil, X76-1240. Gift of Caroline and Howard West.
183. Tzute, Zunil, X76-97d. Museum Purchase.
183. Cinta, Almolonga, X83-75. Gift of Caroline and Howard West.
183. Huipil, Almolonga, X75-61. Gift of Frieda Whitman Ellsworth.
183. Faja, Almolonga, X80-949. Gift of Caroline and Howard West.
183. Corte, Almolonga, X80-948. Gift of Caroline and Howard West.
184. Huipil strip, Almolonga, X83-48. Gift of Caroline and Howard West. Photograph, Andrew West.
185. Huipil, Almolonga, X75-61. Gift of Frieda Whitman Ellsworth.
186. Cinta, Zunil, X76-97c. Museum Purchase.
187. Tzute, Zacualpa, X76-90b. Museum Purchase.
187. Huipil, Zacualpa, X75-813. Gift of Caroline and Howard West.
187. Tzute, Zacualpa, X76-90d. Museum Purchase.
187. Faja, Zacualpa, X76-90c. Museum Purchase.
187. Corte, Zacualpa, X76-90a. Museum Purchase.
188. Tzute, Santa Clara la Laguna, X76-87c. Museum Purchase.
188. Huipil, Santa Clara la Laguna, X76-87a. Museum Purchase.
188. Faja, Santa Clara la Laguna, X76-87b. Museum Purchase.
188. Corte, Santa Clara la Laguna, X76-87d. Museum Purchase.
189. Photograph, Caroline West.
190. Sombrero, Comalapa, X80-1002. Gift of Patricia B. Altman
190. Saco, Comalapa, X86-1218a. Gift of Caroline and Howard West.
190. Camisa, Comalapa, X86-1218c. Gift of Caroline and Howard West.
190. Banda, Comalapa, X86-1218d. Gift of Caroline and Howard West.
190. Rodillera, Comalapa, X86-1218f. Gift of Caroline and Howard West.
190. Pantalones, Comalapa, X86-1218b. Gift of Caroline and Howard West.
191. Banda, Comalapa, X86-1218d. Gift of Caroline and Howard West.
192. Sobrehuipil, Tecpán. Lent by Caroline and Howard West.
192. Corte, Tecpán, X83-32. Gift of Caroline and Howard West.
192. Huipil, Santa Apolonia, X76-810. Anonymous Gift.
192. Faja, Santa Apolonia, X80-936. Gift of Caroline and Howard West.
192. Corte, Santa Apolonia, X83-30. Gift of Caroline and Howard West.
193. Huipil, Tecpán, X76-1157. Gift of Caroline and Howard West.
194. Underhuipil, Santa Apolonia, X76-873. Museum Purchase.
195. Huipil, San Antonio Aguas Calientes. X64-954a. Museum Purchase. Photograph, Andrew West.
196. Huipil, San Martín Jilotepeque, X83-197. Gift of Caroline and Howard West. Photograph, Andrew West.
197. Huipil, Tecpán. Lent by Sarah J. Kennington.
198. Huipil, San Martín Jilotepeque. Lent by Dr. Stacy Schaefer.
199. Photograph, Susan Turner, 1970s.
200. Photograph, Dan Clement, 1970s.
201. Sombrero, San Juan Atitlán, X86-1247. Gift of Caroline and Howard West.
201. Tzute, San Juan Atitlán, X80-1012. Anonymous Gift.
201. Camisa, San Juan Atitlán, X75-797. Gift of Caroline and Howard West.
201. Capixay. San Juan Atitlán, X80-1011. Anonymous Gift.
201. Banda, San Juan Atitlán, X75-800. Gift of Caroline and Howard West.
201. Pantalones, San Juan Atitlán, X80-957. Anonymous Gift.

201. Morral, San Juan Atitlán, X80-1014. Anonymous Gift.
201. Morral, San Juan Atitlán, X80-1016. Anonymous Gift.
201. Tzute, San Juan Atitlán, X76-871c. Museum Purchase.
201. Cinta, San Juan Atitlán, X80-975. Anonymous Gift.
201. Huipil, San Juan Atitlán, X75-796. Gift of Caroline and Howard West.
201. Sombrero, San Juan Atitlán, X86-1239. Gift of Caroline and Howard West.
201. Corte, San Juan Atitlán, X80-1013. Anonymous Gift.
201. Faja, San Juan Atitlán, X75-810. Gift of Caroline and Howard West.
202. Photograph, Susan Turner, 1970s.
203. Camisa, San Juan Atitlán, X75-797. Gift of Caroline and Howard West.
204. Tzute, San Juan Atitlán, X76-871c. Museum Purchase.
205. Sombrero, Todos Santos, X75-30a. Gift of Mrs. Eaton Ballard.
205. Camisa, Todos Santos, X77-1162a. Gift of Caroline and Howard West.
205. Banda, Todos Santos, X80-1039. Anonymous Gift.
205. Sobrepantalones, Todos Santos, X80-971. Anonymous Gift.
205. Pantalones, Todos Santos, X77-1162b. Gift of Caroline and Howard West.
205. Net Bag, Todos Santos, X77-1075. Gift of Caroline and Howard West.
205. Morral, Todos Santos, X80-963. Anonymous Gift.
205. Huipil, Todos Santos, X75-781a. Gift of Caroline and Howard West.
205. Faja, Todos Santos, X75-781c. Gift of Caroline and Howard West.
205. Corte, Todos Santos, X75-781b. Gift of Caroline and Howard West.
205. Baby's Wrap. Todos Santos, X80-1031. Anonymous Gift.
206. Cinta, San Pedro Necta, X80-1025. Anonymous Gift.
206. Huipil, San Pedro Necta, X75-804. Gift of Caroline and Howard West.
206. Faja, San Pedro Necta, X80-994. Anonymous Gift.
206. Corte, San Pedro Necta, X80-1001. Anonymous Gift.
206. Tzute, San Pedro Necta, X80-1026. Anonymous Gift.
206. Cinta, Santiago Chimaltenango, X89-723. Promised Gift of Susan N. Masuoka.
206. Camisa, Santiago Chimaltenango, X75-799. Gift of Caroline and Howard West.
206. Faja, Santiago Chimaltenango, X75-808. Gift of Caroline and Howard West.
206. Corte, Santiago Chimaltenango, X80-993. Anonymous Gift.
207. Photograph, Susan Turner, 1980.
208. Cinta, San Rafael Petzal, X75-776c. Gift of Caroline and Howard West.
208. Chachal. San Rafael Petzal, X80-989. Anonymous Gift.
208. Huipil, San Rafael Petzal, X75-776a. Gift of Caroline and Howard West.
208. Faja, Colotenango, X80-986. Anonymous Gift.
208. Corte, Colotenango, X80-1029b. Anonymous Gift.
208. Morral. Colotenango, X80-1037. Anonymous Gift.
208. Huipil, Ixtahuacán, X80-981a. Anonymous Gift.
208. Corte, Ixtahuacán, X80-981b. Anonymous Gift.
208. Tzute. Ixtahuacán, X80-1034. Anonymous Gift.
208. Cinta, Ixtahuacán, X80-982. Anonymous Gift.
208. Huipil, Ixtahuacán, X80-983. Anonymous Gift.
208. Corte, Colotenango, X80-978. Anonymous Gift.
208. Faja (not visible). Colotenango, X80-979. Anonymous Gift.
208. Cinta, Colotenango. Lent by Caroline and Howard West.
208. Huipil, Colotenango. Lent by Caroline and Howard West.
208. Corte, Colotenango. Lent by Caroline and Howard West.
209. Photograph, Susan Turner, 1976.
210. Corte, Colotenango, X80-1029b. Anonymous Gift.
211. Huipil, Colotenango, X80-1029a. Anonymous Gift.
212. Camisa, San Sebastián Huehuetenango, X80-1032. Anonymous Gift.
212. Tzute. San Sebastián Huehuetenango, X80-984. Anonymous Gift.
212. Banda, San Sebastián Huehuetenango, X83-191. Gift of Caroline and Howard West.
212. Rodillera. San Sebastián Huehuetenango, X80-1030. Anonymous Gift.
212. Pantalones, San Sebastián Huehuetenango, X76-872. Museum Purchase.
212. Cinta, San Sebastián Huehuetenango, X80-974. Anonymous Gift.
212. Huipil, San Sebastián Huehuetenango, X80-977b. Anonymous Gift.
212. Faja, San Sebastián Huehuetenango, X80-977c. Anonymous Gift.
212. Huipil, San Sebastián Huehuetenango, X80-1017. Anonymous Gift.
212. Corte, San Sebastián Huehuetenango, X80-977a. Anonymous Gift.
213. Photograph, Dan Clement, 1970s.
214. Tzute. Sololá, X75-777c. Gift of Caroline and Howard West.
214. Camisa, Sololá, X75-777a. Gift of Caroline and Howard West.
214. Faja, Sololá, X75-777d. Gift of Caroline and Howard West.
214. Tzute, Sololá, X77-1158. Gift of Caroline and Howard West.
214. Corte, Sololá, X75-777b. Gift of Caroline and Howard West.
214. Camisa, Sololá, X66-1134. Gift of Dr. & Mrs. Ralph L. Beals.
214. Saco, Sololá, X84-1175. Gift of Caroline and Howard West.
214. Banda, Sololá, X77-1110. Gift of Caroline and Howard West.
214. Morral. Sololá, X76-1217. Gift of Caroline and Howard West.
214. Pantalones, Sololá, X77-1107. Gift of Caroline and Howard West.
214. Rodillera. Sololá, X76-109a. Gift of Caroline and Howard West.
214. Banda, Sololá, X77-1110. Gift of Caroline and Howard West.
214. Morral, Sololá, X76-1217. Gift of Caroline and Howard West.
214. Pantalones, Sololá, X77-1107. Gift of Caroline and Howard West.
214. Rodillera. Sololá, X76-109a. Museum Purchase.
215. Photograph, Whitman Archive, 1960s.
216. Photograph, Polly Blank, 1949.
217. Camisa, Santa Catarina Palopó, X76-108b. Museum Purchase.
217. Banda, Santa Catarina Palopó, X84-1182. Gift of Caroline and Howard West.
217. Pantalones, Santa Catarina Palopó, X77-1161. Gift of Caroline and Howard West.
217. Tzute, Santa Catarina Palopó, X84-1143. Gift of Caroline and Howard West.

217. Chachal, Santa Catarina Palopó, X76-108c. Museum Purchase.
217. Huipil, Santa Catarina Palopó, X76-108a. Museum Purchase.
217. Faja, Santa Catarina Palopó, X75-783d. Gift of Caroline and Howard West.
217. Corte, Santa Catarina Palopó, X75-783b. Gift of Caroline and Howard West.
218. Photograph, Whitman Archive, late 1940s.
219. Cinta, San Antonio Palopó, X80-1095e. Anonymous Gift.
219. Chachal, San Antonio Palopó, X80-1095f. Anonymous Gift.
219. Faja, San Antonio Palopó, X80-1095c. Anonymous Gift.
219. Corte, San Antonio Palopó, X80-1095b. Anonymous Gift.
219. Tzute, San Antonio Palopó, X80-1095d. Anonymous Gift.
219. Tzute, San Antonio Palopó, X83-52. Gift of Caroline and Howard West.
219. Camisa, San Antonio Palopó, X80-1096. Anonymous Gift.
219. Rodillera, San Antonio Palopó, X81-303. Gift of Caroline and Howard West.
219. Pantalones, San Antonio Palopó, X86-1227. Gift of Caroline and Howard West.
220. Photograph, Susan Turner, 1978.
221. Tzute. Panajachel, X75-40f. Museum Purchase.
221. Capixay, Panajachel, X75-40e. Museum Purchase.
221. Banda, Panajachel, X75-40b. Museum Purchase.
221. Pantalones, Panajachel, X75-40a. Museum Purchase.
221. Cinta, Panajachel, X75-39d. Museum Purchase.
221. Huipil, Panajachel, X86-1257. Gift of Hope Stephenson.
221. Faja, Panajachel, X75-39c. Museum Purchase.
221. Corte, Panajachel, X75-39b. Museum Purchase.
221. Tzute, Panajachel, X75-39e. Museum Purchase.
222. Huipil, Panajachel, X86-1257. Gift of Hope Stephenson.
223. Photograph, 1960s. Panajachel. Whitman Archive.
224. Tzute, Santa Cruz la Laguna, X84-1151. Gift of Caroline and Howard West.
224. Huipil, Santa Cruz la Laguna, X83-44. Gift of Caroline and Howard West.
224. Faja, Santa Cruz la Laguna, X81-302. Gift of Caroline and Howard West.
224. Corte, Santa Cruz la Laguna, X83-185. Gift of Caroline and Howard West.
224. Huipil, San Marcos la Laguna, X84-1125. Gift of Caroline and Howard West.
224. Servilleta. San Marcos la Laguna, X80-1093. Gift of Caroline and Howard West.
224. Faja, San Marcos la Laguna, X80-1094. Gift of Caroline and Howard West.
224. Corte, San Marcos la Laguna, X83-1006. Gift of Caroline and Howard West.
224. Huipil, San Juan La Laguna. Anonymous Loan.
224. Faja, San Juan La Laguna, X83-1011. Gift of Caroline and Howard West.
224. Perraje, San Juan La Laguna, X84-1145. Gift of Caroline and Howard West.
224. Corte, San Juan La Laguna, X81-300. Gift of Caroline and Howard West.
225. Huipil, Santa Cruz la Laguna, X83-44. Gift of Caroline and Howard West.
226. Huipil, San Marcos la Laguna, X84-1125. Gift of Caroline and Howard West.
227. Huipil, San Juan la Laguna. Anonymous Loan.
228. Huipil, Quezaltenango, X69-954. Gift of Richard Oaks.
228. Faja, Quezaltenango,.X84-1173. Gift of Caroline and Howard West.
228. Corte, Quezaltenango, X70-1205. Gift of Eric Barker.
228. Perraje. Quezaltenango, X83-53. Gift of Caroline and Howard West.
228. Cinta, Quezaltenango, X80-1088. Anonymous Gift.
228. Huipil, Quezaltenango, X75-812. Gift of Caroline and Howard West.
228. Corte, Quezaltenango, X76-836a. Museum Purchase.
229. Huipil, Quezaltenango, X75-812. Gift of Caroline and Howard West.
230. Corte, Quezaltenango, X76-836a. Museum Purchase.
231. Huipil, Olintepeque, X76-1232. Gift of Caroline and Howard West.
231. Faja, Olintepeque, X83-82. Gift of Caroline and Howard West.
231. Corte, Olintepeque, X80-938. Gift of Caroline and Howard West.
231. Faja, Olintepeque, X84-1172. Gift of Caroline and Howard West.
231. Cinta, Momostenango, X80-1088. Anonymous Gift.
231. Chachal, Momostenango, X76-1165. Gift of Caroline and Howard West.
231. Huipil, Momostenango, X84-1123. Gift of Caroline and Howard West.
231. Faja, Momostenango, X77-1140. Gift of Caroline and Howard West.
231. Corte, Momostenango, X83-187. Gift of Caroline and Howard West.
231. Cinta, Santa María Chiquimula, X76-1191. Gift of Caroline and Howard West.
231. Chachal, Santa María Chiquimula, X76-1166. Gift of Caroline and Howard West.
231. Huipil, Santa María Chiquimula, X83-41. Gift of Caroline and Howard West.
231. Faja, Santa María Chiquimula, X84-1159. Gift of Caroline and Howard West.
231. Corte, Santa María Chiquimula, X83-28. Gift of Caroline and Howard West.
231. Tzute, Santa María Chiquimula, X86-1684. Gift of Caroline and Howard West.
232. Tzute, Santa María Chiquimula, X86-1684. Gift of Caroline and Howard West.
233. Photograph, Dan Clement, 1970s.
234. Cinta, San Cristóbal Totonicapán, X76-100. Museum Purchase.
234. Huipil, San Cristóbal Totonicapán, X80-1021. Anonymous Gift.
234. Faja, San Cristóbal Totonicapán, X77-1139. Gift of Caroline and Howard West.
234. Corte, San Cristóbal Totonicapán, X83-1007. Gift of Caroline and Howard West.
234. Perraje, San Cristóbal Totonicapán, X83-198. Gift of Caroline and Howard West.
234. Blusa, San Francisco el Alto, X80-929. Gift of Caroline and Howard West.
234. Faja, San Francisco el Alto, X77-1141. Gift of Caroline and Howard West.
234. Corte, San Francisco el Alto, X84-1131. Gift of Caroline and Howard West.
234. Cinta, San Andrés Xecul, X66-3277. Gift of Vilma Matchette.
234. Huipil, San Andrés Xecul, X76-870. Museum Purchase.
234. Perraje, San Andrés Xecul. Lent by Caroline and Howard West.
234. Corte, San Andrés Xecul, X83-189. Gift of Caroline and Howard West.
234. Faja, San Andrés Xecul, X81-315. Gift of Caroline and Howard West.
234. Tzute de cofradía, San Andrés Xecul, X76-874. Museum Purchase.
234. Huipil, San Andrés Xecul, X74-1468. Dr. & Mrs. Aaron Nisenson.
234. Corte, San Andrés Xecul, X76-1137. Gift of Caroline and Howard West.

234. Faja (not visible), San Andrés Xecul, X81-315. Gift of Caroline and Howard West.
235. Corte, San Cristobal Totonicapán, X83-1007. Gift of Caroline and Howard West.
236. Cinta, San Cristobal Totonicapán, X66-3277. Gift of Vilma Matchette.
237. Cinta, San Cristobal Totonicapán, X76-99. Museum Purchase.
237. Huipil, San Cristobal Totonicapán, X80-995. Anonymous Gift.
237. Corte, San Cristobal Totonicapán, X83-29. Gift of Caroline and Howard West.
237. Chachal, San Cristobal Totonicapán, X76-1170. Gift of Caroline and Howard West.
237. Faja (not visible), San Cristobal Totonicapán, X84-1162. Gift of Caroline and Howard West.
237. Cinta, Santa Lucía Utatlán, X83-74. Gift of Caroline and Howard West.
237. Huipil, Santa Lucía Utatlán, X80-1019. Anonymous Gift.
237. Corte, Santa Lucía Utatlán, X81-298. Gift of Caroline and Howard West.
237. Chachal, Santa Lucía Utatlán, X76-1165. Gift of Caroline and Howard West.
237. Cinta, Santa Lucía Utatlán, X83-74. Gift of Caroline and Howard West.
237. Faja (not visible), Santa Lucía Utatlán, X84-1158. Gift of Caroline and Howard West.
237. Tzute de cofradía, San Pedro Sacatepéquez, X76-874. Museum Purchase.
237. Huipil, San Pedro Sacatepéquez, X74-1468. Gift of Dr. & Mrs. Aaron Nisenson.
237. Corte, San Pedro Sacatepéquez, X76-1137. Gift of Caroline and Howard West.
238. Corte, Santa Lucía Utatlán, X81-298. Gift of Caroline and Howard West.
239. Cinta, Aguacatán, X75-806. Gift of Caroline and Howard West.
239. Huipil, Aguacatán, X77-1204a. Gift of Caroline and Howard West.
239. Corte, Aguacatán, X80-1000. Anonymous Gift.
239. Faja (not visible), Aguacatán, X84-1171. Gift of Caroline and Howard West.
239. Cinta, Sacapulas, X80-1007. Anonymous Gift.
239. Huipil, Sacapulas, X76-815. Museum Purchase.
239. Corte, Sacapulas, X83-1009. Gift of Caroline and Howard West.
239. Chachal, Sacapulas, X76-1165. Gift of Caroline and Howard West.
240. Huipil, Sacapulas, X76-815. Museum Purchase.
241. Photograph, Patricia B. Altman, 1970s.
242. Perraje, Santa Cruz del Quiché, X86-1219b. Gift of Caroline and Howard West.
242. Huipil, Santa Cruz del Quiché, X86-1219d. Gift of Caroline and Howard West.
242. Faja, Santa Cruz del Quiché, X86-1219c. Gift of Caroline and Howard West.
242. Refajo, Santa Cruz del Quiché, X86-1219a. Gift of Caroline and Howard West.
243. Tzute, San Mateo Ixtatán, X78-1666. Museum Purchase.
243. Huipil, San Mateo Ixtatán, X75-801. Gift of Caroline and Howard West.
243. Corte, San Mateo Ixtatán, X77-1111. Gift of Caroline and Howard West.
244. Photograph, Whitman Archive, 1960s.
245. Photograph, Whitman Archive, 1960s.
246. Huipil, San Pedro la Laguna, X76-249. Museum Purchase.
246. Faja, San Pedro la Laguna, X77-849. Gift of Leonard G. Field.
246. Corte, San Pedro la Laguna, X83-1008. Gift of Caroline and Howard West.
246. Cortecito, San Pedro la Laguna, X84-1179a. Gift of Caroline and Howard West.
246. Camisa (in hands), San Pedro la Laguna, X80-928. Gift of Caroline and Howard West.
246. Camisa, San Pedro la Laguna, X86-1221a. Gift of Caroline and Howard West.
246. Banda, San Pedro la Laguna, X81-301. Gift of Caroline and Howard West.
246. Pantalones, San Pedro la Laguna, X86-1221b. Gift of Caroline and Howard West.
247. Cinta, Santo Domingo Xenacoj, X75-779d. Gift of Caroline and Howard West.
247. Huipil, Santo Domingo Xenacoj, X76-826. Museum Purchase.
247. Faja, Santo Domingo Xenacoj, X83-77. Gift of Caroline and Howard West.
247. Corte, Santo Domingo Xenacoj, X76-839. Museum Purchase.
247. Cinta, Sumpango, X84-1156. Gift of Caroline and Howard West.
247. Sobrehuipil, Sumpango, X75-779a. Gift of Caroline and Howard West.
247. Corte, Sumpango, X75-779c. Gift of Caroline and Howard West.
247. Faja (not visible), Sumpango, X83-78. Gift of Caroline and Howard West.
248. Huipil, Sumpango, X75-779b. Gift of Caroline and Howard West.
249. Photograph, Whitman Archive, 1960s.
250. Photograph, Polly Blank, 1949.
251. Chachal, Santo Tomás Chichicastenango, X76-107. Museum Purchase.
251. Huipil, Santo Tomás Chichicastenango, X76-1203. Gift of Caroline and Howard West.
251. Faja, Santo Tomás Chichicastenango, X78-753. Gift of Gordon L. Smith.
251. Corte, Santo Tomás Chichicastenango, X79-361b. Gift of Joan Seaver.
251. Tzute, Santo Tomás Chichicastenango, X75-787d. Gift of Caroline and Howard West.
251. Chachal, Santo Tomás Chichicastenango, X76-106. Museum Purchase. 251. Huipil, Santo Tomás Chichicastenango, 76-1201a. Gift of Caroline and Howard West.
251. Faja, Santo Tomás Chichicastenango, X76-1201b. Gift of Caroline and Howard West.
251. Corte, Santo Tomás Chichicastenango, X80-1018. Anonymous Gift.
251. Tzute, Santo Tomás Chichicastenango, X76-1197. Gift of Caroline and Howard West.
251. Chachal, Santo Tomás Chichicastenango, X76-1163. Gift of Caroline and Howard West.
251. Huipil, Santo Tomás Chichicastenango, X75-787a. Gift of Caroline and Howard West.
251. Faja, Santo Tomás Chichicastenango, X76-1200. Gift of Caroline and Howard West.
251. Corte, Santo Tomás Chichicastenango, X75-787b. Gift of Caroline and Howard West.
252. Huipil, Santo Tomás Chichicastenango, X76-1201a. Gift of Caroline and Howard West.
253. Huipil, Santo Tomás Chichicastenango, X75-787a. Museum Purchase.
254. Cinta de cofradía, San Juan Sacatepéquez, X76-823. Museum Purchase.
254. Huipil de cofradía, San Juan Sacatepéquez, X84-1120. Gift of Caroline and Howard West.
254. Corte, San Juan Sacatepéquez, X91-563. Gift of Caroline and Howard West.
254. Huipil, San Juan Sacatepéquez, X76-820. Museum Purchase.
254. Faja, San Juan Sacatepéquez, X64-368. Museum Purchase.
254. Corte, San Juan Sacatepéquez, X83-225. Gift of Frieda Whitman Ellsworth.
254. Huipil, San Juan Sacatepéquez, X76-817. Museum Purchase.
254. Tzute, San Juan Sacatepéquez, X76-1160. Gift of Caroline and Howard West.
255. Photograph, Polly Blank, 1949.
256. Huipil (on head), San Martín Jilotepeque, X83-197. Gift of Caroline and Howard West.
256. Huipil, San Martín Jilotepeque, X83-196. Gift of Caroline and Howard West.
256. Huipil, San Martín Jilotepeque. Lent by Sharon Gordon Donnan.
256. Faja, San Martín Jilotepeque, X83-194. Gift of Caroline and Howard West.
256. Corte, San Martín Jilotepeque, X83-190. Gift of Caroline and Howard West.
257. Huipil, Santa María de Jesús, X80-1085. Anonymous Gift.
257. Faja, Santa María de Jesús, X80-1078c. Anonymous Gift.
257. Corte, Santa María de Jesús, X83-34. Gift of Caroline and Howard West.
257. Tzute, Santa María de Jesús, X80-1086. Anonymous Gift.
257. Camisa, Santa María de Jesús, X80-1080. Anonymous Gift.
257. Pantalones, Santa María de Jesús, X86-1226. Gift of Caroline and Howard West.
257. Banda, Santa María de Jesús, X80-1081. Anonymous Gift.
257. Tzute, Santa María de Jesús, X64-366. Museum Purchase.
257. Huipil, Santa María de Jesús, X80-1079. Anonymous Gift.
257. Corte, Santa María de Jesús, X80-1078b. Anonymous Gift.
257. Huipil, Santa María de Jesús, X75-789. Gift of Caroline and Howard West.
257. Faja, Santa María de Jesús, X75-794. Gift of Caroline and Howard West.
257. Corte, Santa María de Jesús, X80-1084. Anonymous Gift.
257. Tzute, Santa María de Jesús, X75-792. Gift of Caroline and Howard West.
258. Huipil, San Martín Sacatepéquez, X75-789. Gift of Caroline and Howard West.
259. Paya, Patzún. Lent by Caroline and Howard West.
259. Chachal, Patzún, X76-1162. Gift of Caroline and Howard West.
259. Huipil, Patzún, X75-780a. Gift of Caroline and Howard West.
259. Corte, Patzún, X80-924. Gift of Caroline and Howard West.
259. Faja (not visible), Patzún, X76-111. Museum Purchase.
259. Uncut huipil, Patzún, X80-192. Gift of Mr. Gordon Frost.
260. Photograph, Whitman Archive, 1960s.
261. Huipil, San Andrés Semetabaj, X80-931. Gift of Caroline and Howard West.
261. Faja, San Andrés Semetabaj, X81-314. Gift of Caroline and Howard West.
261. Tzute, San Andrés Semetabaj, X83-1012. Gift of Caroline and Howard West.
261. Corte, San Andrés Semetabaj, X80-952. Gift of Caroline and Howard West.
261. Tzute, San Andrés Semetabaj, X84-1148. Gift of Caroline and Howard West.
261. Huipil, San Andrés Semetabaj, X84-1127. Gift of Caroline and Howard West.
261. Parraje, San Andrés Semetabaj, X84-1141. Gift of Caroline and Howard West.
261. Faja, San Andrés Semetabaj, X83-193. Gift of Caroline and Howard West.
261. Corte, San Andrés Semetabaj, X84-185. Anonymous Gift.
262. Faja, San Andrés Semetabaj, X83-193. Gift of Caroline and Howard West.
263. Huipil, San Antonio Aguas Calientes, X76-1181. Gift of Caroline and Howard West.
263. Tzute, San Antonio Aguas Calientes, X78-852. Gift of Gordon L. Smith.
263. Huipil, San Antonio Aguas Calientes, X86-1237. Gift of Caroline and Howard West.
263. Faja, San Antonio Aguas Calientes, X64-954d. Museum Purchase.
263. Corte, San Antonio Aguas Calientes, X80-954. Gift of Caroline and Howard West.
263. Tzute, San Antonio Aguas Calientes, X83-421. Gift of Thomas K. Curtis;.Todd P. Curtis; Caroline C. Bramhall; Sandra G. Lovell; S. Premena in memory of Caroline P. Green.
264. Tzute, San Antonio Aguas Calientes, X83-421. Gift of Thomas K. Curtis;.Todd P. Curtis; Caroline C. Bramhall; Sandra G. Lovell; S. Premena in memory of Caroline P. Green.
265. Photograph, Whitman Archive, 1960s.
266. Huipil, Patzicía, X76-866. Museum Purchase.
266. Corte, Patzicía, X80-924. Gift of Caroline and Howard West.
266. Cerro de Oro, X83-42. Gift of Caroline and Howard West.
266. Cerro de Oro, X84-1130. Gift of Caroline and Howard West.
267. Huipil, Santa María Cauqué, X80-939. Gift of Caroline and Howard West.
267. Faja, Santa María Cauqué, X80-81. Gift of Caroline and Howard West.
267. Corte, Santa María Cauqué, X83-184. Gift of Caroline and Howard West.
267. Tzute, Santa María Cauqué, X84-1137. Gift of Caroline and Howard West.
267. Tzute, Santa María Cauqué, X76-829. Museum Purchase.
267. Child's Huipil, Santiago Sacatepéquez, X76-1154. Gift of Caroline and Howard West.
267. Huipil, Santiago Sacatepéquez, X75-778a. Gift of Caroline and Howard West.
267. Corte, Santiago Sacatepéquez, X75-778b. Gift of Caroline and Howard West.
267. Faja, Santiago Sacatepéquez, X75-778c. Gift of Caroline and Howard West.
267. Tzute, Santiago Sacatepéquez, X75-778d. Gift of Caroline and Howard West.
268. Tzute, Sololá, X77-1158. Gift of Caroline and Howard West.
268. Chachal, Sololá, X76-106. Museum Purchase.
268. Huipil de cofradía, Sololá, X84-1118. Gift of Caroline and Howard West.
268. Corte, Sololá, X75-777b. Gift of Caroline and Howard West.
268. Faja (not visible), Sololá, X76-1209. Gift of Caroline and Howard West.
268. Camisa de Santo, Sololá, X86-1249a. Gift of Caroline and Howard West.
268. Tzute de cofradía, Nebaj, X76-1212. Gift of Caroline and Howard West.
268. Huipil de cofradia, Nebaj, X84-1117. Gift of Caroline and Howard West.
268. Corte, Nebaj, X76-1207. Gift of Caroline and Howard West.
268. Tzute de cofradía, Santa María de Jesús, X80-1089. Anonymous Gift.
268. Chachal, Santa María de Jesús, X76-108c. Museum Purchase.
268. Huipil de cofradía, Santa María de Jesús, X75-788. Gift of Caroline and Howard West.
268. Corte (not visible), Santa María de Jesús, X83-186. Gift of Caroline and Howard West.
269. Photograph, Whitman Archive, 1960s.
270. Huipil, Chuarrancho, X80-951. Gift of Caroline and Howard West.
270. Tzute (on head), Chuarrancho, X84-1147. Gift of Caroline and Howard West.
270. Corte, Chuarrancho, X76-819. Museum Purchase.
270. Faja, Chuarrancho, X76-1190. Gift of Caroline and Howard West.
270. Cinta, San Pedro Sacatepéquez, X84-1155. Gift of Caroline and Howard West.
270. Cinta, San Pedro Sacatepéquez, X81-310. Gift of Caroline and Howard West.
270. Huipil, San Pedro Sacatepéquez, X76-1186. Gift of Caroline and Howard West.
270. Corte, San Pedro Sacatepéquez, X80-926. Gift of Caroline and Howard West.
270. Faja (not visible), San Pedro Sacatepéquez, X84-1154. Gift of Caroline and Howard West.
Page 192. Photograph, © Ann Parker, 1982.

THREADS of IDENTITY